Fly Patterns
Of Umpqua Feather Merchants

For Dennis Black, mentor and friend.

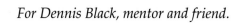

Fly Patterns
Of Umpqua Feather Merchants

1,100 of the World's Best Flies

By Randall Kaufmann

*Introduction by
Dave Whitlock*

UFM II, Inc., dba
Umpqua Feather Merchants
1995

Also By
Randall Kaufmann

American Nymph Fly Tying Manual
Lake Fishing With A Fly
The Fly Tyers Nymph Manual
Tying Dry Flies
Bonefishing With A Fly
Tying Nymphs
Tying Dry Flies, Revised Edition

All photos by Randall Kaufmann unless otherwise noted.

All flies tied by Umpqua Feather Merchants

Published by
Umpqua Feather Merchants
P.O. Box 700
Glide, Oregon 97443
(503) 496-3512
(800) 322-3218
(503) 496-0150 Fax

First Edition, 1995
Printed in Hong Kong
10 9 8 7 6 5 4 3 2 1

Library of Congress Catalog Card Number: 94-061568

International Standard Book Number: 1-885212-10-0 (spiral hardcover)
                                     1-885212-09-7 (softcover)

Contents

Acknowledgments

Book production is a team effort, and this project has allowed me to work with a wonderful group of very special friends. Without these people, there would be no fly patterns, no flies, and no book.

Thanks to the team at Umpqua Feather Merchants, especially Jim Black, for believing in this project since its inception, for keeping it moving over and around the many obstacles, and for encouragement; Dave Hall for helping to assemble the flies, for quality control and proofing; Julie Fay for proofing; Mark Hoy for proofing; Ken Menard for helping to assemble and catalog the flies, pattern information, and proofing; Mryn McCord for typing; Nick Murphy for organization, support, cooperation, and enthusiasm; and all the other Umpqua staff who had a part in this project.

Thanks to the many expert fly tyers and the management at the Umpqua Feather Merchant fly factories: A. Joga Roa at Custom Trout Flies, India; Dunston Athula at Golden Flies and Suresh DeMel at Lanka Fishing Flies, Sri Lanka; and Dan Byford and John Lyons at Thai-A-Fly, Thailand.

Thanks to the Umpqua Feather Merchants family of contract tyers, especially those featured in this book, for providing photographs, autobiographies, and, most important, for creating the many fly patterns and stimulating a passion for the sport: Bob Clouser, Larry Dahlberg, Lefty Kreh, Gary LaFontaine, Mike Lawson, Craig Mathews, Mike Mercer, Bob Popovics, Ed Schroeder, and Dave Whitlock.

In addition, thanks to Tony Capone for photographic consulting; Mary Erickson for encouragement and keeping me calm and happy; Kevin Erickson and Rod Robinson for film pickup; Ian Templeton for editing; my brother, Lance, and mother, Oda, for working around my erratic schedule; Bob Rector for proofing, editing, and cleaning up the inconsistencies that slipped by unnoticed; Joyce Sherman for deciphering my pencil scribbles, editing, formatting, typesetting, and for laughing through the frustrating times; Dave Whitlock for writing the introduction; and Jeff Wyatt for printing production.

Special thanks to Dennis Black, who has had the foresight, energy, and tenacity to assemble and lead this unique team to success.

Lastly, I wish to thank the reader and the many fly tyers and anglers who support our endeavors and make it all worthwhile. Here's to many more enjoyable feather-bending sessions and wild fish adventures!

Introduction

The right fly tackle, cast, and presentation are very important in successful fly fishing, but flies are the focus of our sport. In fact, flies are sort of what gasoline is to driving. . .you can't get far in fly fishing without a good assortment of flies to tempt the palate of the fish we seek to catch.

In the mid 1960s, I witnessed a fast growth in fly fishing in the United States, because of many new, major developments in fly tackle. At the same time, this growth was being limited because there was a shortage of quality flies available commercially. Flies are labor intensive to make, and our fast-rising cost of living was making it difficult to earn a decent living tying flies. During this time, the limited amounts of foreign flies available were poorly tied. . .not necessarily because foreign tyers in Japan, India, Asia, and Africa were not skilled, but because they lacked the training and quality materials to duplicate popular American fresh and saltwater patterns.

I remember my first experiences in the late 1950s trying to fish with foreign flies. I was about 14 and had saved up a couple of dollars for some "store bought" flies, which I purchased at a chain store sporting goods department in Muskogee, Oklahoma. There were about 15 flies in a little red and yellow circular box with a clear flip-up lid. Most were brightly colored and tied on small, long-shanked hooks that looked like the inexpensive ring-eyed offset-bend hooks that I used to cane pole and worm with when I was six. A couple of them had little red cork popper heads. Anyway, each one came apart after a few casts or, if I was lucky enough, with the first fish I hooked. I was disappointed and believe my bad experience was similar to what most fly fishers had with foreign flies at the time. Most fly fishers ended up tying their own, getting them from friends who tied, or purchasing quality American flies from local shops or from professional tyers like Walt Dette, Harry Darbee, Polly Rosborough, and Buz Buszek.

Many years after my experience with foreign flies, during a Federation of Fly Fishers Conclave at SnowMass, Colorado, I was approached by Dennis Black, a handsome young man with long black hair who looked like a cross between a fly fisherman and a reformed hippie. As Dennis told me about himself, I soon sensed he was a very special person, a gifted fly tyer and expert fly fisher. In retrospect, that meeting changed my life and, in my opinion, started a unique revolution in fly fishing and fly tying that's still expanding today!

Dennis' idea was to develop a fly tying factory in India that would use highly skilled and specially trained young Indian women to tie duplicates of flies that other American tyers and I had designed. He planned to use authentic hooks and materials, to maintain correct proportions, and to construct durable flies. To do this, he intended to maintain a residence at the Indian factory to manage the materials and fly production. He showed me some good looking samples.

Dennis knew he had to overcome the bad reputation that foreign flies had earned over the years. He believed that if credible American tyers could be convinced to believe in his idea, to give him exclusive rights to tie their flies commercially, and to endorse his company, he would have a better chance of success. He hoped that the public would at least give him the opportunity to prove himself. He asked me if I would give him an exclusive on producing and marketing my fly patterns. He also asked to use my name for promotion and for my personal endorsements. In return he would pay me a royalty on each fly. This meant, to a certain extent, putting my own reputation on the line, but Dennis had convinced me of his honesty, sincerity, and ability, and I knew there was a definite need for good commercially-tied flies. This was the first offer of its kind but, as it turned out, certainly not the last.

Admittedly, I was initially skeptical of Dennis and his offer. It was a radical and unique idea, but what I feared most was possible damage to my reputation by associating my name with foreign flies. However, the timing was right, as I had all but given up professional tying and was expanding my writing and speaking endeavors. I was also having difficulty getting consistent production from the tyers that worked for me, and I had wholesale commitments to shops and catalogs like Bud Lilly's and Orvis. Dennis presented me with a contract, and, after much discussion and deliberation, I signed it!

I provided Dennis with specific tying instructions, materials, proportions, and fly samples, which included my Whit Hair Bass Bug, Dave's Hopper, Multicolored Marabou Muddler, Whit Stone Nymphs, Eelworm Streamer, Wiggle Leg Frog, Dave's Shrimp, and Dave's Damsel Nymph. It took nearly a year before production samples were perfected to everyone's standards. Dennis never tried to compromise the quality of my flies and just kept trying until he got them right!

During that time, he asked me if I thought we could sell 40 dozen per month of each fly design. That was the minimum amount he had to contract for. It sounded like a huge number to both of us! Because of the big demand for specialty flies that I encountered everywhere I traveled, I thought it was possible, especially if we advertised the flies as the top quality fish-catching "bugs" we knew them to be.

Dennis jumped in and went for it! To our great relief, orders for flies quickly exceeded production. The factory was expanded and other locations were opened. I love to remind Dennis of his initial anxiety over the 40 dozen sales goal, compared to single orders for thousands of dozens today. I'm pleased to watch that process continue as Dennis' Umpqua Feather Merchants expands dramatically every year.

This book is a chronicle of Dennis' fly tying revolution. It gives readers a perspective of what Umpqua has made possible for our sport during the past 20 years. Only a small percentage of these flies would ever have been designed, commercially manufactured, or publicized if Umpqua had not been founded. Interest stimulates creativity, and the family of contract tyers that Umpqua supports is the center of fly tying and fly fishing innovation. Umpqua Feather Merchants has allowed fly fishermen, fly tyers, and fly fishing retailers all over the fly fishing world access to all the flies, materials, and components needed to keep fly fishing healthy and profitable.

Song writers receive royalties from record companies. Inventors receive royalties from manufacturers. Because of Umpqua Feather Merchants, fly tyers receive royalties for their creations and promotional activities, too. Previously, manufacturers, retailers, and other tyers copied and sold these "patterns" without compensating the original creators.

Without Umpqua Feather Merchants, many talented amateur and professional fly tyers would never have been encouraged, recognized, or paid for their contributions and creativity. Creativity that seldom would have progressed past the fly tying bench or local angling waters now flows into the international arena of fly fishing, that Dennis helped create.

My contract with Umpqua Feather Merchants has been the most significant factor in my ability to have time and income for creation of new flies and products, art, photography, teaching, and conservation activities, plus a wonderful way of life. There are many other fly tyers the angling public might not have had the opportunity to learn from and whose contributions would not be available for enjoyment were it not for Dennis' radical ideas, foresight, and courage. . .tyers such as Dan Blanton, Dan Byford, Larry Dahlberg, Randall Kaufmann, Hal Janssen, Lefty Kreh, Mike Lawson. . .the list goes on.

Each year more and more new fly tyers come onto the scene with unique materials, new tying techniques, and fresh fly designs because Umpqua has created so much opportunity for them. Other fly manufacturers have recognized the value in the Umpqua Feather Merchants concept and are now offering tyers royalties for exclusives, too.

There was some initial resentment about Umpqua from some American professional tyers and specialty shops because, understandably, they were worried that they couldn't compete with foreign flies. I do not personally know of any professional tyers who "lost" their job due to foreign flies. Actually, there is more demand than ever for domestic standard and specialty flies. This is true, in my opinion, because Umpqua Feather Merchants' excellent products have helped stimulate fly fishing so much that more people can and do fly fish in more water than ever before. I have also noticed that many of our full-time professional tyers have passed their designs on to Umpqua Feather Merchants when they are no longer able to tie flies full time. By doing so, they continue to receive credit and income after they no longer are able to tie professionally. I truly believe that American fly designs and their commercial production would be lagging decades behind without Umpqua's positive and farsighted impact on the sport.

This book represents much more than an impressive and colorful collection of our sport's best fly tyers' patterns. It's about the seed of a good idea that sprouted roots and is growing into a very special family tree of fly tyers all over the world that includes fly material suppliers, hook and tackle manufacturers, writers, authors, guides, lecturers, and fly fishing specialty shops—an entire industry—and the wonderful fly fishers involved in our fascinating sport.

Dave Whitlock
Mountain Home, Arkansas
January 3, 1995

Chapter 1

Materials

Materials create a fly's animation (action), realism (look and feel), and other specific properties. As an example, you cannot tie a standard style dry fly (Adams) with soft, webby hackle and expect it to float above the water's surface. Conversely, you cannot expect a needlefish imitation to portray the transparent and iridescent colors and the quick-paced animation of the natural if it is constructed with chenille. You would not try to imitate the eye of an adult caddis, but the eye is of paramount importance for a squid pattern. In other words, size, shape, silhouette, color, animation, visual realism, general attractiveness, castability, and fishability are all the direct result of which and how materials are incorporated into a fly.

Standard patterns make this selection for you, but often a new and better material can be incorporated into a standard pattern. Also, you may desire or need to create your own imitations. This is when an understanding of materials becomes very important. This chapter explains materials, what they are used for, and how best to incorporate them into your tying. The list may seem daunting at first, but, as you tie and become familiar with them, you should easily understand their characteristics and usage.

As you shop for materials, always obtain the best. The best may cost a little more or be more difficult to locate, but you will be far better off than trying to tie with junk. Visit your nearest fly fishing specialty store and browse through the material selection. Become familiar with colors, textures, and applications. Ask the clerks questions; they should be happy to help you. If you cannot find good service and a selection of top quality goods locally, shop mail order. Most mail order houses offer excellent merchandise and have experts who can help you over the telephone.

Material procurement is a separate mania. Like flies, you never seem to have enough or exactly what you need when you want it. Collect materials in a systematic manner. I have several dispenser boxes of dubbing material. Some dubbing is only used for one or two patterns and some I have not used at all; but, when I want to tie a specific imitation, I have what I need. Dubbing doesn't take up much space and is relatively inexpensive. In other words, purchase good color selections of various dubbings such as Antron, Superfine, Angora goat, and Hare-Tron.

When you stumble across something special, buy it! This is especially true of hackles. Don't pass up choice quality or rare colors. Remember that fly tying is your dream ticket to the magic of creativity and the instant illusion of exotic angling. Just sit down and tie a couple of bonefish flies, and you are wading the flats of Christmas Island! Consider a

Note that the materials in the fly dressing chapters of this book are given in the order that they are <u>tied</u> onto the hook. This is not necessarily the order in which they are <u>wrapped</u> around the hook or positioned in their final form. As an example, the wingcase material for a Gold-Ribbed Hare's Ear is tied <u>onto</u> the hook before the thorax, but the actual wingcase is not formed or positioned until after the thorax is in place.

permanent location for your fly tying paraphernalia. If you must set up and tear down every time you want to tie a couple of flies, you probably will tie infrequently. Having everything set up and ready allows you to wander in at your leisure, tie a bug or two, and leave. Over a period of a year or two, you may be surprised at your collection and knowledge of flies, fly tying, and fly fishing, to say nothing about your endless enjoyment.

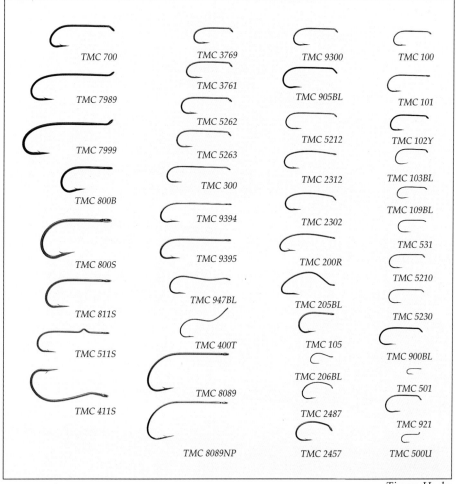

Tiemco Hooks

Hooks

There are several premium hook manufacturers, including Partridge in England and Dai-Riki, Daiichi, and Tiemco in Japan. Premium quality hooks incorporate the latest technology, the strongest tempered steel, and contemporary designs. The hook points are sharp, the eyes are closed tightly without any rough edges, and the finish is blemish free. In relation to lesser quality hooks and the overall value of flies, the cost of premium hooks is negligible. Fishing the best possible hook is another way to maximize your angling success.

My approach to procuring hooks is the same as stocking my fly boxes. Keep it simple. I do not need 10 styles of dry fly hooks any more than I need 10 adult damsel patterns. I prefer Tiemco hooks because I believe they are the best. Tiemco also offers the largest selection of contemporary styles and sizes, and the hooks are easy to obtain. In addition, Tiemco has been responsive to the needs of tyers. Feel free to substitute any other manufacturer or style hook. Note that Umpqua Feather Merchants ties all its flies on Tiemco hooks. The following Tiemco hooks are the most useful, and a selection of sizes allows you to tie most flies.

TMC 900BL, sizes 8-26, *extra fine wire (1X), standard length,* black, barbless, perfect bend (half circle), turned down tapered eye (TDTE). This is the dry fly hook of choice, and it is occasionally used for nymphs.

TMC 100, sizes 8-26, *extra fine wire (1X), standard length,* bronze, turned-down eye. My second choice. Tyers who have the 900BL will not need these.

TMC 101, sizes 8-26, *extra fine wire (1X), standard length,* bronze, straight (ring) eye. Useful for small flies where the open ring eye allows a bit more hooking power in sizes 20-22 and smaller.

TMC 5212, sizes 6-16, *extra fine wire (1X), 2X long,* bronze, down eye. First choice for hoppers and drake patterns.

TMC 200R, sizes 4-22, *standard wire, 3X long,* bronzed, semi-dropped point, slightly humped shank, straight eye. A favorite with both nymph and dry fly tyers (adult stoneflies). Ideal when a slightly curved nymph is desired: caddisflies, stoneflies, mayflies, leeches, scuds.

TMC 2457, sizes 6-18, *2X heavy, 2X wide, 2X short,* bronzed, curved shank, TDTE. Good choice for some scud and caddis nymphs, especially when a curved body is desired. TMC 2487 is the same hook, only fine wire.

TMC 3761, sizes 2-20, *2X heavy, 1X long,* bronze, sproat bend, TDTE. Good for general purpose nymphs, especially mayflies.

TMC 5262, sizes 2-18, *2X heavy, 2X long,* bronze, perfect bend, TDTE. All purpose 2X long hook—many uses, especially nymphs.

TMC 5263, sizes 2-18, *2X heavy, 3X long,* bronze, perfect bend, TDTE. Identical to 5262, but with a longer shank. Many uses: stoneflies (nymphs and adults), dragonflies, leeches, and forage fish (streamers).

TMC 300, sizes 2-14, *1X heavy wire, 6X long,* bronzed, TDTE. Used to tie extra long nymphs (stoneflies), leeches, and forage fish imitations.

TMC 7999, sizes 2/0-8, *1X heavy wire, 2X long,* black, up-turned loop eye. Standard for steelhead and salmon flies. The 7989 is the same hook, only lighter wire, and is perfect for surface flies and low water conditions.

TMC 8089, sizes 2, 6, and 10, *fine wire,* wide gap, straight eye, available in bronze or nickel finish. Standard bass popper hook.

TMC 811S, sizes 4/0-8, *extra strong* (lighter than 800S), *standard length,* straight eye, stainless. Made especially for bonefish, permit, and redfish flies.

TMC 800S, sizes 4/0-8, *heavy wire,* semi-dropped point, straight eye, stainless. Heavy-duty saltwater hook, especially suited for tarpon, striper, etc., and blue-water flies.

Thread

Thread selection is based on size (diameter), breaking strength, color, and whether it is waxed. As a general rule, I like to use the smallest possible size thread in relation to strength that allows me to tightly secure materials onto the hook. Thread sizes are denoted by a letter and number system. Larger thread sizes are labeled with letters. E is larger diameter than A. Size A is used for rod building. Thread sizes smaller than A are denoted with numbers. Threads, from the largest to the smallest, read E, A, 1/0, 2/0, 3/0, 6/0, 8/0, and, the smallest, 15/0.

When wax is added, thread does not unspool or back spool (loosen when you do not want it to). Wax makes dubbing easier because dubbing sticks to the thread before you roll it tightly onto the thread. Waxing thread also seems to make it a bit stronger.

The standard all-purpose thread is Danville 6/0 prewaxed. Danville 6/0 is a special twist of nylon that lies flat so it does not take up much space. It is small enough to tie a size 20 dry fly and strong enough to tie all but the most bulky and largest flies. I use 6/0 for most steelhead, streamer, nymph, and dry flies. Size 3/0 prewaxed monocord is useful for tying hairwing dries and assorted hair and saltwater flies. Another popular and useful thread is single strand nylon floss (SSNF). This is about size 2/0. It is useful for bonefish, saltwater, bass, and large specialty dry patterns where thread coverage and strength are needed. It also lies flat. If super strength is needed, try Kevlar thread. It will cut your fingers before it will break!

As a matter of aesthetics and tying ease, thread should match dubbing color or the overall color of the fly. When thread and dubbing colors match, less dubbing is needed to cover the thread, and it is easier to construct a delicate fly.

Dubbing

Dubbing is the primary ingredient in many flies, especially nymphs. It is both natural (rabbit, muskrat, squirrel) and synthetic (mostly nylon). Natural dubbing is available either on the skin or blended. Synthetic dubbing is usually blended. Blended means the material has been chopped in a blender and is loosely matted.

The word *dubbing* has a dual meaning. Dubbing (the act) is applying any material directly onto a single strand of thread, or between a loop of thread that is twisted to form a single strand, that then is wrapped around the hook shank to help form the fly. Natural fur and blended synthetics are most commonly used, but any soft, smooth material that can be dubbed is referred to as dubbing (the material). There are many name brands, colors, and textures of dubbing. Other than color, important qualities to consider include sparkle, diameter, and texture. Texture is an important consideration, especially in regard to animation qualities and fly size. Smaller flies (16-24) usually need to be more exact and dubbed more tightly with a finer diameter dubbing. Larger and nondescript impressionistic flies (2-12) can often be more animated and shaggy in appearance and dubbed less tightly with a larger diameter dubbing. Most pattern dressings are explicit. If you wish to substitute another dubbing material, feel free to do so, but keep the aforementioned properties in mind.

Tyers do not need every dubbing material, but a general selection of Antron and assorted smooth, coarse, reflective, and natural materials is of value. Many times, procuring additional dubbing is a matter of color. Dubbing is relatively inexpensive; a $1.75 packet of Antron will probably last years. Collect dubbing and colors in a systematic manner. It is frustrating to sit down to tie a specific nymph only to find that you do not have the right color or texture of dubbing.

Oregon-izer Fly Boxes are an excellent way to organize, label, and store dubbing. These small, clear, 12-compartment plastic boxes allow most synthetic dubbing to feed out of holes drilled in the bottom. Dubbing that does not have interconnecting strands does not feed out, but these boxes are still excellent for storage. Lift the lid for easy access.

Note that materials are grouped in alphabetical order in the following groups: **synthetic dubbing**, pages 13-14; **natural dubbing**, pages 14-15; **yarn**, page 15; **chenille**, page 16; **reflectives**, pages 16-17; **eyes**, page 17; **hair**, pages 17-18; **feathers**, pages 18-20; **miscellaneous**, page 20; and **hackle**, page 21.

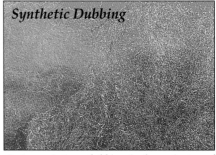

Synthetic Dubbing

Antron: Antron dubbing is the mainstay of every tyer and is called for on almost every style of fly. Its smooth texture, great color selection (45) and sparkle make it indispensable.

Clear Antron: Silvery white Antron fibers that can be used as gills, antennae, wings, and highlights. It is often blended with other dubbing material to create additional sparkle and animation.

Crystal Seal: A tough nylon fiber similar to Salmo Web and Angora goat, only with much more sparkle (but more difficult to blend). I like it for tying leech patterns, but it is also excellent for highlights, wings, bodies, throats, tails, etc.

Flashabou Dubbing: *Finely shredded Flashabou that is available in pure or blended colors. Creates exciting effects. Usage is only limited by your imagination. Try it for highlights, wings, bodies, etc. Mix, use as is, or form dubbing loop.*

Poly: *Commonly called Fly-Rite, this polypropylene is a fine-diameter, smooth-textured fiber popular for dry flies. It is available in dozens of colors and has excellent floating qualities.*

Salmo-Web: *A long, shaggy, somewhat coarse, sparkly, Antron-type fiber. Many uses, but most popular for representing the pupal shuck and air bubble on caddisflies. See Emergent Diving Caddis.*

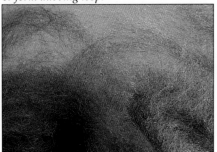

Superfine: *Developed by Wapsi, this smooth, waterproof synthetic is half the diameter of other dubbings. It is perfect for medium to tiny flies. It dubs easily and is the favorite small fly dubbing. Many flies in this book call for Superfine.*

Natural Dubbing

Angora Goat: *Also called African goat. A medium coarse, slightly crinkled fiber that can be used as is or blended with a smoother fur, which creates an animated, light-reflective blend. For additional information, see the Kaufmann Stone Nymph patterns in this book.*

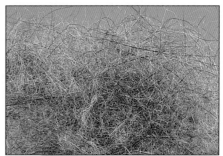

Australian Opossum: *Opossum texture is a cross between guard hair and smoother underfur—it offers the best of both. A skin offers several natural colors. It is easy to work with, and it has wonderful water-retention properties.*

Gray Fox: *Useful for tying nymph bodies and streamer-style wings. The barred black-white-tan hair makes a nice contrast, and the underfur is popular for dubbed bodies.*

Hare-Tron: *Longtime favorite with nymph tyers, Hare-Tron is a blend of rabbit and Antron fibers. It is easy to use, available in several colors, and offers excellent sparkle. Belongs on every tying bench.*

Hare's Ear Dubbing: *This is what blended hare's ear looks like. It seems to be magic on flies. Be certain to trim the ears especially closely. I like to apply additional wax to the tying thread—it helps keep the fur from evaporating into the air as you dub it.*

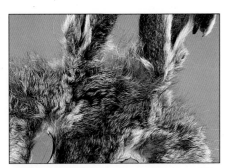

Hare's Mask/Ears: *This makes incredibly effective nymph and dry fly bodies (famed Gold Ribbed Hare's Ear and Parachute Caddis). Blend entire mask and ears, except soft white fur along outside of mask. Save a small patch in the center for tail material.*

Kaufmann Blends: *Hold any "blend" up to the light, and the attraction and advantages become obvious. Angora provides animation, highlights, and contrast, and Antron and rabbit provide the sparkle and smooth texture, making the dubbing process easier.*

Muskrat: *For decades muskrat was the staple gray dubbing material. It is fine diameter, smooth textured, and is easy to dub. It has exceptionally beautiful guard hairs that can be incorporated into a buggy fly or easily pulled out.*

Otter: *A short, dense "water fur" that is popular for tying some nymphs (Matt's Fur, Trueblood Otter). It is usually blended with Angora goat for an amazing effect. Ted Trueblood and Buz Buszek popularized it during the 1960s.*

Rabbit: *For many years this was the only readily available natural dubbing available in several dyed colors. Today it is the basis for many fur blends. Its soft, fine texture blends easily, and it is the basic ingredient for Hare-Tron.*

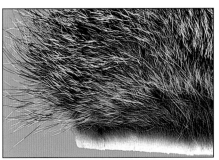

Squirrel: *Similar to hare's ear in color but softer and easier to dub. Makes wonderful nymph bodies and is easy to blend. Its fine, furry texture and mottled appearance have great value. More tyers should use it.*

Yarn

Antron Yarn, Smooth: *Fine diameter, smooth Antron yarn with lots of sparkle and many uses. Perfect for spinner wings, caddis emergers, caddis adults, and midges—tails, shucks, overbodies, wings, and highlights.*

Antron Sparkle Yarn: *Wool yarn with silvery fibers interwoven. Four-ply is easy to separate for smaller flies. Used in lieu of wool yarn.*

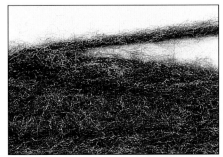

Antron Yarn, Wool-Style: *Beautiful, somewhat fuzzy but smooth and soft four-ply yarn interwoven with silver sparkle fibers. Often used in lieu of wool yarn and for Gary LaFontaine's caddis imitations.*

Egg Yarn: *Commonly called Glo Yarn, this smooth synthetic is used for tying egg flies and other bright steelhead, salmon, and leech flies. It is very easy to work with and is available in many bright colors.*

Fuzzy Wool: *A small diameter, smooth, two-ply fluorescent yarn useful for steelhead and salmon patterns such as the Freight Train.*

Leech Yarn: *Leech and mohair yarn are nearly identical in appearance. Long, free-flowing fibers extend from a woven core. These long fibers breathe well, are well animated, and portray a buggy look. Sweep all fibers backward after each wrap.*

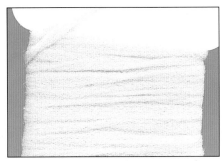

Poly Yarn: *Polypropylene in yarn form. Many long fibers create this yarn, which is easy to divide and work with. It is smooth and flattens out when wrapped. Usually used for spinner, parachute, and thorax-style wings.*

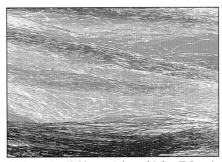

Z-Lon: *Available straight or kinky, Z-Lon is used on a great many contemporary nymphs and dry flies for tails, shucks, bodies, wings, wingcases, legs, and highlights. It looks similar to Antron but varies in fiber structure. Popularized by John Betts.*

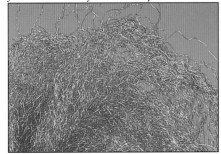

Zelon: *Zelon is a crinkly Antron-style yarn popularized by Craig Mathews. It is used to tie Emergent Sparkle Pupa overbodies, shucks, tails, wingcases, wings, legs, and highlights.*

Chenille: *Chenille is made of rayon wound onto a thread core. It is soft, pliable, easy to work with, and available in several sizes and a multitude of colors. It is used to form bodies for all styles of flies. Sparkle Chenille has tinsel added. Tinsel Chenille is pure tinsel.*

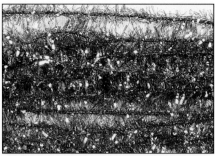

Chenille, Crystal: *A pearlescent, translucent Flashabou-type material that reflects and refracts surrounding light and is ever-changing in color. Use it to form bodies on streamer-style flies, Woolly Buggers, leeches, etc. Ice Chenille is a similar product.*

Chenille, Metallic: *Mini-sized mylar chenille perfect for small bodies. Try it for mini streamer-style flies, Woolly Buggers, and leeches.*

Chenille, Ultra: *Stiffer and smoother than standard chenille. Ultra chenille is popular for small nymphs, San Juan Worms, and low water steelhead and salmon patterns. Available in micro size for mini nymphs and emergers.*

Estaz: *Similar to Crystal Chenille, only larger, which creates more sparkle and animation. Vivid colors make Estaz excellent for big steelhead, bass, leech, and saltwater patterns. Stroke fibers backward after each wrap.*

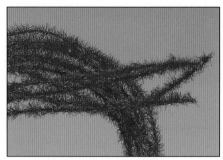

New Dub: *New Dub has a fine mono core and is a tightly twisted synthetic. It looks like mini chenille but is stiffer and not as smooth. Erratic fibers create the illusion of animation. It was popularized by Brett Smith for tying his Palomino Midge series.*

Accent Flash: *Commonly called Krystal Flash (K.F.), the two are interchangeable throughout this book. This is a fine diameter, spiraled mylar that offers a great amount of light reflection. It has been incorporated into every type of fly imaginable.*

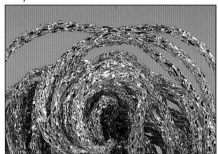

Diamond Braid: *A soft and pliable mylar braid that is perfect for making streamer-style and bonefish bodies (Muddler, Marabou Shrimp). Covers quickly, ties easily, and offers lots of flash.*

Fine Wire: *Used for ribbing small flies and as a reinforcer on many patterns, fine wire is available in three diameters and several colors. It is also referred to as copper, gold, green, brass, silver, or any other color of "wire."*

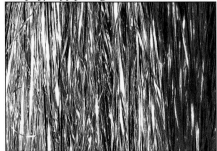

Flashabou: *A strong, narrow, flat mylar that is packaged in a bundle of strips. Its reflective properties are amazing. Used for bodies, tails, wings, and highlights on almost every style of fly. Another "must have."*

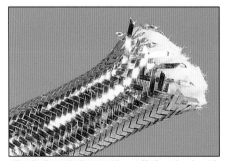

Flashabou Tubing: *Also called mylar braid, tinsel piping, or mylar piping, braided mylar is woven on a thread core. Remove core, slide mylar tube over hook or underbody of Zonker or Lead Tape (adhesive back), and secure. Presto! A perfect minnow body.*

Holographic Fly Fiber: *The shimmering three-color combination creates a 3-D holographic effect. Thin, flat, narrow strips of Flashabou-like material, but stiffer. New this year.*

Holographic Fly Flash: *A true holographic flat tinsel flash, similar to Flashabou and Krystal Flash but slightly stiffer. Incredible reflective properties. New this year.*

Mylar Tinsel: *Commonly referred to as flat tinsel, tinsel, or mylar, it is used for ribbing and to form bodies. This is a soft, non-tarnishing narrow mylar strip that is gold on one side and silver on the other. Available in four widths and packaged on spools.*

Poly Flash: *Also called Flat Braid, it is similar to Diamond Braid, only narrower and flat. Makes beautiful bodies—bonefish, streamer-style flies, both fresh and saltwater. A holographic color of Poly Flash is new this year.*

Eyes

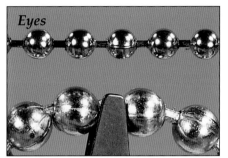

Bead Chain: *Popular on steelhead, Pacific salmon, and saltwater flies, bead chain is available in five sizes and different colors. Stainless or gold plated are nice for saltwater use. Use a cutting pliers to cut two "eyes" off chain, secure with thread, and apply Zap-A-Gap.*

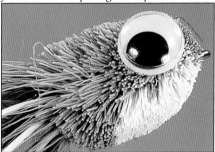

Doll Eyes: *Sometimes called audible eyes because the center eye is free to move about inside the plastic "bubble." Available in different sizes and colors. Popular for bass and saltwater flies. Secure with Zap-A-Gap or Goop.*

Hourglass Eyes: *These are shaped like an hourglass and made of lead, steel, or non-toxic alloys. They are also called barbell eyes, lead eyes, steel eyes, and non-toxic eyes. They add weight and are popular for all types of flies. I like gold plating best. See Christmas Island Special.*

Monofilament Eyes: *Also called monofilament nymph eyes or burned mono eyes, these are heavy monofilament that has been melted to shape. Different sizes are available. They make excellent nymph and dry fly eyes.*

Prismatic Eyes: *Sometimes called Witchcraft or stick-on eyes, these have an adhesive back. Stick onto fly and overcoat with epoxy. Makes realistic eyes on streamer-style, bass, and saltwater flies. Various sizes and colors are available.*

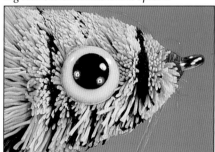

Solid Plastic Eyes: *These three-dimensional eyes look real and are used for bass, saltwater, and streamer-style flies. They come on a short plastic peg. Cut off the peg and attach with epoxy or Zap-A-Gap. Available in several colors and sizes.*

Hair

Antelope: *The largest diameter hair, antelope is sometimes used for flared and trimmed bass bodies and streamer-style or saltwater heads. Natural colors range from white-gray to tan-brown.*

Bucktail: *The standard long-fiber natural material for streamer-style wings, bucktail is called for on so many streamer and saltwater flies that it should be labeled indispensable. Good for everything from mini Clouser Minnows to oversize Lefty's Deceivers.*

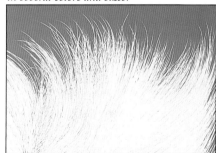

Calf Body: *Much straighter and shorter than calftail. Makes beautiful dense dry-fly wings. The straight hair stacks easier than crinkled or kinky calftail, and more fibers can be packed into a given space.*

Calf Tail: *Used for dry fly and streamer-style wings. The choice hair is found in the center portion of the tail. The top one-third is too coarse and kinky, and the bottom one-third is often black or too short.*

Caribou: *Preferred by most professional tyers for tying small (sizes 8 to 18) clipped hair dry flies such as the Irresistible. Caribou is hollow, fine, and soft, making it easy to tie in place, flare, and pack tightly. Use the center section of the hair.*

Deer Hair: *Used for wings, tails, backs, trimmed heads, and bodies. Many colors and textures are available. Experiment, observing how specific hairs tie in place and react to thread pressure. See* Tying Dry Flies-Revised Edition, *for additional information.*

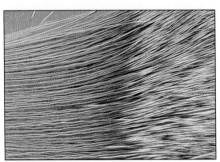

Deer, Natural Dyed: *Natural deer is mottled light to dark gray-brown, even golden-brown. It takes dye differently. The lighter the hair, the brighter the dye. Colors are difficult to match and duplicate. If you find that perfect color, stock up.*

Deer, White Dyed: *Pure white deer takes the brightest dye and does not have any mottling. Some is very coarse, and some (from the belly) is very fine. The coarser hair is used for bass bodies. Use Kevlar or single strand floss to flare and pack it.*

Elk: *Available in many natural colors, textures, and lengths. Short, fine hair is good for caddis-style wings; medium length, straight hair is perfect for Humpy bodies and Wulff-style hair wings; long straight hair is used for stonefly wings and extended bodies.*

Elk, Dyed and Bleached: *Bleached elk is pictured. It is popular for tying light-colored dry fly and caddis wings. Dyed elk is popular for many dry flies. Look for unbroken tips. Elk is usually stiffer than deer. It does not flare as much; ideal for hairwing dry flies.*

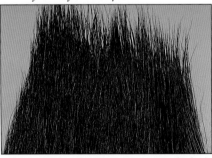

Moose Body: *Good quality moose body is straight with tapered tips. It makes perfect hair wings, tails, and overbodies on Humpies. Moose mane is black and white and is used for some mosquito pattern bodies.*

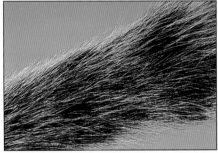

Squirrel Tail, Fox: *Sometimes called fox squirrel or red fox squirrel, this is used for wings and sometimes for tails. Like gray squirrel, it has beautiful natural color barring and can sometimes be found dyed black (Atlantic salmon and steelhead wings).*

Feathers

CDC Feathers: *Called Cul de Canard, these make wonderful nymphs and dry flies (tails, shucks, wingcases, legs, wings, and "hackle"). Creates unique light pattern and excellent animation. Use only CDC from wild ducks. It must have dense fibers (pictured).*

Duck Wing Quill: *Natural gray color is pictured. It is also available in dyed colors. Used for upright, divided quill wing dry flies (Royal Coachman, Blue Dun, Black Gnat, etc.). Select matching left and right feathers. Hold feather over steam to straighten.*

Goose Wing Quill: *Matched "left" and "right" feathers are used to tie Atlantic Salmon fly wings, plus nymph wingcases, bodies, and legs. Available in many colors. Fibers can be "married" together, like most bird wing feathers.*

Golden Pheasant Tippet: *Some flies incorporate it for tails, but it is used mostly for Atlantic salmon patterns (tails, cheeks, wings, or throats). The crest is yellow and is used for topping on Atlantic salmon patterns.*

Grizzly Marabou: *These are secondary body feathers from a Plymouth Rock "grizzly" hen or rooster. Use as tails or legs on nymphs or wings on streamers. Dampen the feathers; they are easier to work with. This works for many other materials, also.*

Guinea: *Used mostly for Atlantic salmon flies—tails, cheeks, throats, toppings, etc. Some nymphs call for it on tails or legs (Black Martinez and Tellico). In jumbo sizes it can be substituted for Spey hackle. Pictured is natural color.*

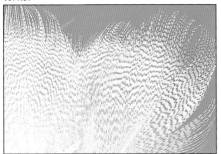

Mallard Flank: *Use on all types of flies for tails, wings, throats, cheeks, legs, etc. Natural feathers are barred black and white. Pictured are choice feathers—note the consistent barring and fine, even tips.*

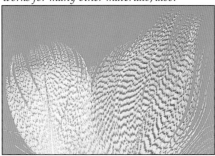

Mallard Flank Dyed Woodduck: *A substitute for real woodduck flank—fish cannot tell the difference and neither can many anglers. Used for tails, wings, legs, and wingcases. Feather size varies from a half-inch to three inches. Barring may vary slightly.*

Marabou: *Comes from turkeys (ostrich also have excellent "marabou"). Use for wings, legs, tails, gills, and bodies. Feathers are four to six inches long and are soft and "breathable." Marabou "flues" come off the side and point toward the tip in a perfect taper.*

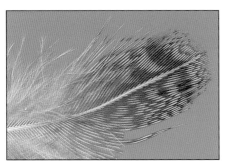

Partridge: *Also referred to as Hungarian partridge, either light, dark, or mottled. Partridge is used for legs and tails, especially on nymphs. Usable portion of the feather is a half to one inch. They are usually tied in at the tip when wound as "hackle."*

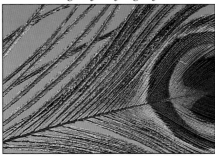

Peacock Herl: *The magical material that has been incorporated into every style of fly imaginable, sailfish to panfish. Buy complete eyed tails. Use only choice herl immediately below eye. In this book, unless otherwise noted, dressings that call for peacock refer to this material.*

Peacock Sword: *These are the shorter, metallic-colored peacock tail feathers without eyes. They are six to 10 inches long and up to two inches wide. They make perfect salt-water wings but are also used for nymph tails and highlights on other flies.*

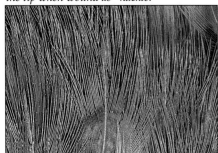

Ringneck Pheasant Body: *The most useful body feathers are on the rump, pictured here. Many applications (legs, wings, wingcases, cheeks). The whimsical feather found at the base of these feathers is called a filoplume; it is used for gills and nymph bodies.*

Ringneck Pheasant Tail: *Available in many dyed colors (green is pictured here) used for tying many of the most popular flies of the day (tails, bodies, legs, wingcases). Unless otherwise noted, reference to pheasant in this book means ringneck pheasant.*

Teal Flank: *Usually referred to simply as teal, these black and white flank feathers are occasionally used for streamer-style flies and some nymphs. Barring varies, as pictured.*

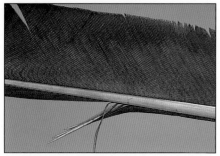

Turkey Biot Quills: *These are the short side of the first flight feather on the wing (one feather per wing). The short, stiff, tapered individual quills make great legs, antennae, tails, and bodies for nymphs and dries. They are larger than "stripped goose."*

Turkey Shoulder: *These turkey body feathers are usually used for thorax-style wings. The fiber tips are fairly even across the top. Trim out the center stem, bunch together, and you have a perfect upright thorax- or parachute-style wing.*

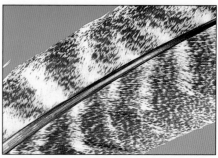

Turkey Wing Quill: *Also called mottled turkey feathers, these are prized for tying streamer (Muddler Minnow) and hopper wings. They come from brown turkeys; U.S. growers only raise white turkeys, hence their short supply and relatively high cost.*

White Tip Turkey Tail, Primary: *Primaries are eight to 10 inches long and are perfect for forming wingcases on nymphs. Stiffen with Flexament and use the tips, which are finer in diameter and do not split as easily as the fibers close to the stem.*

White Tip Turkey Tail, Secondary: *Secondaries are six inches long, soft and flimsy, and, when lacquered, less prone to split. Use for wingcases, bodies, legs, and tails. Apply Flexament as needed.*

Miscellaneous Materials

Betts' Tailing Fibers: *Fine diameter, stiff, tapered synthetic fibers that are perfect for specialty dry fly tails. (It is difficult to find hackle long and stiff enough for split or "V" tails.) Micro Fibetts are nearly identical, have the same use, and are interchangeable.*

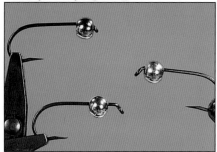

Metal Beads: *Also called bead heads, single beads, bead eyes, Cyclops eyes, and standard beads. The best metal beads are tapered or counter drilled and plated with real gold, copper, or nickel for a more brilliant, rust-proof finish. Glass beads are also available.*

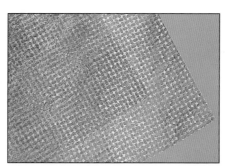

Shimazaki AirThru Fly Wing: *A porous, flexible, soft nylon material with random "veins" that look and feel real. Cut to shape. Makes realistic adult mayfly wings. See the AirThru Dun series.*

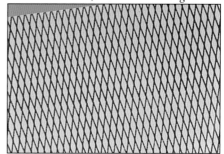

Shimazaki Fly Wing: *Realistic thin plastic sheet material that is somewhat flexible and easy to tie in place. Makes excellent caddisfly and stonefly wings. Many veined patterns and colors available. See Seducer and Giant Caddis.*

Swannundaze: *Flat (half round) stretchable solid plastic that makes excellent segmented and ribbed bodies—everything from bonefish to nymphs. See Kaufmann Stone nymphs. Available in three sizes and many colors.*

Swiss Straw: *A thin and narrow crinkly plastic that is easy to work with and popular on Dave Whitlock's Crayfish, and stone and dragonfly nymphs. Easily marked with Pantone color pens.*

Vinyl Rib: *Also called V Rib, this is similar to Swannundaze, only much smaller in diameter. Perfect for ribbing and small bodies. See Crazy Charlie series.*

Hackle

Hackle is one of the most important materials. Hackle is graded by its size and stiffness, with grade one being the best, followed by grade two and three. Stiff hackle is needed to tie dry flies. Softer hackle is desired when tying subsurface flies. Standard hackle comes from barnyard chickens and roosters—hen and rooster necks. Hen necks have shorter, softer, wider hackle than roosters. Usually, unless otherwise specified, the term hackle denotes rooster hackle. There are two types of hackle, neck and saddle. Neck hackle is shorter and more narrow than saddle hackle, and is necessary to tie small dry flies.

The best hackle is genetically grown. There are several growers. Metz has the largest production and best color selection. Most colors and grades are readily available at your favorite fly fishing specialty store. Domestic and Chinese necks and saddles are useful for some types of flies, but not for dry or those flies tied on small hooks. Tyers interested in learning how to best select and tie hackle should read *Tying Dry Flies, Revised Edition.*

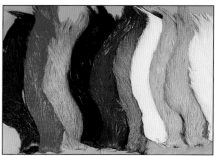

Domestic Necks: *These are big rooster necks with large, soft hackles that are perfect for tying bass, saltwater, and oversized streamer-style flies. All colors are useful. They are easy to find, inexpensive, and last a long time.*

Chinese Strung Saddle Hackle: *This extra-wide hackle is highly prized for tying saltwater, salmon, steelhead, and over-sized streamer-style flies. Length usually runs five to six inches, hackle sizes 2 to 6. Some feathers have more web than others; all are useful.*

Domestic Dyed Saddle Hackle Patches: *Domestic saddle patches offer sizes 2 to 8 hackles, which are ideal for steelhead, salmon, and streamer-style flies. Feathers are pure white before dying, insuring bright colors. Hackle length is usually 4-6 inches.*

Domestic Dyed Grizzly Necks: *The lighter barring takes the brighter dye, creating a beautiful barred effect. Large, soft hackles make wonderful bass, saltwater, and streamer-style flies. Dyed Metz grizzly is the best. I like these for bonefish flies.*

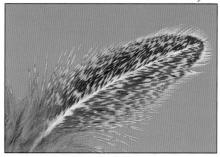

Domestic Hen Saddle: *This color is referred to as mottled brown or dark mottled. Its uses are many, including all styles of wings, hackle, legs, tails, and wingcases. They are inexpensive.*

Metz Hen and Saddle Patches: *Feathers are long, wide, and webby, perfect for Matuka, nymph, and specialty patterns. Some colors can be substituted for partridge. Pictured are ginger, dun, and grizzly.*

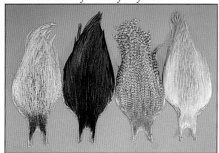

Metz Necks and Saddles: *Pictured are Metz light blue dun, blue dun, barred ginger and natural (light) ginger necks. They offer a complete range of sizes; long, narrow, stiff, feathers; and good coloring. Number one grade is the best; 2 and 3 are also very nice.*

Metz Saddles: *These offer wonderful feathers for sizes 6 to 10 flies. Hackle length ranges from two to six inches. Some are soft, and some are stiff, making them ideal for everything from large dries to long saltwater flies. Available in many dyed colors.*

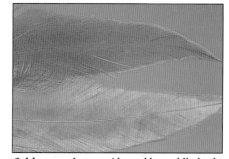

Schlappen: *Long, wide, webby saddle hackles found at the butt of a rooster saddle, there are only a few feathers per bird. These are the best heron substitutes for tying Spey-style flies. Stroke backwards after each wrap.*

Chapter 2

Dry Flies

Ed Schroeder

I started tying flies in 1963. Flyfishers for Conservation in Fresno, California, was giving lessons, and I was fortunate enough to have Dennis Black (now President of Umpqua Feather Merchants) as one of my instructors. With Dennis' help and encouragement, I began to tie simple patterns well enough to fool trout on the King's River. After a year or so, I had honed my tying skills enough to make some extra money selling flies locally.

Once I had mastered the standard fly patterns, I began to develop patterns of my own in search of that elusive fly that would fool trout all the time. While experimenting with various materials and patterns, I was asked by some older fly fishermen (with failing eyesight) to tie a caddis dry fly that they could see during our evening caddis hatch. The popular fly in those days was the late Buz Buszek's King's River Caddis. It worked very well, but it was difficult to see. I took this fly and added a white calf body parachute wing, hare's ear body, and a grizzly hackle. The results were excellent. The trout liked it as well or better than any caddis I had ever fished, and the parachute wing made it much easier to see under any light conditions. In those days, my eyesight was great, but now I am wearing trifocals and can relate to complaints of, "I can't see my fly."

The main attraction of dry fly fishing to me is that everything is visual. After 30 years, the dry fly take is still the most exciting part of fly fishing for me. Spurred on by the success of the Parachute Caddis, I soon added the Parachute Mayfly, Parachute Hare's Ear, Parachute Olive Hare's Ear, Parachute Golden Stone, Parachute Emergent Caddis, Parachute Ant, and Parachute Hopper. This gave me a very visible dry fly to cover almost every conceivable situation.

The Parachute Mayfly, Hare's Ear, and Emergent Caddis are simply wet flies with a parachute wing and grizzly hackle added. With the body moistened and the hackle and wing greased, they are very effective for fussy trout. The Parachute Hopper and Ant caught on quickly with guides in the western states. Guides know how effective terrestrials can be, especially on hot midsummer days when nothing is hatching and the trout are down. The problem was, because most of the artificial hoppers and ants are hard to see, clients were reluctant to fish them.

The other advantage with the parachute series is that guides can teach beginners nymph fishing quickly by using the parachutes as indicators above the nymph. For some reason, beginners will stay focused on the parachute dry fly far better than on cork or yarn indicators. The chances for strikes are also increased because both surface and subsurface are being covered with this method.

The parachutes also work well on lakes, ponds, and spring creeks. The parachute wing is much more visible than conventional flies and can be seen even when you are sitting low in a float tube. For spring creeks, I tie size 20 or 22 flies, and they have consistently fooled even the fussiest spring creek trout. Without the parachute wing, I could no longer see a size 22, and, as I used to tell my fly fishing students, "If you can't see your dry fly, you should be nymph fishing!"

My hobby became my occupation in 1978. I was attending the Ed Rice International Sportsmen's Exposition at San Mateo, California, and bumped into Randall Kaufmann, whom I had met years earlier through Dennis. Randall was expanding his retail business in Tigard, Oregon, and asked me to come to work for him. After 15 years at the Fresno Bee, I had decided that I had no future in the newspaper business, and I jumped at the opportunity to get into the fly fishing business full time. After two years, I moved on to Orvis in San Francisco, California, as their fishing department manager. In 1984, again at the International Sportsmen's Expo, Dennis Black approached me and asked me to come to work for Umpqua Feather Merchants as his West Coast factory representative. This was the job I really wanted. It offered me more freedom than retail. I worked for Dennis Black as he was building Umpqua from a small cottage industry into the major wholesale fly supplier in the country.

My parachute flies were selling well at Orvis, so Dennis signed me to a royalty contract for the rights to all my patterns. From the first time I met Dennis Black, my destiny has been tied to him. I owe him a lot for providing me with the opportunity to make a good living in the fly fishing industry and saving me from the terrible fate of having to get a real job.

For me, the ultimate stillwater experience with a fly rod is fishing over weedbeds in five to 15 feet of water. Each day presents new challenges locating the trout, dealing with changes in the weather, and understanding the trout's ever-changing feeding habits and food preferences. The best way to locate trout in stillwater is to go where the food is, and weedbeds are the cafeteria of any lake fishery. Most weedbeds produce large quantities of mayflies, caddis, scuds, damsels, chironomids, dragonflies, and leeches, all of which trout find irresistible. Weedbeds provide food and shelter for trout and their prey. Do not overlook weedbeds!

To be a consistently successful angler, you must adjust quickly to a trout's finicky feeding habits. There are four important time periods to be aware of during a typical stillwater day. The early morning (6:00 a.m. to 9:00 a.m.) usually starts with calm, cool conditions. Temperatures slowly warm with a gentle breeze (9:00 a.m. to 12:30 p.m.). That's usually followed by continued warming with the wind picking up and often becoming strong after 2:00 p.m. After 6:00 p.m., the temperature cools, and the wind often calms until dark. Of course, all this can be changed by a sudden thunderstorm or summer heat wave. All these factors will affect a trout's feeding habits. Water and air temperature dictate the timing of insect movement in and below the surface of the water. These four fishing periods of the day, coupled with weather variables, help me determine which fly line to use. I may change lines more often than I change flies because even the right fly fished at the wrong depth produces poor results.

The best all-around fly line is the intermediate line with at least 50 yards of backing (I prefer a hundred yards). You should also have extra spools with a Uniform Sink Type II fly line and a floating line. During very windy conditions, use Type IV as wind will cause a fly line to ride up and make it difficult to keep the line down in the feeding zone.

There are many flies that produce in lakes, but begin with what most lake fisheries have in common: mayflies, chironomids, caddis, damsels, dragonflies, scuds, leeches, minnows, and terrestrials. With these imitations, you should be prepared for almost any angling situation and be able to deal with 95 percent of the trout's food preferences.

When fishing shallow weedbeds, I like to cover both surface and subsurface at the same time. To do this, use a floating line, a nine to 12-foot leader, and a 4X or 5X tippet. Slide a visible dry fly (like my Parachute Mayfly, sizes 14 to 16) onto the leader. Then knot a five-foot section of 5X tippet with a double or triple surgeon's knot below the dry fly and tie on the nymph of your choice. (I usually use my Mayfly Nymph in sizes 14 to 16.) Cast both flies (using a wide loop to avoid tangling) to a likely spot over a weedbed and allow the nymph to sink. Be alert at all times as trout will often take the nymph as it sinks. If the dry fly moves or goes under, don't strike, just take the slack out of the line. If you strike, 70 percent of the time you will break off the fish as it surges away from you.

If there is no strike after one to three minutes, slowly pull the dry fly towards you a foot or so and stop. This will cause the nymph to swim towards the surface and often results in a solid strike. Continue stripping the dry fly slowly towards you, pausing often, until the dry fly sinks. Slowly finish stripping the line in and recast. Depending on the clarity of the water, trout can see the suspended nymph many feet away.

This method requires patience but is especially effective with spooky trout in hard-fished waters. There are endless combinations of surface and subsurface flies that can be used. When there are no hatches and you are not familiar with the water you are fishing, try an intermediate fly line with two subsurface flies, such as a Prince Nymph and a leech. Your selection depends on the time of the year and correct insect hatches. This technique can also be executed with a strike indicator, but the dry fly often entices a strike, and you occasionally experience a double hookup.

Stillwater fishing is a constantly changing challenge that rewards observation, patience, and persistence. Another bonus is that most fly fishing lakes are quiet, relatively uncrowded, and offer larger trout than most streams. The next strike could be a 10 pound dream trout! The double fly rig I have explained also works well in moving water. Give it a try.

Author's Note: Ed Schroeder has a well-deserved reputation for being a maniac angler, and a very good one. If there are any fish to be caught, he will catch them—all of them! It is rumored that Ed has, on occasion, launched his float tube in the early morning and fished straight through until starlight, arriving on shore grinning and starved with one wet, but warm, wader foot.

Ed Schroeder
Fresno, California
January, 1995

Mike Lawson

I started tying flies when I was about 14 years old. Growing up in Sugar City, Idaho (population 600), did not offer me many fly tying resources. I had a catalog from Reed Tackle as well as a Herter's catalog. The guy who owned the local mercantile, Emery Thomas, was a fly fisherman. I spent many hours at the Merc talking fly fishing with him. I didn't fish with many different patterns then—mostly wets like Sandy Mite, Lady Mite, Yellow Fizzle, and Triple Bar-X. Most of those flies were made out of horse hair. I got a good supply of various colors from all of the horses that lived around Sugar City.

I never had a book about how to tie flies or owned a fly tying kit. I bought a vise and some basic tools from Herter's and purchased materials as needed for the flies that I tied. I got most of my furs, hair, and some feathers from the local critters (road kills). I purchased flies from the Merc and dissected them. I figured out how to weave the horse hair on my own. I also learned how to wrap hackle, mount wings, etc. from taking flies apart.

My father was also a fly fisherman but was in poor health, and fly fishing was physically demanding for him. He was very knowledgeable, however, and helped me determine what materials I needed to order for the various flies I tied. He and I spent many hours on the streams of southeastern Idaho until he died at the young age of 44.

Soon after I got married in 1971, I became acquainted with Rene' Harrop. He had a commercial fly tying operation underway supplying flies for Orvis and had several fishing friends helping him fill orders. Soon my wife, Sheralee, and I were tying hundreds of dozens of nymphs for the Harrop operation as a supplemental income for my meager school teaching salary.

Rene' and I also became close friends and spent many hours fishing together. We had both grown up fishing wet flies, and the challenge of the dry fly kept us busy trying to understand the insects and develop patterns to match them. Several books came out about that time that changed the way the angling world approached fly patterns for selective trout. *Selective Trout* by Swisher and Richards, *Nymphs* by Schwiebert, and *Hatches* by Caucci and Nastasi had a great influence on me.

The book that has had the greatest impact on my own fly fishing philosophy, however, is *A Modern Dry Fly Code* by Vince Marinaro. Rather than just learning about insects and how to tie flies to match them, Marinaro made something I had considered somewhat of a science into a magnificent pursuit of pleasure. I read it over and over. The *Code* has had a great impact on my own fishing philosophy until this day. One of my great regrets was never having met him. I did have a chance to fish his river and to sit on the bank of the Letort with his close friend Charles Fox.

The Thorax pattern is one of my favorites, and I often use it to represent the mayfly dun. Marinaro's flies were delicate works of art, that required the finest of hackles and perfectly cut, shaped wings. His patterns required two slightly different sizes of hackles, which were crisscrossed around the wing. My thorax patterns are much cruder with a clump post wing and a long single hackle, which is then clipped under the body to get the desired effect. These flies work equally well and are much easier to keep consistent at the commercial level. The Thorax pattern gives trout the perfect silhouette of the natural as it drifts into their window of vision. If trout are feeding on duns, the upright wing is visible first and triggers the initial response.

My years owning and operating a destination fly fishing shop on the banks of the Henry's Fork of the Snake River in Idaho have had a great influence on my fly tying philosophy. I not only see and experience my own frustrations and problems but those of many others. Because of this, I believe I have a better understanding of flies, trout, and fly fishing.

I believe that tying flies for selective trout feeding in difficult situations gives me the most satisfaction. The size, shape, and position the fly rests on, in, or under the surface is far more important than color. Brightness, translucency, and roughness are other factors that can rank higher in importance than color. I have watched hundreds of aquatic insects emerge in my aquarium and have spent countless hours sitting on the bank and watching trout feed. Understanding the biology of the aquatic insects and how the trout sees and feeds on them is much more important than knowing the scientific names of the insects.

Spring creek anglers should be prepared to fish nymphs, floating nymphs, or pupae just under the surface film, emergers or cripples in the surface film, or adults on the surface film. I consider my flies to be generic representations of this biology.

Randomly casting a fly over a fast water stream with runs, riffles and pockets has its rewards. It is exciting to see a trout flash out and grab a high-floating attractor pattern. Such fishing is a guessing game. Anglers "read" the water and hope to put a fly over the holding lie of a hungry trout. If the trout sees the fly, it will likely take it. Fast water trout do not enjoy the luxury of taking their time deciding what is or is not food. If they do not grab it, it is gone and the opportunity is lost. Trout are not selective because they see a wide variety of food forms in this type of water, but not in large concentrations. Trout make decisions on feel after food has been taken into their mouths. Then they either keep or reject it. Anglers who like to cast and move are best suited to this fishing.

Spring creek trout enjoy the luxury of leisurely inspecting their food before taking it into their mouths. Spring creek trout do not see a wide variety of insects, but those available exist in enormous numbers. Trout see the same insects and, over time, visualize them in detail through the clear, smooth surface film. They make their decisions whether to accept or reject food by sight. They determine if the size and color are correct, the shape, and how the fly sits on or in the water, and are selective about the way the fly drifts.

When spring creek trout accept an offering, they do so in a soft, deliberate rise. The sight of a trout feeding, seeing him slowly drift to the surface, inhale the fly, and the sound he makes when he does so, is what sets spring creeks apart from other trout fishing.

Author's Note: Mike Lawson is one of the West's great angler/tyers. His ability to decipher hatches and riseforms and to present natural "drifts" over selective, flat water trout is legendary. Mike is at work on a book about spring creek fishing, which is scheduled for publication in 1996. He has studied most of his life to write it and says it has been one of the greatest learning experiences of his life.

Mike Lawson
Last Chance, Idaho
February, 1995

Craig Mathews

In March, 1979, I accepted the position of police chief in West Yellowstone. My wife, Jackie, and I purchased a home sight unseen over the telephone and moved on a wing and a prayer, "battling blizzards" across North Dakota and Montana on the way.

During 1980 Bud and Greg Lilly, along with Nick Lyons, urged us to start a fly tying operation, especially since no police chief had ever lasted there longer than two years. (West Yellowstone was still the "wild West.") I broke the record of longevity for the job by lasting over three years. Jackie ran Blue Ribbon Flies, established in 1980, using handicapped fly tyers. The company was named for the hundreds of miles of Blue Ribbon rivers and streams in Yellowstone country.

Since then four Blue Ribbon Flies locations have hatched: the headquarters shop is in West Yellowstone, the second is in Mountain Home, Arkansas, and two satellite shops are on the Madison River in Montana.

Fishing the Yellowstone country and operating Blue Ribbon Flies allowed me the insight to develop and promote many new fly patterns. The most popular are the X-Caddis and Sparkle Dun. Both have become standards on the Madison River.

An extensive knowledge of local hatches and fly patterns led to numerous magazine articles, and friends urged me to write a book. *Fly Patterns of Yellowstone, Volume I* was published in 1987 and *Fishing Yellowstone Hatches* followed in 1992, both co-authored with John Juracek. Both are distributed by Lyons and Burford. My work has been featured in many other magazines and books, both fresh and saltwater.

During the winter months Jackie and I can be found lecturing to angling groups around the country, on behalf of the Montana Nature Conservancy and the Montana Trout Foundation, to preserve the fishing wonders of Yellowstone Country.

I serve on the board of directors of the Nature Conservancy of Montana, the Montana Trout Foundation, and the West Yellowstone Cooperative Fisheries Foundation. All of these organizations work to preserve and protect wild trout habitat. Our shop has received a prestigious award from Montana's Nature Conservancy for the business that provides the best support to further its work of protecting Montana and the Yellowstone country. Jackie and I also conduct fly tying and fishing strategy seminars and present slide programs: "Underfished and Overlooked Waters of Yellowstone" and "Bonefish and Permit of Belize."

During the winter we chase bonefish and permit and develop new fly patterns in Belize and the Bahamas. Some of my more popular patterns include Pop's Bonefish Bitters, Famous Reef Crab, Sir Mantis, and Turneffe Crab.

The idea of imitating nymphal shucks trailing behind newly hatched, stillborn, or crippled mayfly or caddis is not new. G. E. M. Skues was the first angling author to point out that trout do take the natural during its metamorphosis from nymph to dun, the hatching nymph, and the dun when emerging but not yet clear of its nymphal shuck. In 1931, Col. E. W. Harding's *The Flyfisher And The Trout's Point Of View* discussed the emerging dun splitting the nymphal envelope. He went on to talk of the importance of the nymphal shuck lying on the surface film like a raft with a rippled undersurface creating an aura of soft light broken by little points of brighter light. Harding said that the emerger moves and that the edges of the light pattern quiver and shimmer. Col. Harding is the first author who talks of "sparkle" in connection with mayflies and caddis.

The evolution of the Sparkle Dun is interesting. Friends and I had used stillborn patterns as first tied by Doug Swisher, Carl Richards, and others with only limited success. One morning while observing emerging pale morning duns on the Henry's Fork in Idaho, we noted a great number of stillborns coming down in the drift. Most stillborns were still attached to the nymphal shuck, which sparkled and shimmered in the light. The shuck, still attached to the abdomen, trapped the tails and legs of the duns. We felt that this sparkle-shimmering feature of the still-attached shuck may have been the trigger to the rise. We are convinced that trout recognize crippled or otherwise impaired duns. Whether or not they are currently feeding on them, they almost always accept an imitation of one. This is the reason Sparkle Duns have been fished with tremendous success in Yellowstone country as well as worldwide.

During caddis emergences on streams like the Madison, Firehole, Yellowstone, and Henry's Fork when emergences are often long and heavy, trout will switch from pupa to cripples and stillborns. While a few smaller trout can be taken on a standard Elk Hair or Fluttering Caddis, most larger fish will key in on the stillborns and cripples. Their rises to these defective naturals are triggered by the shimmering shuck trailing behind. While wing, silhouette, and size are still a concern, imitating the shuck is the key to a successful imitation—hence the Sparkle Dun.

With mayflies, and even more so with caddis, stillborn and cripple patterns are necessary. Pupa rising from the stream's bottom in a gaseous bubble are susceptible to structural problems, causing many caddis to end up caught in their shucks, and trapped in the surface film, an easy grab for trout.

In the Yellowstone area, we fish the Sparkle Dun during the following hatches: Pale Morning Duns (*Ephemerella infrequens* and *E. inermis*), Tiny Western Olives (*Baetis* species), Mahogany Duns (*Paraleptophlebia* sp. and *Heptagenia* sp.), Pink Ladies (*Epeorus albertae*), White Winged Blacks (*Tricorythodes minutus*), Speckled Spinners (*Callibaetis* sp.), Small Green Drakes (*Drunella flavilinea* and *coloradensis*), and Blue-Winged Olives (*Attenalla margarita*, *Serratella tibialies*, and *Rithrogena* sp.). This important mayfly imitation can be fished with confidence the world over during any mayfly emergence, from blue-winged olives and pale morning duns to Hendricksons.

We have been using crippled and stillborn caddis patterns for years, whether fish are feeding on these emergers or not. Trout seem to recognize struggling emergers trapped in their pupal shucks as easy prey. We feel it is this recognition that makes trout so susceptible to X-Caddis.

The X-Caddis is to caddis imitations as the Sparkle Dun is to mayfly patterns. It has proved most effective when trout are extremely selective. A shuck of Zelon with a dubbed body and mottled deer hair wing (no hackle) in a few sizes and colors are all you need. This fly will work anywhere when trout are taking fully emerged adults.

Author's Note: Craig is considered the resident expert on Yellowstone flies and fishing. He lectures widely on Yellowstone fishing and conservation issues. Blue Ribbon Flies is *the* destination shop in the Yellowstone area.

Craig Mathews
West Yellowstone, Montana
May, 1994

Adams
- Hook: TMC 100, sizes 10-22
- Thread: Black, 6/0
- Tail: Grizzly and brown hackle fibers
- Body: Gray muskrat or Superfine
- Wing: Grizzly hen hackle tips
- Hackle: Grizzly and brown

Adams, Moosetail
- Hook: TMC 100, sizes 10-20
- Thread: Gray, 6/0
- Tail: Dark moose body
- Body: Gray muskrat or Superfine
- Wing: Grizzly hen hackle tips
- Hackle: Grizzly and brown

Adams, Female
- Hook: TMC 100, sizes 12-20
- Thread: Gray, 6/0
- Tail: Grizzly hackle fibers
- Butt: Yellow poly dubbing
- Body: Gray muskrat or Superfine
- Wing: Grizzly hen hackle tips
- Hackle: Grizzly and brown

Adult Damsel, Blue (Andy Burk)
- Hook: TMC 100, size 10
- Thread: Blue, 3/0
- Abdomen: Blue Z-lon, twisted, extended style
- Wing: Dun hackle
- Thorax: Bright blue deer hair
- Legs: Three strands of blue 3/0 monocord tied spinner style
- Eyes: Extra small monofilament nymph eyes

Adult Damsel, Tan (Andy Burk)
- Hook: TMC 100, size 10
- Thread: Coffee, 3/0
- Abdomen: Light brown Z-lon, twisted, extended style
- Wing: Dun hackle
- Thorax: Tan deer
- Legs: Three strands of coffee 3/0 monocord tied spinner style
- Eyes: Extra small monofilament nymph eyes

Adult Midge, Dark (Bill Fitzsimmons)
- Hook: TMC 101, sizes 20-24
- Thread: Black, 6/0
- Abdomen: Black thread
- Thorax: Peacock herl and dark dun hackle
- Wing: White Z-Lon

Adult Midge, Light (Bill Fitzsimmons)
- Hook: TMC 101, sizes 20-24
- Thread: Cream, 6/0
- Abdomen: Cream thread
- Thorax: Ginger hackle over ginger dubbing
- Wing: White Z-Lon

Adult Stone (Dave Whitlock)
- Hook: TMC 7989, sizes 6-8
- Thread: Fluorescent fire orange, 6/0
- Tail: Mason 15 lb. monofilament, "V"
- Antennae: Same as tail
- Body: Orange deer, extended and doubled back over top
- Legs: Brown saddle hackle, palmered
- Wing: Natural dark deer
- Head, Collar: Dyed brown deer, reversed bullet head style

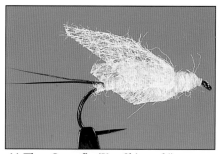

AirThru Cranefly (Ken Shimazaki)
- Hook: TMC 206BL, sizes 14-16
- Thread: Cream, 6/0
- Body: Pale yellow
- Wing: Medium gray AirThru Fly Wing No. 2

AirThru Dun, Baetis (*Ken Shimazaki*)
Hook:	TMC 902BL, sizes 14-18
Thread:	Dark olive, 6/0
Tail:	Dark moose
Body:	Grayish olive dubbing
Wing:	Light gray AirThru Fly Wing No. 1

AirThru Dun, Ephemera (*Ken Shimazaki*)
Hook:	TMC 109BL, sizes 9-13
Thread:	Cream, 6/0
Tail:	Dark moose
Body:	Cream dubbing
Wing:	Dirty yellow AirThru Fly Wing No. 6

AirThru Dun, Ephemerella (*Ken Shimazaki*)
Hook:	TMC 900BL, sizes 12-18
Thread:	Black, 6/0
Tail:	Black moose
Body:	Olive brown rabbit
Wing:	Medium gray AirThru Fly Wing No. 2

Aquatic Moth (*Carl Richards*)
Hook:	TMC 9300, sizes 10-14
Thread:	Tan, 6/0
Body:	Tan Superfine
Wing:	Ginger mottled hen saddle
Hackle:	Ginger mottled hen saddle, beard style

Bivisible, Brown
Hook:	TMC 100, sizes 12-16
Thread:	Black, brown, or white, 6/0
Tail:	Brown hackle fibers
Body:	Brown hackle, tightly palmered, back to front
Hackle:	Cream or white

Black Beetle (*Dave Whitlock*)
Hook:	TMC 100, sizes 14-18
Thread:	Black, 6/0
Back:	Black elk
Body:	Pearl-green Flashabou
Head:	Black elk
Legs:	Black elk
Indicator:	Fluorescent orange egg yarn

Black Gnat
Hook:	TMC 100, sizes 10-20
Thread:	Black, 6/0
Wing:	Natural gray duck quill
Tail:	Black hackle fibers
Body:	Black rabbit or Superfine
Hackle:	Natural or dyed black

Blue Dun
Hook:	TMC 100, sizes 12-22
Thread:	Gray, 6/0
Wing:	Natural gray duck quill
Tail:	Medium blue dun hackle fibers
Body:	Gray muskrat
Hackle:	Medium blue dun

Blue Quill
Hook:	TMC 100, sizes 12-20
Thread:	Gray, 6/0
Wing:	Natural gray duck quill
Tail:	Medium blue dun hackle fibers
Body:	Stripped peacock quill
Hackle:	Medium blue dun

Blue-Winged Olive
  Hook: TMC 100, Sizes 12-22
  Thread: Olive, 6/0
  Wing: Dark blue dun hen hackle tips
  Tail: Dark blue dun hackle fibers
  Body: Medium olive to brown olive
           dubbing
  Hackle: Dark blue dun

Brown Drake, Standard (Mike Lawson)
  Hook: TMC 5212, size 10
  Thread: Tan, 6/0
  Wing: Medium brown elk hair
  Tail: Black moose
  Rib: Yellow floss
  Body: Tan Superfine
  Hackle: Golden grizzly

Brown Paradrake (Mike Lawson)
  Hook: TMC 100, size 10
  Thread: Yellow, 3/0
  Wing: Dark gray elk hair
  Tail: Black moose
  Body: Elk hair
  Hackle: Golden grizzly

Buck Caddis, Dark
  Hook: TMC 100, sizes 8-14
  Thread: Orange, 6/0
  Tail: Moose body or brown hackle
           fibers
  Rib: Orange, 6/0
  Body: Orange wool yarn or dubbing
  Hackle: Brown hackle, palmered
  Wing: Deer

Caddis Cripple, Olive
  Hook: TMC 100, sizes 14-16
  Thread: Olive, 6/0
  Tail: Dark olive marabou
  Rib: Fine copper wire
  Abdomen: Dark olive marabou
  Thorax: Dark olive rabbit
  Wing: Cree hackle tips
  Head: Olive deer, spun and clipped to
           box shape, tips on top form
           overwing

Caddis Variant, Dark (Chuck Stranahan)
  Hook: TMC 921, sizes 14-20
  Thread: Black, 6/0
  Body: Gray Superfine
  Wing: Fine deer, color to blend with
            hackle
  Overwing: White calf body
  Hackle: Grizzly dyed blue dun

Caddis Variant, Dun (Chuck Stranahan)
  Hook: TMC 921, sizes 12-18
  Thread: Gray, 6/0
  Body: Caddis green Superfine
  Wing: Fine deer, color to blend with
            hackle
  Overwing: White calf body
  Hackle: Golden ginger grizzly and blue
            dun grizzly

Caddis Variant, Ginger (Chuck Stranahan)
  Hook: TMC 921, sizes 12-18
  Thread: Tan or medium brown, 6/0
  Body: Cinnamon Superfine
  Wing: Fine deer, color to blend with
            hackle
  Overwing: White calf body
  Hackle: Grizzly dyed golden ginger

Caddis Variant, Light (Chuck Stranahan)
  Hook: TMC 921, sizes 10-16
  Thread: Yellow, 6/0
  Body: Yellow poly dubbing, twisted
  Wing: Fine deer hair, color to blend
           with hackle
  Hackle: Grizzly dyed light ginger

Cahill, Dark
Hook: TMC 100, sizes 12-18
Thread: Tan or gray, 6/0
Wing: Woodduck mallard flank
Tail: Dark ginger hackle fibers
Body: Gray muskrat
Hackle: Dark ginger

Cahill, Light
Hook: TMC 100, sizes 10-20
Thread: Yellow, 6/0
Wing: Woodduck mallard flank
Tail: Dark cream or ginger hackle fibers
Body: Cream Antron
Hackle: Dark cream or ginger

California Mosquito
Hook: TMC 100, sizes 12-20
Thread: Black, 6/0
Tail: Grizzly hackle fibers
Rib: White silk thread
Body: Black floss
Wing: Grizzly hen hackle tips
Hackle: Grizzly

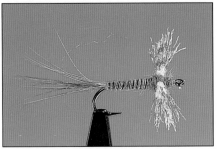

Callibaetis *Spinner* (A. K. Best)
Hook: TMC 100, sizes 14-16
Thread: Light olive, 6/0
Wing: Light, well marked grizzly spade hackle fibers or clear Antron colored with Pantone
Tail: Medium dun stiff spade hackle fibers
Body: Medium dun hackle stem
Thorax: Light medium dun Superfine; color to match stem

Carpenter Ant (Dave Whitlock)
Hook: TMC 100, sizes 12-16
Thread: Black, 6/0
Body: Black elk; three sections—abdomen, thorax, and head
Legs: Black elk
Indicator: Fluorescent orange egg yarn

CDC Ant, Black
Hook: TMC 100, sizes 14-16
Thread: Black, 6/0
Back: Black CDC, over both humps
Abdomen: Black rabbit
Legs: Black CDC
Thorax: Black rabbit

CDC Black Ant (Ken Shimazaki)
Hook: TMC 100, sizes 14-16
Thread: Black, 6/0
Abdomen: Black Superfine
Wing, Rear: Black or dark gray CDC
Legs: Black hackle
Wing, Front: White CDC; tie over top of thorax
Thorax: Black Superfine

CDC Biot Comparadun, Blue-Winged Olive (Shane Stalcup)
Hook: TMC 100, sizes 16-20
Thread: Olive, 6/0
Tail: Dun Betts' Tailing Fibers, split
Abdomen: Olive goose or turkey biot
Thorax: Tan Superfine
Wing: Dun CDC topped with natural mallard

CDC Biot Comparadun, Callibaetis (Shane Stalcup)
Hook: TMC 100, sizes 14-18
Thread: Tan, 6/0
Tail: Dun Betts' Tailing Fibers
Abdomen: Olive-tan goose or turkey biot
Thorax: Callibaetis Superfine
Wing: Light dun CDC topped with natural mallard

CDC Biot Comparadun, Gray Baetis
(*Shane Stalcup*)

Hook:	TMC 100, sizes 16-20
Thread:	Gray, 6/0
Tail:	Dun Betts' Tailing Fibers
Abdomen:	Gray goose or turkey biot
Thorax:	Adams gray Superfine
Wing:	Dun CDC topped with natural mallard

CDC Biot Comparadun, Mahogany
(*Shane Stalcup*)

Hook:	TMC 100, sizes 16-20
Thread:	Rust, 6/0
Tail:	Dun Betts' Tailing Fibers
Abdomen:	Mahogany goose or turkey biot
Thorax:	Mahogany brown Superfine
Wing:	Dun CDC topped with natural mallard

CDC Biot Comparadun, Pale Morning Dun (*Shane Stalcup*)

Hook:	TMC 100, sizes 16-20
Thread:	Yellow, 6/0
Tail:	Ginger Betts' Tailing Fibers
Abdomen:	Yellow-olive goose or turkey biot
Thorax:	Pale morning dun Superfine
Wing:	Dun CDC topped with natural mallard

CDC Biot Comparadun, Pink (*Shane Stalcup*)

Hook:	TMC 100, sizes 16-20
Thread:	Gray, 6/0
Tail:	Dun Betts' Tailing Fibers
Abdomen:	Pink turkey biot
Thorax:	Hendrickson pink Superfine
Wing:	Dun CDC topped with natural mallard

CDC Biot Comparadun, Quill Gordon
(*Shane Stalcup*)

Hook:	TMC 100, sizes 14-20
Thread:	Brown, 6/0
Tail:	Dun Betts' Tailing Fibers
Abdomen:	Medium brown goose or turkey biot
Thorax:	Brown Superfine
Wing:	Dun CDC topped with natural mallard

CDC Biot Comparadun, Red Quill
(*Shane Stalcup*)

Hook:	TMC 100, sizes 14-20
Thread:	Olive, 6/0
Tail:	Dun Betts' Tailing Fibers
Abdomen:	Burnt orange goose or turkey biot
Thorax:	Rusty brown Superfine
Wing:	Dun CDC topped with natural mallard

CDC Biot Comparadun, Trico Female,
(*Shane Stalcup*)

Hook:	TMC 100, sizes 20-24
Thread:	Black, 6/0
Tail:	White Betts' Tailing Fibers
Abdomen:	Yellow-green goose or turkey biot
Thorax:	Black Superfine
Wing:	White CDC topped with natural mallard

CDC Biot Comparadun, Trico Male (*Shane Stalcup*)

Hook:	TMC 100, sizes 20-24
Thread:	Black, 6/0
Tail:	White Betts' Tailing Fibers
Abdomen:	Black goose or turkey biot
Thorax:	Black Superfine
Wing:	White CDC topped with natural mallard

CDC Biot Spinner, Blue-Winged Olive

Hook:	TMC 900BL, sizes 16-20
Thread:	Olive, 6/0
Underwing:	Light blue dun CDC, tied spent (spinner style)
Overwing:	Light blue dun Z-lon
Tail:	Light blue dun Betts' Tailing Fibers, 2-4, split or flared wide
Abdomen:	Olive turkey biot
Thorax:	Medium olive or olive-brown Superfine

CDC Biot Spinner, Callibaetis
Hook: *TMC 900BL, sizes 14-16*
Thread: *Tan, 6/0*
Underwing: *Light blue dun CDC tied spent style*
Overwing: *Brown Z-Lon*
Tail: *Light blue dun Betts' Tailing Fibers, split*
Abdomen: *Tan turkey*
Thorax: *Tan Superfine*

CDC Biot Spinner, Pale Morning Dun
Hook: *TMC 900BL, sizes 16-20*
Thread: *Yellow, 6/0*
Underwing: *Light blue dun CDC, tied spent*
Overwing: *Light blue dun Z-Lon*
Tail: *Light blue dun Betts' Tailing Fibers, split*
Abdomen: *Olive yellow turkey biot*
Thorax: *Yellow olive Superfine*

CDC Biot Spinner, Rusty
Hook: *TMC 900BL, sizes 14-20*
Thread: *Brown, 6/0*
Underwing: *Light blue dun CDC, tied spent*
Overwing: *Light blue dun Z-Lon*
Tail: *Light blue dun Betts' Tailing Fibers, split*
Abdomen: *Rusty turkey biot*
Thorax: *Rusty Superfine*

CDC Biot Spinner, Trico
Hook: *TMC 900BL, sizes 20-22*
Thread: *Black, 8/0*
Underwing: *White CDC, tied spent*
Overwing: *Blue dun Z-Lon*
Tail: *Light blue dun hackle fibers, 2-4 stiff, or Betts' Tailing Fibers, split*
Abdomen: *Black goose or turkey biot*
Thorax: *Black Superfine*

CDC Caddis Adult, Black
Hook: *TMC 100, sizes 14-20*
Thread: *Black, 6/0*
Abdomen: *Black poly*
Wing: *Black CDC over black Z-Lon*
Legs: *Black CDC*
Thorax: *Black poly*

CDC Caddis Adult, Gray
Hook: *TMC 100, sizes 14-20*
Thread: *Gray, 6/0*
Abdomen: *Adams gray Superfine*
Wing: *Natural dun CDC over gray Z-Lon*
Legs: *Natural dun CDC*
Thorax: *Same as abdomen*

CDC Caddis Adult, Olive
Hook: *TMC 100, sizes 14-20*
Thread: *Olive, 6/0*
Abdomen: *Olive poly*
Wing: *Medium dun CDC over light dun Z-Lon*
Legs: *Medium dun CDC*
Thorax: *Olive poly*

CDC Caddis Adult, Tan
Hook: *TMC 100, sizes 14-18*
Thread: *Tan, 6/0*
Abdomen: *Tan poly*
Wing: *Ginger CDC over white Z-Lon*
Legs: *Ginger CDC*
Thorax: *Tan poly*

CDC Comparadun, Ginger Quill (Shane Stalcup)
Hook: *TMC 100, sizes 14-20*
Thread: *Tan, 6/0*
Wing: *Cream CDC with woodduck fibers*
Tail: *Light ginger hackle fibers*
Abdomen: *Tan goose biot*
Thorax: *Light tan Superfine*

CDC Direct Hackled Adams (Ken Shimazaki)
- Hook: TMC 900BL, sizes 12-20
- Thread: Gray, 6/0
- Wing: Grizzly hen hackle tips and white CDC
- Tail: Grizzly hackle fibers and brownish CDC
- Body: Adams gray Superfine
- Hackle: Grizzly and brown

CDC Direct Hackled Baetis (Ken Shimazaki)
- Hook: TMC 101, sizes 16-20
- Thread: Dark olive, 6/0
- Wing: White CDC center; dark dun CDC outside
- Tail: Dun Betts' Tailing Fibers
- Body: Brownish-gray-olive Superfine
- Head: Same as body

CDC Direct Hackled Blue-Winged Olive (Ken Shimazaki)
- Hook: TMC 101, sizes 14-20
- Thread: Yellow, 6/0
- Tail: Dark dun Betts' Tailing Fibers
- Body: Blue-winged olive Superfine
- Wing: White CDC center; dark dun CDC outside
- Head: Same as body

CDC Direct Hackled Light Cahill (Ken Shimazaki)
- Hook: TMC 101, sizes 12-20
- Thread: Pale yellow, 6/0
- Wing: White CDC inside; pale dun CDC outside
- Tail: Cream Betts' Tailing Fibers
- Body: Cream Superfine
- Head: Same as body

CDC Direct Hackled Pale Morning Dun (Ken Shimazaki)
- Hook: TMC 101, sizes 14-20
- Thread: Yellow, 6/0
- Tail: Light dun Betts' Tailing Fibers
- Body: PMD yellow Superfine
- Wing: White CDC center; pale dun CDC outside
- Head: Same as body

CDC Direct Hackled Royal Wulff (Ken Shimazaki)
- Hook: TMC 900BL, sizes 10-20
- Thread: Black, 6/0
- Wing: Dark gray and white CDC
- Tail: Dark gray CDC and moose
- Body: Royal body (peacock, red floss, peacock)
- Hackle: Dark dun CDC

CDC Direct Hackled Yellow, Dry (Ken Shimazaki)
- Hook: TMC 101, sizes 16-20
- Thread: Pale yellow, 6/0
- Wing: White CDC center; dark dun CDC outside
- Tail: Light dun Betts' Tailing Fibers
- Body: Sulphur yellow Superfine

CDC Dun, Blue-Winged Olive
- Hook: TMC 100, sizes 16-20
- Thread: Olive, 6/0
- Tail: Medium dun hackle fibers
- Body: Olive Superfine
- Hackle: Dun CDC
- Wing: Dark dun CDC

CDC Elk Caddis, Brown
- Hook: TMC 900BL, sizes 12-18
- Thread: Brown, 6/0
- Rib: Brown thread, 6/0
- Body: Dark tan Superfine
- Hackle: Dark dun CDC, palmered
- Wing: Elk

CDC Elk Caddis, Dun
Hook: TMC 900BL, sizes 12-18
Thread: Gray, 6/0
Rib: Gray thread, 6/0
Body: Adams gray Superfine
Hackle: Dark dun CDC, palmered
Wing: Elk

CDC Elk Caddis, Olive
Hook: TMC 900BL, sizes 12-18
Thread: Olive, 6/0
Rib: Olive thread, 6/0
Body: Olive Superfine
Hackle: Dark dun CDC, palmered
Wing: Elk

CDC Emergent/Crippled Dun, Blue-Winged Olive
Hook: TMC 100, sizes 18-20
Thread: Olive, 6/0
Tail: Woodduck and olive-brown Z-Lon
Abdomen: Olive-brown Antron
Thorax: Olive Superfine
Wing: Dun Z-Lon and dun CDC

CDC Emergent/Crippled Dun, Pale Morning Dun
Hook: TMC 900BL, sizes 16-18
Thread: Yellow, 6/0
Tail: Wooduck mallard and yellow-brown Z-lon
Abdomen: Brownish-golden yellow Antron
Wing: Light blue dun CDC and dun Z-lon
Thorax: Yellow to yellow-olive Antron

CDC Emerger Parachute, Dark (Shane Stalcup)
Hook: TMC 2487, sizes 18-22
Thread: Black, 6/0
Wing: White poly yarn
Abdomen: Black goose or turkey biot
Thorax: Black Superfine
Hackle: Dark dun CDC

CDC Emerger Parachute, Light (Shane Stalcup)
Hook: TMC 2487, sizes 18-22
Thread: Gray, 6/0
Wing: White poly yarn
Abdomen: Gray goose or turkey biot
Thorax: Adams gray Superfine
Hackle: Dark dun CDC

CDC Extended Body, Blue-Winged Olive
(John Shaner)
Hook: TMC 2487, sizes 14-20
Thread: Olive, 6/0
Tail: Dun hackle, trimmed
Wing: Dark dun CDC

CDC Extended Body, Pale Morning Dun
(John Shaner)
Hook: TMC 2487, sizes 14-20
Thread: Yellow, 6/0
Tail: Light ginger hackle, trimmed
Wing: Pale yellow CDC

CDC Green Drake Parachute (Shane Stalcup)
Hook: TMC 2312, sizes 10-12
Thread: Olive, 6/0
Wing: Gray poly yarn
Tail: Dun Betts' Tailing Fibers
Rib: Wine or brown monofilament
Abdomen: Olive dubbing
Hackle: Natural gray CDC

CDC Little Yellow Stone (*Andy Burk*)
Hook: TMC 100, sizes 14-16
Thread: Yellow, 6/0
Body: Yellow deer or elk extended to form tail; red Pantone last quarter of body
Legs: Yellow CDC
Wing: Yellow and white CDC, one each, lying flat, and yellow Accent Flash

CDC Midge Adult, Black
Hook: TMC 100, sizes 20-22
Thread: Black, 6/0
Abdomen: Stripped black ostrich herl
Wing: Black Z-Lon and white CDC
Legs: Black CDC
Thorax: Black Superfine

CDC Midge Adult, Gray-Olive
Hook: TMC 100, sizes 20-22
Thread: Olive, 6/0
Abdomen: Gray goose biot
Wing: Dun Z-Lon, white CDC, and gray CDC
Legs: White Z-Lon and dark gray CDC
Thorax: Gray-olive Superfine

CDC Spent Caddis, Gray (*Shane Stalcup*)
Hook: TMC 101, sizes 14-18
Thread: Gray, 6/0
Underwing: Dun CDC
Overwing: Dun Z-lon
Abdomen: Gray goose biot
Thorax: Gray Superfine
Antennae: Dun Betts' Tailing Fibers

CDC Spent Caddis, Olive (*Shane Stalcup*)
Hook: TMC 101, sizes 14-18
Thread: Olive, 6/0
Underwing: Dun CDC
Overwing: Dun Z-Lon
Abdomen: Olive goose or turkey biot
Thorax: Gray-olive Superfine
Antennae: Dun Betts' Tailing Fibers

CDC Spent Caddis, Tan (*Shane Stalcup*)
Hook: TMC 101, sizes 14-18
Thread: Tan, 6/0
Underwing: Tan CDC
Overwing: Ginger Z-Lon
Abdomen: Tan goose or turkey biot
Thorax: Callibaetis Superfine
Antennae: Ginger Betts' Tailing Fibers

CDC Spinner, Black and White
Hook: TMC 101, sizes 20-22
Thread: Black, 6/0
Wing: White CDC
Tail: Dun Betts' Tailing Fibers
Body: Black Superfine

CDC Spinner, Red Quill
Hook: TMC 100, sizes 16-18
Thread: Black, 6/0
Wing: Dun and white CDC
Tail: Dun Betts' Tailing Fibers
Body: Stripped brown hackle stem

CDC Tailwater Dun, Blue-Winged Olive
Hook: TMC 100, sizes 16-20
Thread: Olive, 6/0
Tail: Dun Betts' Tailing Fibers
Abdomen: Olive Superfine
Wing: Dun Z-Lon and dun CDC
Thorax: Same as abdomen

CDC Tailwater Dun, Light Cahill
Hook: TMC 100, sizes 14-16
Thread: Cream, 6/0
Tail: Cream Betts' Tailing Fibers
Abdomen: Cahill Superfine
Wing: White Z-Lon and white CDC
Thorax: Same as abdomen

CDC Tailwater Dun, Pale Morning Dun
Hook: TMC 100, sizes 16-20
Thread: Yellow, 6/0
Tail: Dun Betts' Tailing Fibers
Abdomen: PMD Superfine
Wing: Cream Z-Lon and dun CDC
Thorax: Same as abdomen

Cicada (Clark Reid)
Hook: TMC 200R, sizes 8-10
Thread: Olive, 6/0 or 3/0
Eyes: Monofilament
Body: Olive deer
Wing: Shimazaki Fly Wing over pearl Krystal Flash
Collar: Olive deer
Head: Olive deer
Note: Originated in New Zealand.

Cicada (Shane Stalcup)
Hook: TMC 5212, size 8
Thread: Black, 6/0
Body: Black poly yarn
Wing: Calftail with pearl Accent Flash
Overwing: Orange deer
Head: Black deer, bullet style; tips form collar
Legs: Fine black rubber

Clear-Winged Spinner, Black (Gary LaFontaine)
Hook: TMC 5230, sizes 18-22
Thread: Black, 6/0
Wing: Clear Antron fibers
Tail: Two grizzly hackle fibers
Body: Black Antron or Superfine

Clear-Winged Spinner, Reddish Brown (Gary LaFontaine)
Hook: TMC 5230, sizes 14-18
Thread: Tan, 6/0
Wing: Clear Antron fibers
Tail: Two dun hackle fibers
Body: Reddish Brown Antron or Superfine

Colorado Green Drake
Hook: TMC 100, size 12
Thread: Dark olive, 6/0
Wing: Medium blue dun hen hackles
Tail: Dark moose
Rib: Dark olive floss
Body: Olive-brown rabbit
Hackle: Olive grizzly and brown

Comparadun, Baetis
Hook: TMC 100, size 16
Thread: Olive, 6/0
Tail: Pale blue dun hackle fibers, split
Body: Medium olive
Wing: Natural grayish-tan deer

Comparadun, Green Drake
Hook: TMC 100, size 10
Thread: Olive, 6/0
Tail: Pale blue dun hackle fibers, split
Body: Green olive
Wing: Natural dark deer

Comparadun, Hendrickson
- Hook: TMC 100, size 14
- Thread: Tan, 6/0
- Tail: Pale blue dun hackle fibers, split
- Body: Tan spectrumized dubbing
- Wing: Natural tan deer

Comparadun, Pale Morning Dun
- Hook: TMC 100, size 16
- Thread: Olive, 6/0
- Tail: Pale blue dun hackle fibers, split
- Body: Pale olive
- Wing: Natural grayish-tan deer

Comparadun, Sulphur
- Hook: TMC 100, size 14
- Thread: Cream, 6/0
- Tail: Pale blue dun hackle fibers, split
- Body: Pale yellow
- Wing: Bleached deer

Cranefly, Adult (Shane Stalcup)
- Hook: TMC 100 or 101, size 14
- Thread: White, 6/0
- Eyes: Burned monofilament
- Wing: Gray Z-Lon
- Legs: Brown Maxima monofilament, 4 lb.
- Abdomen: Closed cell foam, Pantone tan, pull over top of body from behind and secure at head
- Body: Tan dubbing

Cricket (Dave Whitlock)
- Hook: TMC 5263, sizes 6-14
- Thread: Black, 6/0
- Tail: Black deer and dark brown poly yarn
- Body: Dark brown poly yarn and palmered black hackle, trimmed
- Wing: Black turkey wing
- Legs: Black turkey wing quill section, trimmed and knotted
- Collar: Black deer
- Head: Black deer

Cripple, Pale Morning Dun (Mike Lawson)
- Hook: TMC 100, sizes 16-18
- Thread: Pale yellow, 6/0
- Shuck: Brown Z-Lon and brown Filoplume
- Rib: Fine red copper wire
- Abdomen: Natural ringneck pheasant tail
- Thorax: Pale morning dun Superfine
- Wing: Natural light gray deer
- Hackle: Natural light dun

Crowe Beetle
- Hook: TMC 100, sizes 14-18
- Thread: Black, 6/0
- Overbody: Black deer
- Body: Black thread (dub if you like)
- Legs: Black deer

Daddy Long Legs, Dry (Alice Conba)
- Hook: TMC 2302, size 10
- Thread: Pale yellow 6/0
- Rib: Golden pheasant center tail fibers
- Body: Natural raffia
- Legs: Pheasant tail fibers, knotted
- Hackle: Dark ginger
- Wing: Dark ginger hackle tips

Damsel, Adult (Shane Stalcup)
- Hook: TMC 100 or 101, size 14
- Thread: White, 6/0
- Eyes: Burned monofilament
- Wing: Gray Z-Lon
- Legs: Brown Maxima monofilament, 4 lb.
- Abdomen: Closed cell foam, Pantone blue, pull over top of body from behind and secure at head
- Body: Blue dubbing

Dave's Hopper (Dave Whitlock)
Hook: TMC 5263, sizes 4-14
Thread: Yellow, 6/0
Tail: Red deer and yellow poly yarn
Body: Yellow poly yarn, palmered with brown hackle, trimmed
Underwing: Pale yellow or gold deer
Overwing: Brown mottled oak turkey wing quill
Legs: Yellow grizzly hackle stem, trimmed and knotted
Head: Natural deer; tips form collar

Divided Hackle Mayfly, Callibaetis (Dan Byford)
Hook: TMC 100, sizes 14-18
Thread: Gray, 6/0
Wing: Woodduck mallard flank
Tail: Blue dun hackle fibers
Body: Adams Superfine
Hackle: Blue dun, trimmed flush on bottom

Divided Hackle Mayfly, Light Cahill (Dan Byford)
Hook: TMC 100, sizes 14-18
Thread: Cream, 6/0
Wing: Woodduck mallard flank
Tail: Cream hackle fibers
Body: Cream Superfine
Hackle: Cream, trimmed flush on bottom

Eastern Green Drake Dun (Dave Lucca)
Hook: TMC 100, size 8
Thread: Pale yellow, 6/0
Wing: Deer
Tail: Pale yellow elk
Abdomen: Pale yellow elk, extended
Hackle: Brown, grizzly, and olive

Eastern Green Drake Spinner (Dave Lucca)
Hook: TMC 100, sizes 8-10
Thread: White, 6/0
Body: Bleached elk, extended
Wing: Deer
Wingcase: Turkey
Thorax: Cream Superfine

Elk Hair Caddis, Black
Hook: TMC 100, sizes 10-18
Thread: Black, 6/0
Rib: Copper wire
Body: Black Antron or Superfine
Hackle: Black, palmered
Wing: Black or dark elk

Elk Hair Caddis, Brown
Hook: TMC 100, sizes 10-20
Thread: Brown, 6/0
Rib: Fine gold wire
Body: Brown Antron or Superfine
Hackle: Brown, palmered
Wing: Light tan elk

Elk Hair Caddis, Dun
Hook: TMC 100, sizes 10-18
Thread: Gray, 6/0
Rib: Fine copper wire
Hackle: Dun, palmered
Body: Adams gray Superfine
Wing: Light natural elk

Elk Hair Caddis, Olive
Hook: TMC 100, sizes 10-20
Thread: Olive, 6/0
Rib: Fine gold wire
Body: Olive Antron or Superfine
Hackle: Olive grizzly, palmered
Wing: Light elk

Elk Hair Caddis, Tan
Hook: TMC 100, sizes 10-18
Thread: Tan, 6/0
Rib: Fine gold wire
Body: Tan Antron or Superfine
Hackle: Ginger, palmered
Wing: Light elk

Elk Hair Caddis, Yellow
Hook: TMC 100, sizes 10-20
Thread: Yellow, 6/0
Rib: Fine gold wire
Body: Yellow Antron or Superfine
Hackle: Light ginger or pale yellow grizzly, palmered
Wing: Light elk

E-Z Caddis, Olive (Mike Lawson)
Hook: TMC 100, sizes 14-16
Thread: Olive, 8/0
Rib: Gold wire
Wing: White calf, parachute style
Body: Olive hare's ear, blended
Underwing: Olive Z-lon
Overwing: Brown partridge hackle tips, two, tied one on top of the other with dull sides down
Hackle: Grizzly, tied parachute style
Thorax: Same as body

E-Z Caddis, Tan (Mike Lawson)
Hook: TMC 100, sizes 14-16
Thread: Camel, 8/0
Rib: Gold wire
Wing: White calf, parachute style
Body: Blended natural hare's ear
Underwing: Tan Z-lon
Overwing: Brown partridge hackle tips, two, tied one on top of the other with dull sides down.
Hackle: Grizzly, tied parachute style
Thorax: Same as body

Elk Hair Hopper
Hook: TMC 5212, sizes 8-14
Thread: Black, 6/0
Tail: Red deer and yellow foam
Body: Yellow foam with palmered brown hackle, trimmed
Wing: Elk
Hackle: Grizzly and brown

Extended Body Mayfly, Blue-Winged Olive (Brett Smith)
Hook: TMC 2487, sizes 14-18
Thread: Olive, 6/0
Wing: Dark dun Z-Lon
Tail: Blue dun Betts' Tailing Fibers
Abdomen: Light olive Ultra Chenille
Hackle: Blue dun
Thorax: Blue-winged olive Superfine

Extended Body Mayfly, Pale Morning Dun (Brett Smith)
Hook: TMC 2487, sizes 16-18
Thread: Yellow, 6/0
Wing: Light dun Z-Lon
Tail: White Betts' Tailing Fibers
Abdomen: Yellow Ultra Chenille
Hackle: Blue dun
Thorax: Sulphur orange Superfine

Firefly (Harrison R. Steeves III)
Hook: TMC 5212, size 14
Thread: Black or orange, 6/0
Back: Black closed cell foam, 1/8 inch wide strip
Body: Peacock
Butt: Glow-in-the-dark yellow Kreinik braid
Wingcase: Black Kreinik 1/8 inch flat ribbon, over entire back
Wing: Black Kreinik flat ribbon, unraveled; pearl Krystal Flash

Fluttering Caddis, Black
Hook: TMC 100, sizes 16-18
Thread: Black, 6/0
Body: Black rabbit
Wing: Black mink tail guard hairs
Hackle: Dark rusty dun

Fluttering Caddis, Blue Dun
  Hook: TMC 100, sizes 14-18
  Thread: Black, 6/0
  Body: Gray muskrat
  Wing: Dun hackle fibers
  Hackle: Rusty dun

Fluttering Caddis, Ginger
  Hook: TMC 100, sizes 14-18
  Thread: Tan, 6/0
  Body: Ginger rabbit
  Wing: Ginger mink tail guard hairs
  Hackle: Ginger

Fluttering Stone
  Hook: TMC 5262, sizes 4-8
  Thread: Orange, 6/0
  Body: Orange Polypro yarn, woven
             and extended
  Wing: Natural light elk
  Overwing: Dark elk, short
  Hackle: Brown saddle
  Antennae: Stripped brown hackle stems,
             or mono

Flying Ant, Black
  Hook: TMC 100, sizes 10-16
  Thread: Black, 6/0
  Overbody: Black deer
  Body: Black Antron or Superfine
  Wing: Dark blue dun hackle tips tied
             delta wing style
  Hackle: Brown, furnace, blue dun, or
             black
  Head: Black Antron or Superfine,
             shaped and rounded into small
             mound

Flying Ant, Cinnamon
  Hook: TMC 100, sizes 14-18
  Thread: Cream, 6/0
  Body: Cinnamon Superfine
  Wing: Natural duck quill
  Legs: Blonde elk, two hairs on each
           side
  Hackle: Ginger
  Head: Cinnamon Superfine

Foam Ant (Gary LaFontaine)
  Hook: TMC 5230, size 10
  Thread: Black, 6/0
  Body: Foam, colored with permanent
           marker; form loop at front and
           back
  Hackle: Black

Foam Beetle (Mike Lawson)
  Hook: TMC 100, sizes 14-18
  Thread: Black, 3/0
  Back: Black foam
  Underbody: Peacock herl; optional
  Legs: Black deer

Foam Cricket, Black
  Hook: TMC 5212, size 8
  Thread: Black, 6/0
  Body: Black foam preformed bug body
  Legs: Black rubber and black Accent
             Flash
  Antennae: Black Accent Flash

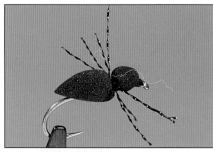

Foam Spider, Black
  Hook: TMC 100, size 12
  Thread: Black, 6/0
  Body: Black foam preformed bug body
  Legs: Black Accent Flash

Fur Ant, Black
> Hook: TMC 100, sizes 12-20
> Thread: Black, 6/0
> Abdomen: Black rabbit
> Hackle: Black
> Thorax: Black rabbit

Fur Ant, Cinnamon
> Hook: TMC 100, sizes 12-20
> Thread: Brown, 6/0
> Abdomen: Cinnamon rabbit
> Hackle: Brown
> Thorax: Cinnamon rabbit

Giant Caddis *(Ken Shimazaki)*
> Hook: TMC 109BL, size 9
> Thread: Dark olive, 6/0
> Rib: Tan thread, 6/0
> Body: Natural gray ostrich herl, palmered with grizzly hackle
> Underwing: Light brown CDC
> Overwing: Speckled brown Fly Wing No. 9
> Hackle: Brown partridge and white hen

Giant Sedge *(Nori Tashiro)*
> Hook: TMC 2312, size 6
> Thread: Cream, 6/0
> Body: Bleached deer or elk
> Rib: Same as tying thread
> Wing: Mottled grouse or pheasant
> Head: Clipped deer (leave some long as "hackle")
> Antennae: W00dduck mallard flank

Ginger Quill
> Hook: TMC 100, sizes 12-18
> Thread: Yellow, 6/0
> Wing: Natural gray duck quill
> Tail: Golden ginger hackle fibers
> Body: Stripped peacock quill
> Hackle: Golden ginger

Goddard Caddis
> Hook: TMC 100, sizes 10-18
> Thread: Tan, 6/0
> Body: Natural caribou, spun and trimmed to resemble a winged adult caddisfly
> Antennae: Brown hackle stems
> Hackle: Brown

Gray Caddis *(Ken Shimazaki)*
> Hook: TMC 902BL, sizes 12-14
> Thread: Dark olive, 6/0
> Body: Greenish olive dubbing
> Underwing: Dun CDC
> Overwing: Speckled gray Fly Wing No. 11
> Hackle: Grizzly

Gray Fox
> Hook: TMC 100, sizes 12-14
> Thread: Primrose, 6/0
> Wing: Mallard flank fibers
> Tail: Golden ginger hackle fibers
> Body: Light red fox
> Hackle: Golden ginger and light grizzly

Gray Fox Variant
> Hook: TMC 100, sizes 12-14
> Thread: Yellow, 6/0
> Tail: Golden ginger hackle fibers
> Body: Ginger hackle stem
> Hackle: Ginger or dark ginger, and grizzly

Gray Hackle, Peacock
- Hook: TMC 900BL or TMC 100, sizes 12-16
- Thread: Black, 6/0
- Tail: Red hackle fibers
- Rib: Fine gold wire
- Body: Peacock
- Hackle: Grizzly

Gray Hackle, Yellow
- Hook: TMC 100, sizes 12-16
- Thread: Black, 6/0
- Tail: Red hackle fibers
- Rib: Flat gold mylar
- Body: Yellow floss
- Hackle: Grizzly

Green Drake, Standard (Mike Lawson)
- Hook: TMC 5212, size 12
- Thread: Olive, 6/0
- Wing: Dark gray elk
- Tail: Black moose
- Rib: Yellow floss
- Body: Olive Superfine
- Hackle: Yellow-chartreuse grizzly

Green Paradrake (Mike Lawson)
- Hook: TMC 100, sizes 10-12
- Thread: Yellow, 3/0
- Wing: Dark gray elk
- Tail: Black moose tail fibers
- Body: Olive elk
- Hackle: Yellow-chartreuse grizzly, parachute style

Griffith's Gnat
- Hook: TMC 101, sizes 14-22
- Thread: Olive, 6/0
- Rib: Fine gold wire
- Body: Peacock herl
- Hackle: Grizzly hackle, palmered

Gulper Special, Brown
- Hook: TMC 100, sizes 14-18
- Thread: Dark brown, 6/0
- Wing: White poly yarn
- Tail: Natural grizzly or bronze blue dun hackle fibers
- Body: Dark brown poly dubbing
- Hackle: Grizzly

Gulper Special, Olive
- Hook: TMC 100, sizes 14-20
- Thread: Black, 6/0
- Wing: White poly yarn
- Tail: Grizzly hackle fibers
- Body: Olive rabbit
- Hackle: Grizzly

Gulper Special, Tan
- Hook: TMC 100, sizes 14-18
- Thread: Black, 6/0
- Wing: White poly yarn
- Tail: Grizzly hackle fibers
- Body: Tan rabbit
- Hackle: Grizzly

H & L Variant
- Hook: TMC 100, sizes 10-18
- Thread: Black, 6/0
- Wing: White calf
- Rib: Fine gold wire, reverse wrapped
- Tail: White calf
- Body: Rear half, stripped peacock herl; front half, peacock herl
- Hackle: Brown

Hairwing Caddis, Light Brown
  Hook: TMC 100, sizes 14-18
  Thread: Tan, 6/0
  Body: Light tan rabbit
  Wing: Light deer or elk
  Hackle: Cream

Hairwing Caddis, Light Olive
  Hook: TMC 100, sizes 14-18
  Thread: Olive, 6/0
  Body: Light olive rabbit
  Wing: Light deer or elk
  Hackle: Ginger

Hairwing Dun, Adams
  Hook: TMC 100, sizes 14-16
  Thread: Gray, 6/0
  Tail: Brown hackle fibers, split
  Body: Gray Antron or muskrat
  Hackle: Brown and grizzly mixed, tied
           thorax style in center of body,
           trimmed on underside
  Wing: Medium gray elk

Hairwing Dun, Blue-Winged Olive
  Hook: TMC 100, sizes 16-20
  Thread: Olive, 6/0
  Tail: Dark blue dun hackle fibers,
           split
  Body: Olive rabbit
  Hackle: Dark blue dun, clipped on the
           bottom
  Wing: Dyed dark gray deer

Hairwing Dun, Colorado Green Drake
  Hook: TMC 5212, sizes 10-12
  Thread: Olive, 6/0
  Tail: Fine black moose, split
  Rib: Brown floss
  Body: Gray olive Superfine
  Hackle: Grizzly and dyed olive grizzly
  Wing: Deer

Hairwing Dun, Green Drake
  Hook: TMC 100, sizes 10-12
  Thread: Olive, 6/0
  Tail: Olive grizzly hackle fibers,
           split
  Rib: Bright olive floss
  Body: Olive rabbit
  Hackle: Olive grizzly, clipped on the
           bottom
  Wing: Black moose body

Hairwing Dun, Pale Morning Dun
  Hook: TMC 100, sizes 16-20
  Thread: Pale yellow, 6/0
  Tail: Light ginger hackle fibers, split
  Body: Pale yellow poly
  Hackle: Ginger, clipped on bottom
  Wing: Natural light elk

Hairwing Dun, Trico
  Hook: TMC 100, sizes 18-20
  Thread: Black, 6/0
  Tail: Dun hackle fibers
  Body: Black Superfine
  Hackle: Black
  Wing: Bleached deer or elk

Hairwing No-Hackle, Gray Yellow
  Hook: TMC 100, sizes 16-20
  Thread: Yellow, 6/0
  Wing: Fine blue dun elk
  Tail: Medium blue dun hackle
           fibers, split
  Body: Sulphur yellow Antron or
           Superfine

Hairwing No Hackle, Slate Gray
Hook: TMC 100, sizes 14-18
Thread: Gray, 6/0
Wing: Natural light deer
Tail: Dark dun hackle fibers
Body: Slate gray poly

Hairwing No-Hackle, Slate Olive
Hook: TMC 100, sizes 14-20
Thread: Olive, 6/0
Wing: Deer
Tail: Dun hackle fibers
Body: Olive Superfine

Hairwing No-Hackle, Slate Tan
Hook: TMC 100, sizes 16-20
Thread: Coffee, 6/0
Wing: Deer
Tail: Dun hackle fibers
Body: Tan Superfine

Hairwing No-Hackle, Trico
Hook: TMC 100, sizes 20-22
Thread: Black, 6/0
Wing: Bleached deer
Tail: Dun hackle fibers
Body: Black Superfine

Hatching Midge (Randall Kaufmann)
Hook: TMC 900BL, sizes 12-20
Thread: Black, 6/0
Tail: Dark dun CDC
Rib: White silk thread
Abdomen: Black thread
Wingcase: Dark dun CDC
Hackle: Natural grizzly
Thorax: Peacock herl
Antennae: Same as wingcase
Note: Other colors to suit.

Hatching Mayfly, PMD (Randall Kaufmann)
Hook: TMC 900BL, sizes 12-20
Thread: Yellow, 6/0
Tail: Light dun CDC
Rib: White silk thread
Abdomen: Yellow thread
Wingcase: Light dun CDC
Hackle: Natural grizzly
Thorax: Peacock herl
Antennae: Same as wingcase

Hemingway Caddis (Mike Lawson)
Hook: TMC 100, sizes 12-18
Thread: Olive, 6/0
Body: Olive Superfine palmered with medium dun hackle
Wing: Mallard quill segments
Underwing: Woodduck mallard flank
Thorax: Peacock
Hackle: Medium dun

Hendrickson, Dark
Hook: TMC 100, sizes 12-18
Thread: Gray, 6/0
Wing: Woodduck mallard flank
Tail: Dark blue dun hackle fibers
Body: Dark gray muskrat
Hackle: Dark blue dun

Hendrickson, Light
Hook: TMC 100, sizes 12-16
Thread: Tan, 6/0
Wing: Woodduck mallard flank
Tail: Medium blue dun hackle fibers
Body: Light fox belly
Hackle: Medium blue dun

Henryville Special
Hook: TMC 100, sizes 12-18
Thread: Black, 6/0
Rib: Fine gold wire
Body: Olive rabbit
Hackle: Grizzly, undersized, palmered
Underwing: Woodduck mallard flank
Overwing: Natural gray duck quill, tent style
Hackle: Dark ginger

Henry's Fork Cricket (Mike Lawson)
Hook: TMC 5212, sizes 10-14
Thread: Black, 3/0
Body: Dark brown elk, reverse style, extended
Underwing: Brown elk
Overwing: Black hen saddle feather coated with Dave's Flexament
Head: Black elk, tied bullet head style; tips form collar
Legs: Black rubber, knotted

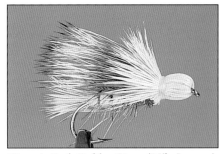

Henry's Fork Golden Stone (Mike Lawson)
Hook: TMC 5262, sizes 8-10
Thread: Tan, 3/0
Tail: Dark tan elk
Hackle: Brown, palmered and trimmed
Body: Yellow-tan elk
Wing: Light tan elk
Head: Dark tan elk, tied bullet head style

Henry's Fork Hopper (Mike Lawson)
Hook: TMC 5212, sizes 6-14
Thread: Yellow, 3/0
Body: Natural cream elk rump, reverse style, extended
Underwing: Yellow elk
Overwing: Mottled brown hen saddle feather coated with Dave's Flexament
Head: Natural gray elk, tied bullet head style
Legs: Light yellow rubber

Henry's Fork Salmonfly (Mike Lawson)
Hook: TMC 5262, sizes 4-6
Thread: Fluorescent fire orange, 6/0
Tail: Black moose
Hackle: Brown, palmered and trimmed
Body: Brownish orange elk
Wing: Dark gray elk
Head: Black elk tied bullet head style

Henry's Fork Yellow Sally (Mike Lawson)
Hook: TMC 5212, sizes 14-16
Thread: Yellow, 6/0
Tail: Medium dun hackle fibers
Abdomen: Light yellow-olive dubbing
Wing: Medium gray elk
Hackle: Medium dun, clipped top and bottom
Thorax: Same as abdomen

Henspinner, Black and White (Mike Lawson)
Hook: TMC 100 or 5210, sizes 18-22
Thread: Black, 6/0
Wing: White hen hackle tips, tied spent
Tail: Medium dun hackle fibers, split
Body: Black Superfine

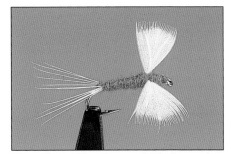

Henspinner, Dun Brown (Mike Lawson)
Hook: TMC 100 or 5210, sizes 14-18
Thread: Brown, 6/0
Wing: Light dun hen hackle tips, tied spent
Tail: Medium dun hackle fibers, split
Body: Rusty brown Superfine

Henspinner, Dun Cream (Mike Lawson)
Hook: TMC 100 or 5210, sizes 14-18
Thread: Cream, 6/0
Wing: Light dun hen hackle tips, tied spent
Tail: Medium dun hackle fibers, split
Body: Cream brown Superfine

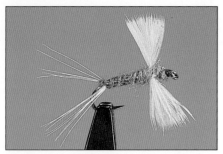

Henspinner, Slate Olive *(Mike Lawson)*
Hook: TMC 100 or 5210, sizes 16-20
Thread: Olive, 6/0
Wing: Light dun hen hackle tips, tied spent
Tail: Medium dun hackle fibers, split
Body: Olive Superfine

Henspinner, White and Yellow *(Mike Lawson)*
Hook: TMC 100 or 5210, sizes 18-20
Thread: Pale olive, 6/0
Wing: Light dun hen hackle tips, tied spent
Tail: Medium dun hackle fibers, split
Body: Pale yellow olive Superfine

Hexagenia Limbata, Dun *(Dave Lucca)*
Hook: TMC 5212, size 6
Thread: Yellow, 6/0
Wing: Natural gray elk
Tail: Natural gray (2) and dyed yellow (1) elk hair fibers
Rib: Yellow tying thread, crisscrossed over body
Body: Yellow elk, extended beyond hook shank 3/8"
Hackle: Light ginger

Hexagenia Spinner *(Dave Lucca)*
Hook: TMC 100, size 8
Thread: Pale yellow, 6/0
Body: Pale yellow elk, extended
Wing: Pale yellow elk and yellow Krystal Flash
Wingcase: Yellow foam
Thorax: Pale yellow Superfine

Humpy, Adams
Hook: TMC 100, sizes 12-16
Thread: Gray, 6/0
Wing: Deer
Tail: Dark moose
Back: Same as tail
Body: Gray thread
Hackle: Brown and grizzly

Humpy, Black
Hook: TMC 100, sizes 10-16
Thread: Black, 6/0
Wing: Dark elk
Tail: Dark moose
Back: Dark moose
Body: Black thread
Hackle: Natural or dyed black

Humpy, Blonde
Hook: TMC 100, sizes 10-16
Thread: Yellow, 6/0
Wing: Bleached light elk
Tail: Bleached light elk
Back: Bleached light elk
Body: Yellow thread
Hackle: Ginger

Humpy, Green
Hook: TMC 100, sizes 10-18
Thread: Fluorescent green, 6/0
Wing: Elk
Tail: Moose
Back: Moose
Body: Fluorescent green thread
Hackle: Brown

Humpy, Olive
Hook: TMC 100, sizes 12-16
Thread: Olive, 3/0
Wing: Deer
Tail: Deer
Back: Deer
Body: Olive thread
Hackle: Medium to dark dun

Humpy, Orange
Hook:	TMC 100, sizes 10-16
Thread:	Fluorescent fire orange, 6/0
Wing:	Elk
Tail:	Moose
Back:	Moose
Body:	Fluorescent fire orange thread
Hackle:	Brown or furnace

Humpy, Red
Hook:	TMC 100, sizes 10-20
Thread:	Bright red, 6/0
Wing:	Elk
Tail:	Elk
Back:	Elk
Body:	Bright red thread
Hackle:	Badger

Humpy, Royal
Hook:	TMC 100, sizes 10-18
Thread:	Red, 6/0
Wing:	White calf
Tail:	Dark moose
Back:	Dark moose
Body:	Red thread
Hackle:	Brown

Humpy, Royal Green
Hook:	TMC 100, sizes 10-16
Thread:	Fluorescent green, 6/0, or single strand floss
Wing:	White calf
Tail:	Moose
Back:	Moose
Body:	Fluorescent green thread
Hackle:	Brown—or try Adams

Humpy, Royal Yellow
Hook:	TMC 100, sizes 10-18
Thread:	Bright yellow, 6/0
Wing:	White calf
Tail:	Light elk
Back:	Light elk
Body:	Bright yellow thread
Hackle:	Brown

Humpy, Yellow
Hook:	TMC 100, sizes 8-20
Thread:	Bright yellow, 6/0
Wing:	Elk
Tail:	Elk
Back:	Elk
Body:	Bright yellow thread
Hackle:	Brown and grizzly

Improved Golden Stone
Hook:	TMC 200R, sizes 6-10
Thread:	Pale yellow, 6/0
Tail:	Bleached deer
Rib:	Same as thread
Body:	Cream wool yarn
Hackle:	Light ginger, palmered
Wing:	Natural light elk
Hackle:	Light ginger

Improved Sofa Pillow
Hook:	TMC 200R, sizes 4-8
Thread:	Black or orange, 6/0
Tail:	Elk
Rib:	Orange thread or fine gold wire
Body:	Burnt orange yarn or dubbing
Hackle:	Brown or furnace, palmered
Wing:	Elk
Hackle:	Brown

Inchworm (Dave Whitlock)
Hook:	TMC 100, size 12
Thread:	Yellow, 6/0
Abdomen:	Green elk, tied bullet or reverse style and extended
Indicator:	Fluorescent orange egg yarn

Irresistible, Adams
- Hook: TMC 100, sizes 10-16
- Thread: Black, 6/0
- Tail: Moose
- Body: Caribou
- Wing: Grizzly hen hackle tips
- Hackle: Brown and grizzly

Irresistible, Rat Face
- Hook: TMC 100, sizes 12-16
- Thread: Tan, 6/0
- Tail: Yellow elk
- Body: Caribou
- Wing: Grizzly hen hackle tips
- Hackle: Grizzly and brown

Irresistible, Wulff
- Hook: TMC 100, sizes 10-16
- Thread: Black, 6/0
- Tail: Moose
- Body: Caribou
- Wing: White calf
- Hackle: Brown

Jacklin's Hopper (Bob Jacklin)
- Hook: TMC 5212, sizes 8-12
- Thread: Yellow, 6/0
- Tail: Red deer
- Butt: Fluorescent green fuzzy wool
- Body: Fluorescent green fuzzy wool, with palmered brown hackle, trimmed short
- Wing: Natural gray goose quill
- Head: Natural light elk, bullet style; tips form collar

Japanese Beetle (Dave Whitlock)
- Hook: TMC 100, sizes 12-14
- Thread: Yellow, 6/0
- Back: Light gold deer
- Body: Flat gold tinsel
- Antennae: Light gold deer
- Thorax: Light gold deer
- Legs: Light gold deer
- Indicator: Fluorescent orange deer
- Markings: Black Pantone pen

Joe's Hopper
- Hook: TMC 5212, sizes 6-14
- Thread: Yellow, 6/0
- Tail: Red hackle fibers with loop of yellow poly yarn on top
- Body: Yellow poly yarn, dubbing or foam, palmered with brown hackle, trimmed closely on sides and short top and bottom
- Wing: Mottled turkey wing quills, treated with Flexament
- Hackle: Brown and grizzly

King's River Caddis
- Hook: TMC 100, sizes 12-18
- Thread: Brown, 6/0
- Body: Tannish-brown rabbit
- Wing: Mottled turkey wing quill, "V" (tent style)
- Hackle: Brown

Lempke's Hopper (Bing Lempke)
- Hook: TMC 900 BL, sizes 8 and 12
- Thread: Tan, 6/0
- Rib: Fine gold mylar tinsel
- Body: Tan dubbing, extended style
- Rear Legs: Knotted ringneck pheasant tail fibers
- Wing: Woodduck mallard overwing; orange calf underwing
- Front Legs: Natural elk
- Head: Spun antelope

Little Yellow Stone, Female
- Hook: TMC 100, sizes 12-16
- Thread: Yellow, 6/0
- Tail: Bright yellow deer or elk
- Butt: Fluorescent fire orange thread or Antron
- Rib: Fine gold wire
- Body: Yellow poly dubbing palmered with light dun or ginger hackle
- Wing: Bright yellow deer or elk tied downwing style and trimmed
- Hackle: Light dun or ginger

Loop Wing Caddis, Dun (Nori Tashiro)
Hook: TMC 5210, sizes 14-16
Thread: Gray, 6/0
Body: Dyed gray deer
Rib: Same as tying thread
Wing: Dun hackle (butt end)
Hackle: Light to medium dun

Loop Wing Caddis, Ginger (Nori Tashiro)
Hook: TMC 5210, sizes 12-14
Thread: Olive, 6/0
Body: Dyed olive deer
Rib: Same as tying thread
Wing: Dun hackle (butt end)
Antennae: Woodduck mallard flank
Hackle: Ginger

Madam X
Hook: TMC 5263, sizes 6-10
Thread: Yellow Kevlar or single strand nylon floss
Tail: Deer
Body: Yellow thread
Head: Deer tied reverse style, natural ends forming wing
Legs: White round rubber adjusted to an "X" pattern

March Brown, American
Hook: TMC 100, sizes 12-16
Thread: Orange, 6/0
Wing: Woodduck mallard flank
Tail: Dark brown hackle fibers
Rib: Yellow thread or floss
Body: Brown rabbit
Hackle: Brown and grizzly

March Brown, Flick
Hook: TMC 100, sizes 12-14
Thread: Tan, 6/0
Wing: Woodduck mallard flank
Tail: Dark ginger hackle fibers
Body: Tan rabbit or poly dubbing
Hackle: Brown and grizzly

Mayfly Cripple, Callibaetis
Hook: TMC 100, sizes 14-18
Thread: Gray, 6/0
Tail: Gray ostrich plumes or marabou
Abdomen: Gray ostrich
Thorax: Gray Antron
Wing: Grayish-tan deer
Legs: Grizzly hackle

Mayfly Cripple, Green Drake
Hook: TMC 100, sizes 10-12
Thread: Olive or tan, 6/0
Tail: Olive ostrich plumes or marabou
Abdomen: Olive ostrich
Thorax: Dark olive Antron
Wing: Tan deer
Legs: Olive grizzly hackle

Mayfly Cripple, Limestone
Hook: TMC 100, size to match natural
Thread: Tan, 6/0
Tail: Tan or olive-brown marabou
Abdomen: Stripped hackle stem, light brown or color to match natural
Thorax: Tan Superfine or color to match natural
Wing: Light tan deer or elk or color to match natural
Legs: Light ginger dun hackle, or color to match natural

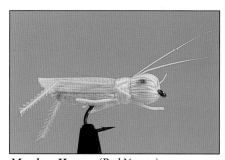

Meadow Hopper (Rod Yerger)
Hook: TMC 100, size 16
Thread: White, 6/0
Underbody: Shaped balsa wood cylinder
Body: Chartreuse deer
Wing: White turkey wing quill dyed chartreuse, lacquer and trim
Rear legs: Chartreuse hackle stem, trimmed close to quill and bent
Front Legs: Chartreuse coarse deer
Antennae: Chartreuse fine deer
Eyes: Red lacquer

Melon Quill *(A.K. Best)*
Hook: TMC 100, sizes 14-18
Thread: Pale yellow, 6/0
Wing: Dyed medium dun hen hackle tips
Tail: Medium dun hackle fibers
Body: One cream and one pink stripped neck hackle stem
Hackle: Medium ginger

Midge, Adams
Hook: TMC 101, sizes 20-28
Thread: Gray, 6/0
Tail: Brown and grizzly hackle fibers
Body: Muskrat or dark dun Superfine
Hackle: Brown and grizzly

Midge, Black
Hook: TMC 101, sizes 20-26
Thread: Black, 8/0
Tail: Black hackle fibers
Body: Black Superfine
Hackle: Black

Midge, Blue Dun
Hook: TMC 101, sizes 20-26
Thread: Black, 8/0
Tail: Dun hackle fibers
Body: Adams gray Superfine
Hackle: Blue dun

Midge, Brown
Hook: TMC 101, sizes 20-28
Thread: Gray, 6/0
Tail: Brown hackle fibers
Body: Medium brown Superfine
Hackle: Brown

Midge, Cream
Hook: TMC 101, sizes 20-28
Thread: Cream, 6/0
Tail: Dark cream hackle fibers
Body: Cream Superfine
Hackle: Dark cream

Midge, Grizzly
Hook: TMC 100 or 101, sizes 20-26
Thread: Gray, 8/0
Tail: Grizzly hackle fibers
Body: Adams gray Superfine
Hackle: Grizzly

Midge, Olive
Hook: TMC 100 or 101, sizes 20-26
Thread: Olive, 8/0
Tail: Olive hackle fibers
Body: Olive Superfine
Hackle: Olive

Mosquito
Hook: TMC 100, sizes 10-20
Thread: Black, 6/0
Tail: Grizzly hackle fibers
Wing: Grizzly hackle tips
Body: One light and one dark strand of moose mane, wound together
Hackle: Grizzly

Mr. Rapidan (Harry Murray)
Hook: TMC 100, sizes 12-18
Thread: Tan or olive, 6/0
Wing: Yellow calf tail
Tail: Dark moose
Body: Yellowish tan dubbing
Hackle: Brown and grizzly

No-Hackle, Gray Olive (Mike Lawson)
Hook: TMC 100 or 5210, sizes 20-24
Thread: Pale olive, 6/0
Tail: Light dun hackle fibers
Body: Blue wing olive Superfine
Wing: Medium gray mallard quill

No-Hackle, Gray Yellow (Mike Lawson)
Hook: TMC 100 or 5210, sizes 16-20
Thread: Pale olive, 6/0
Tail: Light dun hackle fibers
Body: Pale morning dun Superfine
Wing: Medium gray mallard quill

No-Hackle, Pink Cahill (Mike Lawson)
Hook: TMC 100 or 5210, sizes 16-20
Thread: Cream, 6/0
Tail: Light dun hackle fibers
Body: Hendrickson pink Superfine
Wing: Medium gray mallard quill

No-Hackle, Slate Gray (Mike Lawson)
Hook: TMC 100 or 5210, sizes 18-22
Thread: Gray, 6/0
Tail: Dark dun hackle fibers
Body: Gray Superfine
Wing: Dark gray mallard quill

No-Hackle, Slate Olive (Mike Lawson)
Hook: TMC 100 or 5210, sizes 14-18
Thread: Dark olive, 6/0
Tail: Dark dun hackle fibers
Body: Gray Superfine
Wing: Dark gray mallard quill

No-Hackle, Slate Tan (Mike Lawson)
Hook: TMC 100 or 5210, sizes 14-18
Thread: Dark brown, 6/0
Tail: Dark dun hackle fibers
Body: Tan Superfine
Wing: Dark gray mallard quill

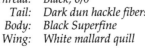

No-Hackle, White Black (Mike Lawson)
Hook: TMC 100 or TMC 5210, sizes 20-24
Thread: Black, 6/0
Tail: Dark dun hackle fibers
Body: Black Superfine
Wing: White mallard quill

Olive Dun, Extended Body (Bing Lempke)
Hook: TMC 100, size 16
Thread: Black, 6/0
Tail: Light dun tailing fibers, three
Rib: Yellow 3/0 thread
Body: Gray olive Superfine
Wing: Dun goose primary fibers
Hackle: Ginger

Olive Dun Quill *(A.K. Best)*
Hook:	TMC 100, sizes 16-22
Thread:	Olive, 6/0
Wing:	Blue dun hen hackle tips
Tail:	Medium dun hackle fibers
Body:	Olive hackle stem
Hackle:	Blue dun

Ovipositing Caddis, Black *(Brett Smith)*
Hook:	TMC 2457, sizes 14-18
Thread:	Olive, 6/0
Abdomen:	Black; ultra chenille, size 14; micro chenille, size 16; mini chenille, size 18
Abdomen Taper:	Black Superfine
Wing:	Black deer mixed with black Salmo-Web
Head:	Black Superfine
Egg:	Green-gold Tulip Pearl brand fabric paint

Pale Evening Dun
Hook:	TMC 100, sizes 14-20
Thread:	Cream, 6/0
Wing:	Natural gray duck quill
Tail:	Light blue dun hackle fibers
Body:	Pale yellow rabbit
Hackle:	Medium blue dun

Pale Morning Dun *(Mike Lawson)*
Hook:	TMC 100 or 5210, sizes 14-20
Thread:	Pale olive, 6/0
Wing:	Medium dun hackle tips
Tail:	Light dun hackle fibers
Body:	Pale yellow olive Superfine
Hackle:	Light dun

Pale Morning Dun, Extended Body *(Bing Lempke)*
Hook:	TMC 100, size 18
Thread:	Pale yellow, 6/0
Tail:	Clear tailing fibers, three
Body:	Pale yellow poly dubbing, extended
Wing:	Natural gray duck quill
Hackle:	Light ginger hackle, clipped on bottom

Parachute, Adams
Hook:	TMC 100, sizes 12-22
Thread:	Gray, 6/0
Wing:	White calf
Tail:	Grizzly hackle fibers
Body:	Gray muskrat
Hackle:	Brown and grizzly

Parachute Ant *(Ed Schroeder)*
Hook:	TMC 900 BL, sizes 14-20
Thread:	Black, 6/0
Wing:	White calf body
Abdomen:	Black rabbit or Antron
Hackle:	Grizzly
Head:	Black rabbit or Antron

Parachute, Baetis
Hook:	TMC 100, sizes 16-22
Thread:	Olive, 6/0
Wing:	Mallard fibers
Tail:	Blue dun tailing fibers, split
Body:	Olive to olive-brown Antron or Superfine
Hackle:	Olive grizzly or natural grizzly

Parachute, Black
Hook:	TMC 100, sizes 14-18
Thread:	Black, 6/0
Wing:	White calf
Tail:	Black hackle fibers
Body:	Black Antron or Superfine
Hackle:	Black

Parachute, Caddis *(Ed Schroeder)*
  Hook: TMC 102Y, sizes 11-19
  Thread: Cream, 6/0
  Wing: White calf, parachute style
  Body: Blended hare's ear
  Wing: Mottled oak turkey quill, tent
          style
  Hackle: Grizzly

Parachute, Cahill
  Hook: TMC 100, sizes 12-20
  Thread: Yellow, 6/0
  Wing: White calf
  Tail: Light ginger or cream hackle
          fibers
  Body: Cream Antron or Superfine
  Hackle: Light ginger or cream

Parachute, Coachman
  Hook: TMC 100, sizes 14-18
  Thread: Black, 6/0
  Wing: White calf
  Tail: White calf
  Rib: Gold wire
  Body: Peacock
  Hackle: Brown

Parachute Damsel, Blue
  Hook: TMC 5212, size 12
  Thread: Black 6/0
  Rib: Black thread
  Body: Medium blue bucktail, tied
          extended
  Head: Medium blue bucktail, butts
          from wingcase
  Hackle: Light dun, wound around base
          of wingcase
  Wingcase: Medium blue bucktail, twisted

Parachute Damsel, Dark Olive
  Hook: TMC 5212, size 12
  Thread: Black, 6/0
  Rib: Black thread
  Body: Olive bucktail, tied extended
  Head: Olive bucktail, butts from
          wingcase
  Hackle: Dark blue dun, wound around
          base of wingcase
  Wingcase: Olive bucktail, twisted

Parachute Damsel, Tan
  Hook: TMC 5212, size 12
  Thread: Black, 6/0
  Rib: Tying thread
  Body: Tan deer or bucktail
  Head: Tan deer or bucktail
  Hackle: White
  Wingcase: Tan deer or bucktail, twisted

Parachute, Dun
  Hook: TMC 100, sizes 12-22
  Thread: Gray, 6/0
  Wing: White calf
  Tail: Dun hackle fibers
  Body: Adams gray Superfine
  Hackle: Dun

Parachute, Emergent Caddis *(Ed Schroeder)*
  Hook: TMC 900BL, sizes 12-18
  Thread: Gray, 6/0
  Wing: White calf
  Tail: Deer
  Rib: Monofilament, 7X
  Body: Gray ostrich herl
  Hackle: Grizzly

Parachute, Golden Stone *(Ed Schroeder)*
  Hook: TMC 900BL, sizes 12-16
  Thread: Yellow, 6/0
  Wing: White calf, parachute style
  Body: Golden yellow Antron
  Wing: Yellow oak turkey
  Hackle: Grizzly

Parachute, Hare's Ear (Ed Schroeder)
- Hook: TMC 102Y, sizes 11-19
- Thread: Cream, 6/0
- Wing: White calf
- Tail: Deer
- Body: Blended hare's ear
- Hackle: Grizzly

Parachute Hopper (Ed Schroeder)
- Hook: TMC 5212, sizes 8-14
- Thread: Cream, 6/0
- Parachute Wing: White calf body
- Abdomen: Golden-tan Antron
- Tent Wing: Mottled oak turkey quill
- Legs: Pheasant tail fibers, knotted
- Hackle: Grizzly

Parachute, Light Orange
- Hook: TMC 100, sizes 16-18
- Thread: Rust, 6/0
- Wing: White calf
- Tail: Dark ginger hackle fibers
- Body: Light orange rabbit
- Hackle: Ginger

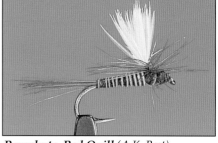

Parachute, Olive Hare's Ear (Ed Schroeder)
- Hook: TMC 102Y, sizes 11-19
- Thread: Olive, 6/0
- Wing: White calf
- Tail: Deer
- Rib: Yellow 3/0 monocord
- Body: Blended olive hare's ear
- Hackle: Grizzly

Parachute, Olive Quill (A.K. Best)
- Hook: TMC 100, sizes 16-20
- Thread: Light olive, 6/0
- Tail: Dun hackle fibers
- Body: Green hackle stem
- Wing Post: White turkey
- Hackle: Medium dun

Parachute, Red Quill (A.K. Best)
- Hook: TMC 100, sizes 16-18
- Thread: Brown, 8/0
- Tail: Brown hackle fibers
- Body: Light brown hackle stem
- Wing: Medium dun hen hackle tips
- Hackle: Brown

Parachute, Royal Coachman
- Hook: TMC 100, sizes 12-18
- Thread: Black, 6/0
- Wing: White calf
- Tail: Golden pheasant tippet or brown hackle fibers
- Body: Three-part royal body; peacock, red floss, and peacock
- Hackle: Brown or Coachman brown

Parachute, Trico (A.K. Best)
- Hook: TMC 100 or 101, sizes 18-22
- Thread: White to thorax, black for thorax forward, 8/0
- Tail: White hackle fibers
- Body: Pale green rooster hackle stem
- Thorax: Black dubbing
- Wing: White turkey
- Hackle: Black

Paranymph, Callibaetis
- Hook: TMC 100, sizes 14-18
- Thread: Gray, 6/0
- Tail: Mottled hen hackle fibers
- Abdomen: Adams gray Superfine
- Rib: Fine copper wire
- Wingcase: Deer; butt ends form wing
- Thorax: Same as abdomen
- Hackle: Grizzly

Peacock Caddis
Hook: TMC 100, sizes 12-18
Thread: Black, 6/0
Body: Peacock herl
Wing: Tan elk
Hackle: Brown and grizzly

Pink Cahill
Hook: TMC 100, sizes 14-20
Thread: Tan, 6/0
Wing: Woodduck mallard flank
Tail: Pale ginger hackle fibers
Body: Tannish pink poly
Hackle: Pale ginger

Pocket Water (Cal Bird)
Hook: TMC 100, sizes 12-16
Thread: Black, 6/0
Wing: White calf
Tail: Golden pheasant tippets
Body: Claret yarn
Hackle: Furnace or brown

Quill Gordon
Hook: TMC 100, sizes 12-18
Thread: Black, 6/0
Wing: Woodduck mallard flank
Tail: Dark blue dun hackle fibers
Body: Stripped peacock quill, lacquered
Hackle: Dark blue dun

Red Quill
Hook: TMC 100, sizes 12-20
Thread: Gray, 6/0
Wing: Woodduck mallard flank
Tail: Medium bronze dun hackle fibers
Body: Coachman brown hackle stem
Hackle: Medium bronze dun

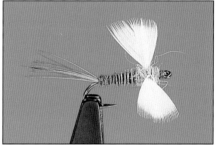

Red Quill Spinner (A. K. Best)
Hook: TMC 100, sizes 14-18
Thread: Tan, 6/0
Tail: Ginger or light brown hackle fibers
Body: Light brown or dark ginger hackle stem
Wings: White hen hackle tips
Thorax: Tan Superfine

Renegade
Hook: TMC 100, sizes 10-18
Thread: Black, 6/0
Rib: Fine gold wire
Tag: Gold mylar tinsel
Rear Hackle: Brown
Body: Peacock herl
Front Hackle: White

Rio Grande King
Hook: TMC 100, sizes 12-16
Thread: Brown, 6/0
Wing: White duck quill
Tail: Golden pheasant tippet fibers
Body: Black chenille or dubbing
Hackle: Brown

Royal Coachman
Hook: TMC 100, sizes 10-18
Thread: Black, 6/0
Tail: Golden pheasant tippet
Wing: White duck quill
Body: Peacock, red floss, and peacock
Hackle: Coachman brown

RS2 Emerger *(Bill Fitzsimmons)*
  Hook: TMC 101, sizes 16-20
  Thread: Gray, 8/0
  Wing: Dark dun CDC
  Tail: Muskrat guard hairs
  Body: Muskrat

Salmon Fly *(Bing Lempke)*
  Hook: TMC 5263, sizes 4-6
  Thread: Black, 6/0
  Tail: Dark elk tied along entire
            shank to form level underbody
  Rib: Fluorescent fire orange SSNF
  Body: Cassette tape, lacquered after
            floss is in place
  Wing: Light elk in center; dark elk
            along outside
  Hackle: Grizzly and brown, trimmed
            even with body on underside

Seducer, Black *(Randall Kaufmann)*
  Hook: TMC 200R, sizes 8-18
  Thread: Fluorescent fire orange, 6/0
  Tail: Black elk
  Rib: Fine copper wire
  Abdomen: Black Antron
  Hackle: Dark blue dun
  Wing: Black and pearl Krystal Flash
            under Fly Wing, under black
            elk
  Hackle: Grizzly
  Thorax: Peacock

Seducer, Green *(Randall Kaufmann)*
  Hook: TMC 200R, sizes 8-16
  Thread: Fluorescent fire orange, 6/0
  Tail: Moose
  Rib: Fine green or copper wire
  Hackle: Brown
  Body: Bright green Antron
  Hackle: Brown or furnace
  Wing: Shimazaki Fly Wing No. 14 w/10
            strands light olive Krystal Flash
  Hackle: Grizzly
  Thorax: Peacock

Seducer, Orange *(Randall Kaufmann)*
  Hook: TMC 200R, sizes 6-16
  Thread: Fluorescent fire orange, 6/0
  Tail: Dark elk
  Rib: Fine gold wire
  Abdomen: Fluorescent fire orange Antron
  Hackle: Furnace
  Wing: Fluorescent orange Krystal
            Flash, under Fly Wing, under
            dark elk
  Hackle: Grizzly
  Thorax: Peacock

Seducer, Yellow *(Randall Kaufmann)*
  Hook: TMC 200, sizes 8-16
  Thread: Fluorescent fire orange, 6/0
  Tail: Bleached elk
  Rib: Fine gold wire
  Abdomen: Fluorescent yellow Antron
  Hackle: Badger
  Wing: Fluorescent yellow Krystal
            Flash, under Fly Wing, under
            bleached elk
  Hackle: Grizzly
  Thorax: Peacock

Sinking/Jumping Beetle *(Harrison R. Steeves III)*
  Hook: TMC 3769, size 10
  Thread: Olive or green, 6/0
  Back: Copper colored Swiss Straw
  Body: Mallard and emerald color
            Kreinik heavy round braid
  Wing: Mallard color Kreinik flat rib-
            bon, 1/8 inch wide, unraveled
  Head: Kreinik fine round braid, cad-
            dis larva green

Slow Water Caddis, Black
  Hook: TMC 100, sizes 14-18
  Thread: Black, 6/0
  Antennae: Black hackle stems, optional
  Body: Black poly dubbing
  Hackle: Black, tied thorax style and
              clipped flush with body on
              underside
  Underwing: Black deer or elk
  Overwing: Black hen saddle, treated with
              Flexament; two feathers are
              tied downwing tent style

Slow Water Caddis, Brown
  Hook: TMC 100, sizes 14-18
  Thread: Brown, 6/0
  Body: Brown rabbit or poly
  Hackle: Brown
  Wing: Dark brown hen hackle feath-
            ers

Slow Water Caddis, Ginger
  Hook: TMC 100, sizes 14-18
Thread: Olive, 6/0
  Body: Light olive rabbit or poly
Hackle: Ginger
  Wing: Light tan hen hackle

Slow Water Caddis, Gray
  Hook: TMC 100, sizes 14-18
Thread: Gray, 6/0
  Body: Gray rabbit
Hackle: Gray
  Wing: Gray hen saddle

Sparkle Dun, Baetis (Craig Mathews)
  Hook: TMC 100, sizes 18-20
Thread: Olive, 6/0
  Wing: Grayish black-tipped deer
Shuck: Olive Z-Lon
  Body: Gray-olive Antron

Sparkle Dun, Baetis Olive (Craig Mathews)
  Hook: TMC 100, sizes 18-22
Thread: Olive, 6/0
  Wing: Grayish black-tipped deer
Shuck: Olive Z-Lon
  Body: Olive Antron

Sparkle Dun, Black and White (Craig Mathews)
  Hook: TMC 100, sizes 18-22
Thread: Black, 6/0
  Wing: Bleached deer
Shuck: Olive Z-Lon
  Body: Black Antron

Sparkle Dun, Callibaetis (Craig Mathews)
  Hook: TMC 100, size 16
Thread: Tan, 6/0
  Wing: Grayish black-tipped deer
Shuck: Olive Z-Lon
  Body: Grayish-tan Antron

Sparkle Dun, Mahogany (Craig Mathews)
  Hook: TMC 100, size 16
Thread: Brown, 6/0
  Wing: Medium black-tipped deer
Shuck: Olive Z-Lon
  Body: Mahogany Antron

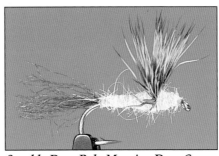

Sparkle Dun, Pale Morning Dun, Cream Yellow (Craig Mathews)
  Hook: TMC 100, sizes 16-20
Thread: Olive, 6/0
  Wing: Golden black-tipped deer
Shuck: Olive Z-Lon
  Body: Cream-olive Antron

Sparkle Dun, Pale Morning Dun, Yellow Olive (Craig Mathews)
  Hook: TMC 100, size 16
Thread: Yellow, 6/0
  Wing: Golden black-tipped deer
Shuck: Olive Z-Lon
  Body: Yellow Antron

Sparkle Dun, Pale Morning Dun, Yellow Orange (Craig Mathews)
    Hook: TMC 100, sizes 16-20
    Thread: Yellow, 6/0
    Wing: Golden black-tipped deer
    Shuck: Golden yellow Z-Lon
    Body: Yellow-orange Antron

Sparkle Dun, Slate Olive (Craig Mathews)
    Hook: TMC 100, sizes 14-20
    Thread: Olive, 6/0
    Wing: Black-tipped deer
    Shuck: Olive Z-Lon
    Body: Pale olive Antron

Sparkle Dun, Slate Tan (Craig Mathews)
    Hook: TMC 100, sizes 14-20
    Thread: Tan, 6/0
    Wing: Black-tipped deer
    Shuck: Olive Z-Lon
    Body: Tan Antron

Sparkle Dun, Sulphur (Craig Mathews)
    Hook: TMC 100, sizes 16-20
    Thread: Cream, 6/0
    Wing: Bleached deer
    Shuck: Golden yellow Z-Lon
    Body: Creamy yellow Antron

Spent Hopper (Andy Burk)
    Hook: TMC 5212, sizes 8-10
    Thread: Yellow, 3/0
    Body: Bleached elk, reverse style
    Wing: Mottled turkey and Zing, col-
             ored brown with black edges;
             use Pantone
    Legs: Knotted pheasant tail fibers
    Head: Natural deer; tips form collar

Spent Partridge Caddis, Olive (Mike Lawson)
    Hook: TMC 100, sizes 14-18
    Thread: Olive, 6/0
    Body: Dark olive rabbit
    Wing: Dark brown mottled partridge
             feathers
    Thorax: Peacock herl
    Hackle: Brown and grizzly

Spent Partridge Caddis, Peacock (Mike Lawson)
    Hook: TMC 100, sizes 14-18
    Thread: Olive, 6/0
    Body: Peacock herl
    Wing: Dark brown mottled partridge
             feathers
    Hackle: Brown and grizzly

Spent Partridge Caddis, Tan (Mike Lawson)
    Hook: TMC 100, sizes 14-18
    Thread: Tan, 6/0
    Body: Tan Superfine
    Wing: Dark brown mottled partridge
             feathers, two, tied spent
    Hackle: Grizzly and brown, one each,
             wound over base of peacock
             herl, clipped on bottom

Stimulator, Black (Randall Kaufmann)
    Hook: TMC 200R, sizes 6-18
    Thread: Fluorescent fire orange, 6/0
    Tail: Black elk
    Rib: Fine gold wire
    Hackle: Dark blue dun
    Abdomen: Black; blend of goat (black,
              purple, claret, blue, rust,
              orange) and black Hare-Tron
    Wing: Black elk
    Hackle: Grizzly
    Thorax: Fluorescent fire orange Antron

Stimulator, Gold (Randall Kaufmann)
Hook: TMC 200R, size 8
Thread: Fluorescent fire orange, 6/0
Tail: Golden-brown elk
Rib: Fine gold wire
Hackle: Blue dun
Abdomen: Golden blend of goat (gold, ginger, amber, yellow) and golden brown Hare-Tron
Wing: Golden-brown elk
Hackle: Furnace
Thorax: Fluorescent fire orange Antron

Stimulator, Green (Randall Kaufmann)
Hook: TMC 200R, sizes 8-18
Thread: Fluorescent fire orange, 6/0
Tail: Gray elk
Rib: Fine gold wire
Hackle: Brown
Abdomen: Bright green Antron
Wing: Gray elk
Hackle: Grizzly
Thorax: Amber goat

Stimulator, Orange (Randall Kaufmann)
Hook: TMC 200R, sizes 6-16
Thread: Fluorescent fire orange, 6/0
Tail: Dark elk
Rib: Fine gold wire
Hackle: Furnace
Abdomen: Fluorescent fire orange Antron
Wing: Dark elk
Hackle: Grizzly
Thorax: Amber goat

Stimulator, Royal (Randall Kaufmann)
Hook: TMC 200R, sizes 8-18
Thread: Fluorescent fire orange, 6/0
Tail: Light natural elk
Rib: Fine copper wire
Hackle: Brown
Abdomen: Peacock herl (rear), fluorescent red floss (middle), peacock herl (front)
Wing: Light natural elk
Hackle: Grizzly
Thorax: Fluorescent fire orange Antron

Stimulator, Tan (Randall Kaufmann)
Hook: TMC 200R, sizes 10-16
Thread: Fluorescent fire orange, 6/0
Tail: Light elk and copper Krystal Flash
Rib: Fine gold wire
Abdomen: Tan Antron
Hackle: Furnace
Wing: Light elk, topped with white calf body
Hackle: Grizzly
Thorax: Fluorescent fire orange Antron

Stimulator, Yellow (Randall Kaufmann)
Hook: TMC 200R, sizes 6-16
Thread: Fluorescent fire orange, 6/0
Tail: Light elk
Rib: Fine gold wire
Hackle: Light brown
Abdomen: Fluorescent yellow Antron
Wing: Light elk
Hackle: Grizzly
Thorax: Amber goat

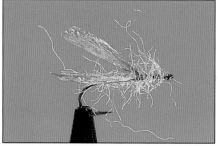

The Fly, Gray (John Betts)
Hook: TMC 101, sizes 14-22
Thread: Gray, 6/0
Body: Dun Z-Lon
Wing: Zing, colored with Pantone gray
Head: Same as body
Note: John ties this pattern all white and uses Pantone markers to color them at streamside, always being able to closely match the hatch.

The Fly, Tan (John Betts)
Hook: TMC 101, sizes 14-22
Thread: Tan, 6/0
Body: Tan Z-Lon
Wing: Zing, colored with Pantone gray
Head: Same as body

The Mess (Gary LaFontaine)
Hook: TMC 100, size 12
Thread: Black, 6/0
Tag: Black thread
Tail: Brown hackle fibers, two, split
Shellback: White foam, thin
Body: Bright green Antron
Hackle: Teal (rear) and brown (front)

Thorax, Baetis *(Mike Lawson)*
Hook:	TMC 100, sizes 18-22
Thread:	Dark olive, 6/0
Wing:	Light dun turkey flats
Tail:	Dun-gray hackle or Betts' Tailing Fibers
Body:	Gray-olive Superfine
Hackle:	Light dun, clipped on bottom

Thorax, Callibaetis *(Mike Lawson)*
Hook:	TMC 100 or 5210, sizes 16-20
Thread:	Cream, 6/0
Wing:	Gray partridge
Tail:	Grizzly hackle fibers
Body:	Cream-gray Antron
Hackle:	Grizzly wound through the wing and clipped on the bottom

Thorax, Mahogany Dun *(Mike Lawson)*
Hook:	TMC 100 or 5210, sizes 16-18
Thread:	Brown, 6/0
Wing:	Dark gray turkey flat
Tail:	Dark dun hackle fibers
Body:	Dark tan Antron
Hackle:	Dark dun wound through the wing and clipped on the bottom

Thorax, Pale Morning Dun *(Mike Lawson)*
Hook:	TMC 100 or 5210, sizes 16-20
Thread:	Pale olive, 6/0
Wing:	Medium gray turkey flat
Tail:	Light dun hackle fibers
Body:	Pale yellow olive Antron
Hackle:	Light dun wound through wing and clipped on bottom

Thorax, Slate Olive *(Mike Lawson)*
Hook:	TMC 100 or 5210, sizes 14-22
Thread:	Olive, 6/0
Wing:	Dark gray turkey flat
Tail:	Dark dun hackle fibers
Body:	Dark olive Antron
Hackle:	Dark dun wound through wing and clipped on bottom

Thorax, White Black *(Mike Lawson)*
Hook:	TMC 100 or 5210, size 18
Thread:	Black, 6/0
Wing:	White turkey flat
Tail:	Dark dun hackle fibers
Body:	Black Antron
Hackle:	Grizzly wound through wing and clipped on bottom

Trailing Shuck Midge, Dark *(Bill Fitzsimmons)*
Hook:	TMC 101, sizes 20-22
Thread:	Black, 8/0
Tail:	Brown Z-Lon
Back:	White Z-Lon
Abdomen:	Black thread
Legs:	Black hackle
Thorax:	Peacock

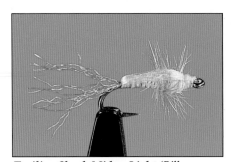

Trailing Shuck Midge, Light *(Bill Fitzsimmons)*
Hook:	TMC 101, sizes 20-22
Thread:	Cream, 8/0
Tail:	Gold Z-lon
Back:	White Z-Lon
Abdomen:	Cream thread
Legs:	Ginger hackle
Thorax:	Cream Superfine

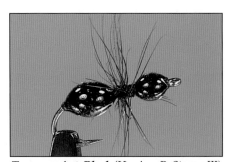

Transpar-Ant, Black *(Harrison R. Steeves III)*
Hook:	TMC 101, sizes 12-16
Thread:	Black, 3/0
Body:	Black thread with epoxy coating
Hackle:	Black

Transpar-Ant, Black and Red (*Harrison R. Steeves III*)
- Hook: TMC 101, sizes 12-16
- Thread: Black and red, 3/0
- Body: Red and black thread with epoxy coating
- Hackle: Black

Transpar-Ant, Red (*Harrison R. Steeves III*)
- Hook: TMC 101, sizes 12-16
- Thread: Red, 3/0
- Body: Red thread with epoxy coating
- Hackle: Brown or furnace

Trico Dun (*A.K. Best*)
- Hook: TMC 100, sizes 18-22
- Thread: White for tail; black for all else; 6/0
- Wing: White hen hackle tips
- Tail: White hackle fibers
- Abdomen: Light green hackle stem, one
- Thorax: Black Superfine
- Hackle: Black

Trico Poly Spinner, Female
- Hook: TMC 100, sizes 18-20
- Thread: Black, 6/0
- Wing: Light gray poly yarn
- Tail: Dark dun hackle fibers
- Abdomen: Light olive
- Thorax: Black Superfine

Trico Spinner, Dark (*John Betts*)
- Hook: TMC 101, sizes 18-22
- Thread: Gray, 6/0
- Wing: White Z-Lon
- Tail: Light dun tailing fibers
- Body: Light olive goose or turkey biot
- Thorax: Black Superfine

Trico Poly Spinner, Male
- Hook: TMC 5230, sizes 18-20
- Thread: Black, 6/0
- Wing: White poly yarn
- Tail: Dark dun Micro-Fibetts, split
- Abdomen: White Superfine, or light hackle stem
- Thorax: Black Superfine

Trude, Adams
- Hook: TMC 100, sizes 12-18
- Thread: Black, 6/0
- Tail: Golden pheasant tippets
- Body: Adams gray Superfine
- Wing: White calf
- Hackle: Brown

Trude, Hare's Ear (*Chuck Stranahan*)
- Hook: TMC 5212, sizes 8-16
- Thread: Gray, 6/0
- Tail: Deer, tied along entire hook shank
- Rib: Rainbow Accent Flash
- Body: Hare's ear dubbing mixed with bright white Antron yarn
- Wing: White calf
- Hackle: Grizzly and golden ginger grizzly

Trude, Lime
- Hook: TMC 100, sizes 12-18
- Thread: Black, 6/0
- Tail: Golden pheasant tippets
- Body: Fluorescent green Superfine
- Wing: White calf
- Hackle: Brown

Trude, Peacock *(Chuck Stranahan)*
Hook: TMC 5212, sizes 8-12
Thread: Olive, 6/0
Tail: Olive deer
Body: Peacock
Wing: White calf
Hackle: Golden ginger grizzly and olive grizzly

Trude, Pink
Hook: TMC 100, sizes 12-18
Thread: Black, 6/0
Tail: Golden pheasant tippets
Body: Pink rabbit
Wing: White calf
Hackle: Ginger

Trude, Rio Grande
Hook: TMC 100, sizes 10-16
Thread: Black, 6/0
Tail: Golden pheasant tippets
Body: Black rabbit
Wing: White calf
Hackle: Coachman brown

Trude, Royal Coachman
Hook: TMC 100, sizes 8-16
Thread: Black, 6/0
Tail: Golden pheasant tippets
Rib: Fine wire, optional
Body: Equal thirds: peacock, red floss, peacock
Wing: White calf
Hackle: Brown

Trude, Yellow *(Chuck Stranahan)*
Hook: TMC 5212, sizes 10-16
Thread: Yellow, 6/0
Tail: Deer
Tag: Fluorescent fire orange, single strand nylon floss
Body: Yellow poly Antron
Wing: White calf
Hackle: Grizzly

Wasp *(Harrison R. Steeves III)*
Hook: TMC 5212, size 14
Thread: Fluorescent yellow, 6/0
Back: Black closed cell foam, 1/8 inch wide strip
Body: Fluorescent yellow thread
Thorax: Black Superfine
Legs: Moose
Wing: Black mallard wing quill segment treated with Flexament

White Miller
Hook: TMC 100, sizes 12-16
Thread: White, 6/0
Wing: White duck quill
Tail: White hackle fibers
Rib: Silver mylar
Body: White floss
Hackle: White

Whitlock's Hopper *(Dave Whitlock)*
Hook: TMC 5263, sizes 4-12
Thread: Pale yellow, 6/0
Body: Light elk, extended
Underwing: Pale yellow deer
Wing: Speckled oak turkey wing quill
Legs: Pale yellow grizzly hackle stem, trimmed and knotted
Indicator: Fluorescent fire orange egg yarn
Head: Natural gray-brown and white deer, bullet head style; gray tips form overwing

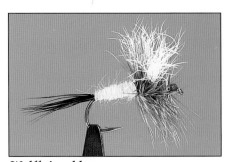

Wulff, Ausable
Hook: TMC 100, sizes 10-18
Thread: Red, 6/0
Wing: White calf
Tail: Moose body
Body: Bleached Australian opossum
Hackle: Brown and grizzly

Wulff, Blonde
Hook:	TMC 100, sizes 12-16
Thread:	Black, 6/0
Wing:	Natural tan elk
Tail:	Natural tan elk
Body:	Light tan rabbit
Hackle:	Light ginger

Wulff, Gray
Hook:	TMC 100, sizes 10-16
Thread:	Gray, 6/0
Tail:	Natural brown bucktail
Wing:	Brown bucktail
Body:	Gray muskrat
Hackle:	Blue dun

Wulff, Grizzly
Hook:	TMC 100, sizes 10-16
Thread:	Black, 6/0
Wing:	Natural brown bucktail
Tail:	Natural brown bucktail
Body:	Yellow floss
Hackle:	Brown and grizzly

Wulff, Royal
Hook:	TMC 100, sizes 8-20
Thread:	Black, 6/0
Wing:	White calf
Tail:	Elk
Rib:	Fine gold wire
Body:	Peacock, red floss, peacock
Hackle:	Coachman brown

Wulff, White
Hook:	TMC 100, sizes 8-18
Thread:	White, 6/0
Wing:	White calf
Tail:	White calf
Body:	White dubbing or yarn
Hackle:	Badger

X-Caddis, Olive *(Craig Mathews)*
Hook:	TMC 100, sizes 14-18
Thread:	Olive, 6/0
Shuck:	Amber Z-Lon
Body:	Olive Antron
Wing:	Mottled natural deer

X-Caddis, Tan *(Craig Mathews)*
Hook:	TMC 100, sizes 14-18
Thread:	Tan, 6/0
Shuck:	Amber Z-Lon
Body:	Tan Antron
Wing:	Mottled natural deer

Yellow Hopper *(Rod Yerger)*
Hook:	TMC 100, sizes 10-12
Thread:	Yellow, 6/0
Underbody:	Shaped balsa wood cylinder
Body:	Yellow deer, tied bullet head style and extended
Wing:	Mottled turkey wing quill
Rear legs:	Grizzly hackle stem, trimmed closely and bent
Front Legs:	Light moose
Antennae:	Dark moose
Eyes:	Red lacquer

Yellow Jacket *(Andy Burk)*
Hook:	TMC 5263, size 10
Thread:	Black, 6/0
Eyes:	Extra small monofilament nymph eyes
Body:	Yellow and black Antron, alternating bands
Wing:	Furnace hackle tips
Head:	Black Antron
Legs:	Brown hackle

Chapter 3

Nymphs

Gary LaFontaine

I can't remember a time when I wasn't fascinated with fishing—or, to be more accurate, fascinated with anything involving water. In later years my hobbies have included whitewater rafting, surfing and scuba diving, not just fishing. Doing any of these things still leaves me feeling a deep respect for water. Those activities also leave me feeling a bit jealous of mermaids and mermen.

My childhood was the perfect situation for someone who loved fishing. My stepfather, John Gaudreau, took me to a lake or stream every weekend from opening day until the end of the season. He was not only a superb all-around angler but also incredibly patient with a high-energy brat who, in his words, "Asked more questions than there could ever possibly be answers for."

Johnny and his friends took me with them to all the great fly fishing waters of the east. By the time I was 12 years old, I was a veteran on streams from the Penobscot in Maine to the White in Arkansas—and I had been skunked at least a couple of times on each of them.

Another great influence in my life was an old curmudgeon, Harry Ramsey, the caretaker of a private stretch of Mill Brook. I was a catch-and-release poacher on Harry's trout stream, and he had a grudging respect for my angling skills. He would fish with me occasionally, always giving a constant barrage of advice, but, better than that, he would invite me over to his house to read his incredible library of fly fishing books. All the great English and American authors were there for me. I didn't read those books—I memorized them by the hundreds.

As a child, one of the greatest advantages for me as an angler was a basement full of aquariums. My stepfather raised freshwater fish, primarily Jack Dempseys, for pet stores. There were more than 60 tanks in the cellar and at any given time a couple of them would be empty. This was where I put my fish. I kept sunfish, bass, trout, etc. I fed them, trained them, and watched them for hours. Their behavior never stopped surprising and delighting me.

Fishing was never my hobby. It was too much a part of my life to be that. It was natural for me to combine fishing and my other great love, writing, and try to sell articles to magazines. I started submitting articles when I was 10 years old, and at that age I never even thought of making money. I just wanted to share all the excitement inside me anytime I found out something about fish and fishing.

Five years and several "no thank you" rejection letters later, my first article appeared in the November, 1963 issue of *Fur-Fish-Game*. During the ensuing years I have written over a hundred articles on fly fishing, mostly for *Field & Stream, Sports Afield, Fly Rod & Reel*, and *Fly Fisherman* magazines.

I consider myself a writer—not an outdoor writer— and have published two books of poetry, more than 200 short stories and poems in literary magazines, and articles on psychology in professional and popular magazines. I've sold movie rights and am currently working on a screen play for one of my novellas, *The Last of the Great 130-Pound Linebackers.*

My first book, *Challenge of the Trout*, was published in 1976 and became the main selection of the *Field & Stream* Book Club. *Caddisflies* followed in 1981 and received the Book of the Year Award from the United Fly Tyers. It was selected by Robert Berls in *Trout* magazine as one of the best 15 books of the last 30 years (1959-1989). *The Dry Fly— New Angles* arrived in 1990 and was selected by United Fly Tyers as their 1990 Book of the Year. I published *Trout Flies—Proven Patterns* in 1993 and it was the 1993 main selection of the Outdoor Life Book Club. I created and interviewed for the River Rap audio series (eight are currently available). I co-authored the Pocket Guide series, which currently includes *Fly Fishing, Emergency First Aid, Fly Fishing the Lakes, Outdoor Photography, Backpacking, Steelhead Fly Fishing, Saltwater Fly Fishing, Nymph Fishing,* and *Dry Fly Fishing.*

I love to tie flies and fish them, but investigation into why and how trout see them and what triggers them to accept or reject my imitation holds the most fascination.

Nymphs

Are trout more selective or less selective to nymphs than to dry flies? Dry flies float in a world of light. That light, and the way it affects color, size, shape, and brightness, gives a trout a precise view of items on the surface. When there is more than one of any particular item—for example, when an important insect species hatches on a stream—the fish, from it's specific vantage point, see the same image over and over again. In the right conditions, mainly slow and clear water, the fish develops a search sequence, looking for various characteristics to appear in a certain order, and it rigidly selects a specific food form (or a matching fly).

Nymphs also depend on light to define color, size, shape, and brightness. But there is a major difference—a trout does not see nymphs in direct light. The strength of this diffused light depends partly on how deep nymphs are drifting. In shallow water, one or two feet, objects are bathed in light; in deep water, beyond two feet, the light gets progressively weaker.

The sequence of selecting or rejecting an item remains the same with a nymph or a dry fly. The trout looks forward for sunken food or up for floating food, but in either situation it searches for the first trait that tells it that this item is the one it is feeding on at the moment. This triggering characteristic (it triggers recognition) is the one the trout can see further away than any other. It is something unique to the food item. On a floating object, that trigger (and this applies only to an object on top of the meniscus, not an emerger half out and half in it) is the first one to appear in the circular window of vision. On a sunken object, that trigger is usually size—and the deeper the insect or the fly the more certain that will be so. In weak light any item drifting in the current loses a lot of detail; the silhouette itself is blurred by movement, but size remains a constant. When the insect or fly gets close to the fish, secondary characteristics such as color and shape become more important.

Once on the Green River in Utah a fish snubbed all my nymphs (including the fly that hooked every trout Emmett Heath sighted for me the previous day). Emmett and Steve Horton stood high on the rocks watching the movements of this fussy gourmet. Jack Dennis, my ghillie for the moment, stood next to me in the current, making suggestions and handing me imitations. The pattern kept getting smaller and smaller, and the leader tippets kept getting thinner and thinner. After more than 70 drifts, with all of us reading his intentions each time, the trout made a serious move at the ninth fly, a size 22 olive mayfly match. He broke off from the pass at the last moment when the nymph slipped into a faster current to his side. He sipped the fly on the next drift as if he had been waiting for it.

Maybe this 23-inch brown was wise from a few catch-and-release moments. Or maybe he was simply involved in a period of very heavy feeding. No trout before or since in my fishing ever worked that selectively on bottom-drifting nymphs, but there was no doubt in my mind that size was the characteristic he locked onto in accepting or rejecting my flies.

At times trout feed as selectively on nymphs as they do on dry flies. In conditions with high visibility—shallow, clear, and slow water—they want impressionistic imitations ("perfect" being much different from "exact") of the drifting naturals. It is not possible to fish tough rivers effectively with just a few general nymphs—it is no fun trying to cover even easy waters without a good selection of subsurface flies.

Emergers

Harry Ramsay, the old caretaker of the club water on Connecticut's Mill Brook, was my first fly fishing teacher. He never said a lot to me at one time; maybe he had a 25-word limit with all 10-year-old boys and not just me.

He watched me cast to a brown trout feeding on a nice hatch of mayflies. That fish refused the best floats of my Light Cahill. Finally Harry got disgusted waiting for me and snapped, "Spit on the fly."

I did and on the next cast the imitation drifted half drowned, and the trout sucked it in. "Why did he take it?" I asked.

"You figure it out," Harry said, and he left me there.

I used that trick on fussy fish for the next year, and it worked often enough to keep me wondering about the why of it. My own observations didn't solve the mystery—it wasn't until my steady progress through Harry's massive library of English fly fishing books brought me to *Minor Tactics of the Chalk Stream*, the G. E. M. Skues classic, that the reason became clear.

The emerger fly and the dry fly are so closely bound that it is impossible to discuss one without mentioning the other. Only the slimmest of barriers, the meniscus (or surface film), separates the two types of flies, one mired in it and the other riding on top of it, but to a feeding trout the imitations are entirely different.

Without the surface film (a compressed layer of molecules created by the uneven electrical charges of water and air) nymphs and larvae could not emerge in open water. They would all have to crawl out onto the bank. The surface film helps in two ways: it gives the emerging insect something to grab onto, a roof that the rising nymph or larva can hump its back into to stabilize itself; and, once the skin along the back splits and the insect starts to struggle out, the surface film holds and pins the skin while the adult pulls free.

The escape through the surface film takes only minutes, sometimes only seconds, but this brief stage in the insect's life is one of its most vulnerable periods. With mayflies, trout take as many emergers as duns during most hatches; with midges and caddisflies, trout take many more pupae than adults.

There are three major things that distinguish the emerging nymph or pupa from the fully free, floating adult form. The emerging insect is half in and half out of the old skin. That "beast in transition" is larger than either the before or after forms because the skin, or sheath, is dangling below the surface film. And, an emerger is bright with air bubbles inside the old skin.

The imitation of an emerger has to have a trailing shuck to match the shape and size of the insect in transition and the bright body parts. It also has to float half in and half out of the water. And, it needs to mimic the budding, unfolding wings of the natural.

The fact that trout typically feed more selectively on emerging insects than any other food form means that the imitations of them are the most important patterns in this series of flies. Those imitations work in the most critical feeding situations—times when other flies not only fail but fail badly.

In my experience, the Emergent Sparkle Pupa outfishes a drab imitation six to one. The Halo Mayfly Emerger outfishes a drab imitation three to one. The Halo Midge Emerger falls somewhere in between these two. These rough figures are based on my experiences (a lot of them). The differences in these ratios are linked to the brightness of the naturals, the air bubbles surrounding the caddisfly being much more visible because the insect has a thin, transparent sheath, rather than the thicker, nymphal skin of the mayfly.

The major step in a fly fisherman's education occurs when he can tell the difference between the bulging and splashy rise forms of trout taking emerging nymphs or pupae in the film and the simple sucking rise forms of trout taking adult insects off the surface. He saves himself many hours of frustrating flogging over fishing fish.

Author's Note: Gary was too modest to write his autobiography, so I wrote it. The section in *Nymphs* and *Emergers* is excerpted from Gary's book, *Trout Flies*. Gary enjoys the lecture circuit, photography, fishing and traveling with his daughter, Heather, and researching and publishing books. He is a partner in Greycliff Publishing and is currently working on a book about bass fishing. Gary thinks and fishes on the edge and loves to go over the wall. Because of him, fly fishing is much more enlightened and interesting.

Mike Mercer

At age five, I began to fish for hatchery trout on upper Hat Creek. In those days it was strictly "catch and kill," although even then I felt the first stirrings of what would bloom into a full-fledged love affair with fish and their environments. I was introduced to fly fishing at about age 12. Living in Chico, California, I was fortunate to count as tutors such anglers as Denton Hill, Lani Waller, Dave Stammet, Walton Powell, John Andrews, and a host of other friends too numerous to mention.

Under the watchful tutelage of Earline Powell, I learned to tie flies and soon began to tie commercially at a local level. At this point I cannot give enough credit to my mother and father, who unflaggingly provided me with transportation, not just to local bass and panfish waters, but to the much more exotic and desired trout streams of the area. How they understood my intense need for this sport or found the time in their busy, stressful lives to accommodate my passion is something I may never understand. I *do* know that this was yet another gift for which I owe them a tremendous debt of gratitude.

They also financed my first venture into the fly fishing retail picture, a short-lived but worthwhile endeavor, Mike Mercer's Rod and Fly Shop. Located in the basement of their house, it became the site of innumerable late night rod building and fly tying sessions as I struggled to acquire orders, then fill them.

Not long after this came a momentous turning point in my fly fishing life: I passed my driving test and was gifted a beautiful old relic, a column shift Ford Falcon Ranchero, by my grandfather. Seven years and five clutches later, I finally retired that old gem, but not before logging incredible mileage and a lifetime of angling experiences.

I constantly fished the local waters and came to know and go to work for the owners of The Fly Shop in Redding, California. For several years I *was* the guide service for the shop, then the head guide, and, eventually, the retail manager. Along the way I've been most fortunate to have fit in 10 lifetimes of angling, both locally and around the world. This plentiful and diverse exposure has permanently etched my thoughts regarding fish behavior and influenced the way I now design flies.

During my guiding days I ate, slept, and breathed fly fishing. There was scarcely a moment that I wasn't dreaming up new schemes to enable my clients to catch more and larger fish. I began finding trout that would refuse my best dead drifts, my most realistic retrieves, my favorite old standby patterns. What was happening—was I losing the touch?

Fortunately, I began to realize that it wasn't the presentation that was lacking but the flies themselves, particularly the subsurface patterns. I was struck by the fact that I had myriad selections of floating and in-the-film patterns that allowed me to successfully match any hatch, but my ability to hook angler-wise fish beneath the water was much less consistent. Most anglers, myself included, were relying on three or four basic nymph patterns to cover a wide and varied spectrum of available aquatic insects. Some trout, however, particularly in spring creek environments, owned Ph.D.'s in selectivity, and a size 16 Pheasant Tail just wasn't the answer anymore. It was time to learn more.

Incorporating a "seine before fish" approach, I slowly began to piece together an intriguing picture of the trout's subsurface dinner plate. Most aquatic insects, for instance, acquire some marked visual traits during that stage of emergence between stream bottom and surface. I call these triggering features, as they seem to be the incentive to trigger a trout's feeding response. Attention to seemingly minute detail at this stage led to the development of such patterns as the Z-Wing Caddis.

Examining the stomach contents of a large rainbow caught during a blizzard caddis hatch allowed me to closely examine several still-wiggling caddis pupa. I immediately noticed the insect's curled, undulating profile and the distinctly contrasting dark dorsal and light ventral coloration. The narrow intersegmental banding was quite pronounced and several shades lighter than the abdomen. The wingpads had a shiny, opaque appearance. Finally, the head was slightly iridescent and messy-looking while the antennae were beautifully speckled and prominent. I headed for my tying desk.

For some tyers, form follows function. To me, form *is* function. Though not an elaborate tyer by nature, I go to great lengths to incorporate as many triggering features as possible into every pattern I design. If the fly looks and behaves more like the natural *beneath* the water, the trout's interest *will* be aroused. In designing a caddis pupa pattern to imitate my samples, I started with the all-important hook selection. I use Tiemco hooks exclusively because of their overall quality and exceptional model selection. In this case the Tiemco 2457 matched the desired short, curled body profile I sought. I dubbed the body with an Antron dubbing blend, as I knew this would sparkle and help simulate the trapped air inherent on emerging caddis bodies. The dark dorsal carapace (back) was achieved with a strip of richly mottled, golden brown turkey tail feather. When the body was ribbed with a thread that was a fluorescent shade of the body dubbing, the intersegmental banding jumped to life. Z-Lon clumps mimicked the milky, semi-translucent wingpads, and a matched pair of lemon woodduck fibers served as antennae. I decided on mottled marabou to give the nymph its unkempt forward appearance. Sometimes I incorporate a small gold bead head for additional shine.

The Z-Wing Caddis succinctly demonstrates important aspects of tying that I feel are important in designing successful flies:

1. Contrast. I do not like homogenous color schemes. Give me a dark wingcase and spectrumized or mottled dubbing any day.

2. I like to combine natural and synthetic materials in a fly. They each have distinctly unique properties that often complement each other.

3. Hook design is important when creating a realistic fraud.

4. Go to whatever lengths necessary to accurately simulate both the visual appearance and the movement of the natural being imitated.

5. Know insects intimately and anatomically. This means you must observe live samples.

6. Finally, don't be afraid to try something radically different in your tying. Search everywhere for materials that will best fit your desired effect—don't just settle for what everyone else is doing. Remember, simply showing a fish something new can, in itself, be a triggering feature.

Author's Note: Mike Mercer has travelled throughout the fishing world and is a thinking man's angler/fly tyer. He has developed several very effective flies and angling strategies for difficult flat water trout. Mike lives in Redding, California and can be reached at The Fly Shop, (916) 222-3555.

Mike Mercer
Redding, California
June, 1994

A. P. Beaver *(Andre' Puyans)*
- Hook: *TMC 3761, sizes 12-16, weighted*
- Thread: *Black, 6/0*
- Tail: *Dark moose*
- Rib: *Fine copper wire*
- Abdomen: *Beaver*
- Wingcase: *Dark moose*
- Thorax: *Same as abdomen*
- Legs: *Same as wingcase*
- Head: *Same as abdomen*

A. P. Black *(Andre' Puyans)*
- Hook: *TMC 3761, sizes 10-18, weighted*
- Thread: *Black, 6/0*
- Tail: *Dark moose*
- Rib: *Fine copper wire*
- Abdomen: *Black beaver or Haretron*
- Wingcase: *Dark moose*
- Thorax: *Same as abdomen*
- Legs: *Same as wingcase*
- Head: *Same as abdomen*

A. P. Hare's Ear *(Andre' Puyans)*
- Hook: *TMC 3761, sizes 10-18, weighted*
- Thread: *Tan, 6/0*
- Tail: *Woodduck mallard*
- Rib: *Fine copper wire*
- Abdomen: *Hare's ear*
- Wingcase: *Woodduck mallard*
- Thorax: *Same as abdomen*
- Legs: *Same as wingcase*
- Head: *Same as abdomen*

A. P. Hendrickson *(Andre' Puyans)*
- Hook: *TMC 3761, sizes 12-18, weighted*
- Thread: *Brown, 6/0*
- Tail: *Dark moose*
- Rib: *Fine copper wire*
- Abdomen: *Dark sooty brown beaver*
- Wingcase: *Dark moose*
- Thorax: *Same as abdomen*
- Legs: *Same as wingcase*
- Head: *Same as abdomen*

A. P. Muskrat *(Andre' Puyans)*
- Hook: *TMC 3761, sizes 10-16, weighted*
- Thread: *Gray, 6/0*
- Tail: *Dark moose*
- Rib: *Fine gold wire*
- Abdomen: *Dark muskrat*
- Wingcase: *Dark moose*
- Thorax: *Same as abdomen*
- Legs: *Same as wingcase*
- Head: *Same as abdomen*

A. P. Olive *(Andre' Puyans)*
- Hook: *TMC 3761, sizes 10-18, weighted*
- Thread: *Olive, 6/0*
- Tail: *Woodduck mallard*
- Rib: *Fine copper wire*
- Abdomen: *Olive beaver*
- Wingcase: *Mallard flank*
- Thorax: *Same as abdomen*
- Legs: *Same as wingcase*
- Head: *Same as abdomen*

A. P. Pheasant *(Andre' Puyans)*
- Hook: *TMC 3761, sizes 10-18, weighted*
- Thread: *Black, 6/0*
- Tail: *Dark ringneck pheasant tail fibers*
- Rib: *Fine copper wire*
- Abdomen: *Bronze peacock herl*
- Wingcase: *Dark ringneck pheasant tail*
- Thorax: *Same as abdomen*
- Legs: *Same as wingcase*
- Head: *Same as abdomen*

Articulated Leech, Black
- Hook: *TMC 7999, sizes 2-8*
- Thread: *Black, 3/0*
- Tail: *Black marabou*
- Wing: *Black marabou*
- Overwing: *Black Accent Flash*
- Eyes: *Nickel bead chain*

Note: Connect 7999 hook behind another 7999 hook with braided dacron. Remove hook bend and point. Tie marabou onto hook shank.

Articulated Leech, Purple
- Hook: *TMC 7999, sizes 2-8*
- Thread: *Black, 3/0*
- Tail: *Purple marabou*
- Wing: *Purple marabou*
- Overwing: *Purple Accent Flash*
- Eyes: *Nickel bead chain*

Note: Connect 7999 hook behind another 7999 hook with braided dacron. Remove hook bend and point. Tie marabou onto hook shank.

Bead Head A. P. Black (*Andre' Puyans*)
Hook: TMC 3761, sizes 10-16
Head: Gold bead, small to medium
Thread: Black, 6/0
Tail: Moose
Rib: Fine copper wire
Abdomen: Black Antron
Wingcase: Moose
Thorax: Same as abdomen
Legs: Moose; leftover tips from wingcase

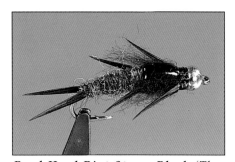

Bead Head Biot Stone, Black (*Theo Bakelaar*)
Hook: TMC 2312, sizes 4-8
Head: Gold bead
Thread: Black, 6/0
Tail: Black goose biot
Abdomen: Black Paxton's Buggy Nymph
Legs: Black goose biots
Wingcase: Black Flexibody
Thorax: Same as body

Bead Head Biot Stone, Dark Peacock (*Theo Bakelaar*)
Hook: TMC 2312, sizes 6-10
Head: Gold bead
Thread: Brown, 6/0
Tail: Brown goose biots
Abdomen: Peacock
Thorax: Peacock
Legs: Brown goose biots
Antennae: Brown goose biots; leftover butts from legs

Bead Head Biot Stone, Golden (*Theo Bakelaar*)
Hook: TMC 2312, sizes 6-10
Head: Gold bead
Thread: Brown, 6/0
Tail: Brown goose biots
Abdomen: Lava brown Paxton's Buggy Nymph
Legs: Brown goose biots
Wingcase: Brown Flexibody
Thorax: Dark hare's ear Paxton's Buggy Nymph

Bead Head Biot Stone, Tan (*Theo Bakelaar*)
Hook: TMC 2312, sizes 10-14
Head: Gold bead
Thread: Brown, 6/0
Tail: Brown goose biots
Rib: Fine oval gold tinsel
Abdomen: Cream Fly-Rite
Legs: Brown goose biots
Wingcase: Brown Flexibody
Thorax: Dark hare's ear Paxton's Buggy Nymph

Bead Head Black Devil (*Theo Bakelaar*)
Hook: TMC 3761, sizes 10-14
Head: Gold bead
Thread: Black, 6/0
Rib: Fine oval gold tinsel
Abdomen: Black thin chenille
Legs: Black hackle
Thorax: Chartreuse wool

Bead Head Blacky (*Theo Bakelaar*)
Hook: TMC 2312, sizes 8-14
Head: Gold bead
Thread: Black, 6/0
Tail: Black pheasant or hackle fibers
Abdomen: Black ostrich
Wingcase: Black Flexibody
Thorax: Black Paxton's Buggy Nymph, picked out

Bead Head Bomber (*Theo Bakelaar*)
Hook: TMC 3761, sizes 8-12
Head: Gold bead
Thread: Black, 6/0
Tail: Golden pheasant tippets and red wool
Rib: Fine gold wire
Abdomen: Peacock
Legs: Black hackle

Bead Head Brer Possum, Green Butt (*Harrison R. Steeves III*)
Hook: TMC 2302, sizes 10-14
Head: Gold bead
Thread: Black, 6/0
Tag: Chartreuse Kreinik braid, or substitute dubbing
Body: Copper Kreinik braid, small, with light opossum; twist tightly
Collar: Light opossum guard hairs

Bead Head Brer Possum, Orange Butt
(Harrison R. Steeves III)
Hook: TMC 2302, sizes 10-14
Head: Gold bead
Thread: Tan, 6/0
Tag: Fluorescent orange Kreinik braid, or substitute dubbing
Body: Yellow-orange Kreinik braid with light opossum; twist tightly
Collar: Honey opossum, spun

Bead Head Bull Stone, Black (Theo Bakelaar)
Hook: TMC 5263, sizes 2-6
Head: Gold bead
Thread: Black, 6/0
Antennae: Wild boar; substitute anything
Tail: Black goose biots
Rib: Heavy gold wire
Abdomen: Black Flexibody over black dubbing
Wingcase: Black Flexibody
Thorax: Black Paxton's Buggy Nymph
Legs: Black goose biots

Bead Head Caddis Pupa, Brown
Hook: TMC 3769, sizes 12-16
Head: Gold bead
Thread: Brown, 6/0
Abdomen: Chocolate brown rabbit
Legs: Mottled brown hen hackle
Antennae: Same as legs

Bead Head Caddis Pupa, Cream
Hook: TMC 3769, sizes 12-16
Head: Gold bead
Thread: Cream, 6/0
Abdomen: Cream rabbit
Legs: Mottled brown hen hackle
Antennae: Same as legs

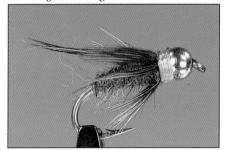

Bead Head Caddis Pupa, Dark Gray
Hook: TMC 3769, sizes 12-16
Head: Gold bead
Thread: Gray 6/0
Abdomen: Gray rabbit
Legs: Mottled brown hen hackle
Antennae: Same as legs

Bead Head Caddis Pupa, Olive
Hook: TMC 3769, sizes 12-16
Head: Gold bead
Thread: Olive, 6/0
Abdomen: Olive rabbit
Legs: Mottled brown hen hackle
Antennae: Same as legs

Bead Head Dream, Amber (Theo Bakelaar)
Hook: TMC 3769, sizes 10-12
Head: Gold bead
Thread: Brown, 6/0
Tag: Shiny copper brown Flexibody
Abdomen: Amber hare's ear
Legs: Light partridge

Bead Head Dream, Hare's Ear (Theo Bakelaar)
Hook: TMC 3769, sizes 10-12
Head: Gold bead
Thread: Brown, 6/0
Tag: Shiny copper brown Flexibody
Abdomen: Natural hare's ear
Legs: Light partridge

Bead Head Emerger, Black Head (Brett Smith)
Hook: TMC 2457, sizes 14-18
Thorax: Small silver bead
Thread: Black, 6/0
Rib: Gold embossed tinsel
Abdomen: Olive sparkle dubbing
Legs: Light dun Salmo-Web
Collar: Dark natural dun or black hackle
Head: Black Salmo-Web

**Bead Head Flashback Pheasant Tail,
Brown** (Randall Kaufmann)
> Hook: TMC 3761, sizes 10-18
> Head: Copper bead
> Thread: Brown, 6/0
> Tail: Brown pheasant tail
> Back: Pearl Flashabou
> Rib: Copper wire
> Abdomen: Brown pheasant tail
> Wingcase: Pearl Flashabou
> Thorax: Peacock
> Legs: Brown pheasant tail
> Head: Cover thread head w/copper wire

**Bead Head Flashback Pheasant Tail,
Olive** (Randall Kaufmann)
> Hook: TMC 3761, sizes 10-18
> Head: Gold bead
> Thread: Olive, 6/0
> Tail: Green pheasant tail
> Back: Pearl Flashabou
> Rib: Gold wire
> Abdomen: Green pheasant tail
> Wingcase: Pearl Flashabou
> Thorax: Peacock
> Legs: Green pheasant tail
> Head: Cover thread head w/gold wire

Bead Head Hare's Ear (Theo Bakelaar)
> Hook: TMC 3761, sizes 10-16
> Head: Gold bead
> Thread: Brown, 6/0
> Tail: Hare's mask
> Rib: Fine oval gold tinsel
> Abdomen: Hare's ear
> Legs: Mottled brown hen hackle

Bead Head Marabou Damsel, Olive
(Randall Kaufmann)
> Hook: TMC 200R , size 12
> Head: Gold bead
> Thread: Olive, 6/0
> Tail: Olive marabou
> Rib: Copper wire
> Abdomen: Olive marabou
> Wingcase: Olive marabou

Bead Head Metallic Caddis, Copper
(Randall Kaufmann)
> Hook: TMC 2457, sizes 12-16
> Head: Copper bead
> Thread: Olive, 6/0
> Abdomen: Copper wire
> Legs: Natural dark gray CDC
> Thorax: Peacock

Bead Head Metallic Caddis, Green
(Randall Kaufmann)
> Hook: TMC 2457, sizes 12-16
> Head: Gold bead
> Thread: Olive, 6/0
> Abdomen: Green wire
> Legs: Natural dark gray CDC
> Thorax: Peacock

Bead Head Mini Leech, Black (Randall
Kaufmann)
> Hook: TMC 200R, size 10
> Head: Gold bead
> Thread: Black, 6/0
> Tail: Black marabou and red and
>   black Krystal Flash
> Body: Black goat and red Krystal
>   Flash (use dubbing loop)

Bead Head Mini Leech, Brown (Randall
Kaufmann)
> Hook: TMC 200R, size 10
> Head: Gold bead
> Thread: Brown, 6/0
> Tail: Brown marabou and pearl
>   Krystal Flash
> Body: Rusty brown goat and pearl
>   Krystal Flash (use dubbing
>   loop)

Bead Head Mini Leech, Olive (Randall
Kaufmann)
> Hook: TMC 200R, size 10
> Head: Gold bead, small
> Thread: Olive, 6/0
> Tail: Olive marabou and olive
>   Krystal Flash
> Body: Olive goat and peacock Krystal
>   Flash (use dubbing loop)

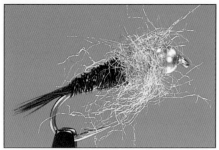

Bead Head Pheasant Tail (Theo Bakelaar)
Hook: TMC 3761, sizes 12-16
Head: Gold bead
Thread: Brown, 6/0
Tail: Dyed brown pheasant tail fibers
Rib: Fine gold wire
Abdomen: Same as tail
Thorax: Hare's ear

Bead Head Possie Bugger (Dennis Black)
Hook: TMC 5262, sizes 8-12, weighted
Head: Gold bead
Thread: Black, 6/0
Tail: Dark Australian opossum and pearl Flashabou
Rib: Pearlescent flat tinsel
Abdomen: Australian opossum
Legs: Mottled dark partridge
Thorax: Black Australian oppossum

Bead Head Possie, Dark
Hook: TMC 3761, sizes 8-16
Head: Gold bead
Thread: Black, 6/0
Tail: Australian opossum guard hairs
Rib: Fine to medium copper wire
Abdomen: Natural dark Australian opossum
Thorax: Australian opossum guard hairs

Bead Head Possie, Light
Hook: TMC 3761, sizes 8-16
Head: Gold bead
Thread: Black, 6/0
Tail: Australian opossum guard hairs
Rib: Fine to medium copper wire
Abdomen: Australian opossum, light shades
Thorax: Australian opossum guard hairs

Bead Head Prince
Hook: TMC 3761, sizes 8-16
Head: Gold bead
Thread: Black, 6/0
Tail: Brown turkey biots
Rib: Flat gold tinsel
Abdomen: Peacock
Legs: Brown
Wing: White turkey biot

Bead Head Rubber Legs, Black (Deke Meyer)
Hook: TMC 5263, sizes 6-10
Head: Gold bead
Thread: Black, 6/0
Tail: Black marabou
Legs: White round rubber
Body: Black Paxton's Buggy Nymph
Hackle: Black

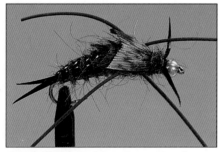

Bead Head Rubber Legs Kaufmann Stone, Black (Randall Kaufmann)
Hook: TMC 300, sizes 4-10, weighted
Head: Gold bead
Thread: Black, 6/0
Tail: Black turkey biot
Antennae: Same as tail
Rib: Black Swannundaze
Abdomen: Black Haretron
Wingcase: Dark turkey tail
Legs: Black rubber
Thorax/Head: Same as abdomen

Bead Head Rubber Legs Kaufmann Stone, Golden (Randall Kaufmann)
Hook: TMC 300, sizes 8-12, weighted
Head: Gold bead
Thread: Brown, 6/0
Tail: Golden brown turkey biot
Antennae: Same as tail
Rib: Transparant gold Swannundaze
Abdomen: Golden Kaufmann Stone mix
Wingcase: Golden brown turkey
Legs: Black round rubber
Thorax/Head: Same as abdomen

Bead Head Rubber Legs, Olive (Deke Meyer)
Hook: TMC 5263, sizes 6-10
Head: Gold bead
Thread: Olive, 6/0
Tail: Dark olive marabou
Legs: White round rubber
Body: Brownish olive Paxton's Buggy Nymph
Hackle: Olive grizzly

Bead Head Rubber Legs, Squirrel *(Dave Whitlock)*

Hook:	TMC 5263, sizes 6-12, weighted
Head:	Gold bead
Thread:	Brown, 6/0
Tag:	Pearlescent flat tinsel
Tail:	Red fox squirrel
Rib:	Same as tag
Abdomen:	Squirrel Antron, picked out
Legs:	Golden green rubber Sililegs
Thorax:	Black Antron
Collar:	Dark mottled hen saddle

Bead Head Rubber Legs Woolly Bugger, Black *(Randall Kaufmann)*

Hook:	TMC 5263, sizes 2-10, weighted
Head:	Gold bead
Thread:	Black, 6/0
Tail:	Black marabou, and black, red, and pearl Krystal Flash
Rib:	Red wire
Body:	Black Crystal Chenille or black chenille
Legs:	Black or white round rubber
Hackle:	Black

Bead Head Rubber Legs Woolly Bugger, Brown *(Randall Kaufmann)*

Hook:	TMC 5263, sizes 2-10, weighted
Head:	Copper or gold bead
Thread:	Black, 6/0
Tail:	Brown or black marabou; black, red, and pearl Krystal Flash
Rib:	Red wire
Body:	Black Crystal Chenille or brown chenille
Legs:	Black or white round rubber
Hackle:	Black or brown dyed grizzly

Bead Head Rubber Legs Woolly Bugger, Olive *(Randall Kaufmann)*

Hook:	TMC 5263, sizes 2-10, weighted
Head:	Gold bead
Thread:	Black, 6/0
Tail:	Olive or black marabou; olive, red, and pearl Krystal Flash
Rib:	Green wire
Body:	Olive Crystal Chenille or olive chenille
Legs:	Black or white round rubber
Hackle:	Black, olive, or olive dyed grizzly

Bead Head Scud, Olive-Gray *(Randall Kaufmann)*

Hook:	TMC 2487, sizes 10-16
Head:	Gold bead
Thread:	Olive, 6/0
Tail:	Olive hackle fibers
Antennae:	Same as tail
Back:	Clear plastic with pearl Flashabou
Rib:	Gray-olive thread
Abdomen:	Gray-olive Antron

Bead Head Scud, Orange *(Randall Kaufmann)*

Hook:	TMC 2487, sizes 10-16
Head:	Gold bead
Thread:	Fluorescent fire orange, 6/0
Tail:	Orange hackle fibers
Antennae:	Same as tail
Back:	Clear plastic, heavy mil, with pearl Flashabou underneath
Rib:	Fluorescent fire orange thread
Abdomen:	Fluorescent orange Antron

Bead Head Scud, Tan *(Randall Kaufmann)*

Hook:	TMC 2487, sizes 10-16
Head:	Gold bead
Thread:	Tan, 6/0
Tail:	Tan hackle fibers
Antennae:	Same as tail
Back:	Clear plastic, heavy mil, with pearl Flashabou underneath
Rib:	Clear monofilament
Abdomen:	Tan Haretron and ginger, amber and cream goat, blended

Bead Head Serendipity, Brown *(Craig Mathews)*

Hook:	TMC 2457, sizes 14-18
Head:	Silver bead
Thread:	Brown, 6/0
Abdomen:	Brown Z-Lon
Thorax:	Dark Australian opossum

Bead Head Serendipity, Copper *(Craig Mathews)*

Hook:	TMC 2457, sizes 14-18
Head:	Copper bead
Thread:	Brown, 6/0
Abdomen:	Copper Z-Lon
Thorax:	Light Australian opossum

Bead Head Serendipity, Olive (*Craig Mathews*)

Hook:	TMC 2457, sizes 14-18
Head:	Gold bead
Thread:	Brown, 6/0
Abdomen:	Olive Z-Lon
Thorax:	Dark Australian opossum

Bead Head Squirrel (*Dave Whitlock*)

Hook:	TMC 5262, sizes 10-16
Head:	Gold bead
Thread:	Black, 6/0
Tail:	Red fox squirrel
Rib:	Fine wire
Abdomen:	Red fox squirrel, belly fur
Thorax:	Red fox squirrel, mixed 50-50 with charcoal Antron
Hackle:	Mottled golden brown hen saddle

Bead Head Stonefly, Brown (*Theo Bakelaar*)

Hook:	TMC 2312, sizes 8-14
Head:	Gold bead
Thread:	Brown, 6/0
Tail:	Pheasant tail fibers
Rib:	Fine oval gold tinsel
Abdomen:	Same as tail
Wingcase:	Brown Flexibody
Thorax:	Brown Paxton's Buggy Nymph, picked out

Bead Head Thorax, Dark (*Andre' Puyans*)

Hook:	TMC 3761, sizes 10-16
Head:	Gold bead, small to medium
Thread:	Black, 6/0
Tail:	Moose
Rib:	Fine copper wire
Abdomen:	Black Antron
Wingcase:	Moose
Thorax:	Same as abdomen
Legs:	Moose; leftover tips from wingcase

Bead Head Zug Bug

Hook:	TMC 3761, sizes 10-16
Head:	Gold bead
Thread:	Black, 6/0
Tail:	Peacock sword
Rib:	Fine silver mylar
Abdomen:	Peacock
Legs:	Brown
Wing:	Woodduck mallard

Big Horn Shrimp, Orange

Hook:	TMC 3761, sizes 10-12, weighted
Thread:	Orange, 6/0
Tail:	Ringneck tail fibers
Back:	Clear plastic
Rib:	Fine copper wire
Abdomen:	Orange Antron, picked out on underside

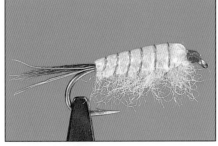

Big Horn Shrimp, Pink

Hook:	TMC 3761 or 2457, sizes 10-12, weighted
Thread:	Pink, 6/0
Tail:	Pink hackle fibers or ringneck tail fibers
Back:	Clear plastic
Rib:	Clear or dyed pink monofilament
Abdomen:	Pink Antron

Bird's Nest, Black (*Cal Bird*)

Hook:	TMC 3761, sizes 10-18
Thread:	Black, 6/0
Tail:	Black mallard flank
Rib:	Copper wire
Abdomen:	Black Australian opossum
Legs:	Same as tail
Thorax:	Same as abdomen
Hackle:	Black mallard flank

Bird's Nest, Brown (*Cal Bird*)

Hook:	TMC 3761, sizes 10-18, weighted
Thread:	Brown, 6/0
Tail:	Brown mallard
Rib:	Fine copper wire
Abdomen:	Dyed brown Australian opossum
Legs:	Same as tail
Thorax:	Same as abdomen

Bird's Nest, Light Cahill (Cal Bird)
Hook: TMC 3761, sizes 10-18, weighted
Thread: Cream, 6/0
Tail: Woodduck mallard
Rib: Fine gold wire
Abdomen: Bleached (cream) Australian opossum
Legs: Same as tail
Thorax: Same as abdomen

Bird's Nest, Natural (Cal Bird)
Hook: TMC 3761, sizes 10-18, weighted
Thread: Tan, 6/0
Tail: Golden brown teal
Rib: Fine copper wire
Abdomen: Australian opossum
Legs: Same as tail
Thorax: Same as abdomen

Bird's Nest, Olive (Cal Bird)
Hook: TMC 3761, sizes 10-18, weighted
Thread: Olive, 6/0
Tail: Olive teal or mallard
Rib: Fine copper wire
Abdomen: Olive Australian opossum
Legs: Same as tail
Thorax: Same as abdomen

Bird's Stone (Cal Bird)
Hook: TMC 5262, sizes 4-10, weighted
Thread: Orange, 3/0
Tail: Brown goose biots
Rib: Orange floss
Abdomen: Coachman brown Antron or rabbit
Wingcase: Mottled turkey
Thorax: Peacock
Hackle: Furnace saddle

Bitch Creek
Hook: TMC 5263, sizes 2-10, weighted
Thread: Black, 6/0
Tail: White rubber
Antennae: White rubber
Abdomen: Black and orange chenille, woven
Rib: Fine gold wire
Thorax: Black chenille
Hackle: Brown, palmered through thorax

Black Martinez
Hook: TMC 5262 or 3761, sizes 10-12, weighted
Thread: Black, 6/0
Tail: Natural guinea
Rib: Fine silver wire
Abdomen: Black rabbit or Angora goat
Wingcase: Green raffia or Swiss Straw
Thorax: Black rabbit
Legs: Gray partridge

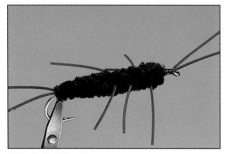

Black Rubber Legs
Hook: TMC 300, sizes 4-8, heavily weighted
Thread: Black, 6/0
Tail: Black rubber
Antennae: Black rubber
Legs: Black rubber
Body: Black chenille

Braided Bitch Creek (Harrison R. Steeves III)
Hook: TMC 5262, sizes 6-10, weighted
Thread: Black, 6/0
Tail: Black round rubber
Antennae: Black round rubber
Abdomen: Beetle black and high luster yellow Kreinik medium round braid
Hackle: Brown or furnace, palmered
Thorax: Black Kreinik Micro Ice Chenille

Brassie
Hook: TMC 200R, sizes 16-22
Thread: Black, 6/0
Abdomen: Copper wire
Head: Peacock herl

Brer Rabbit, Black (Harrison R. Steeves III)
Hook: TMC 5262, sizes 6-10, weighted
Thread: Fluorescent yellow, 6/0
Tail: Black rabbit fur, with gold Flashabou
Body: Black Kreinik braid
Hackle: Black rabbit fur, spun

Brer Rabbit, Tan (Harrison R. Steeves III)
Hook: TMC 5262, sizes 6-10, weighted
Thread: Fluorescent yellow, 6/0
Tail: Black rabbit with green Flashabou
Body: Green Kreinik braid
Hackle: Ginger rabbit fur, spun

Brown Drake (Mike Lawson)
Hook: TMC 5262 or 2302, size 8 or 10
Thread: Brown, 3/0
Tail: Brown partridge
Rib: Fine gold wire
Gills: Gray marabou
Abdomen: Light yellowish tan Antron
Wingcase: Mottled turkey
Legs: Brown partridge
Thorax: Same as abdomen

Brown Hackle Peacock
Hook: TMC 3769, sizes 8-16, weighted
Thread: Black, 6/0
Tail: Brown hackle fibers
Body: Peacock
Hackle: Brown

Brown Stone (George Anderson)
Hook: TMC 5262, sizes 8-14, weighted
Thread: Dark brown, 3/0
Tail: Medium brown mink or otter guard hair
Body: Woven fuzzy yarn, cream on bottom, medium brown on top
Legs: Mink or otter

Brooks' Stone
Hook: TMC 5263, sizes 4-8, weighted
Thread: Black, 6/0
Tail: Black stripped goose fibers
Rib: Copper wire
Abdomen: Black wool yarn
Hackle: Brown and grizzly
Gills: White ostrich herl

Buckskin Caddis (Bill Fitzsimmons)
Hook: TMC 5262, sizes 12-16
Thread: Black, 6/0
Body: Light chamois
Head: Peacock

Bunny Leech, Black
Hook: TMC 300, sizes 2-6, weighted
Thread: Black, 3/0
Tail: Black rabbit strip and red Flashabou
Body: Black cross-cut rabbit strip

Bunny Leech, Olive
Hook: TMC 300, sizes 4-6, weighted
Thread: Black, 3/0
Tail: Olive rabbit strip and red Flashabou
Body: Olive cross-cut rabbit strip

Bunny Leech, Purple
Hook: TMC 300, sizes 2-6, weighted
Thread: Black, 3/0
Tail: Purple rabbit strip and red Flashabou
Body: Purple cross-cut rabbit strip

Caddis Emerger, Olive (Mike Lawson)
Hook: TMC 100, sizes 14-16
Thread: Olive, 8/0
Shuck (Tail): Olive Z-Lon; leave forward section for underwing
Rib: Fine copper wire
Abdomen: Olive Antron
Underwing: Olive Z-Lon
Wing: Brown partridge hackle tips, two, tied with concave side facing down
Thorax: Peacock

Caddis Emerger, Tan (Mike Lawson)
Hook: TMC 100, sizes 14-16
Thread: Camel, 8/0
Abdomen: Tan Antron
Underwing: Tan Z-Lon
Wing: Brown partridge
Thorax: Peacock

Caddis Larva, Bright Green (Gary LaFontaine)
Hook: TMC 200R, sizes 12-16, weighted
Thread: Dark olive, 6/0
Rib: Brown hackle stem
Abdomen: Bright green Antron
Thorax: Dark brown Antron
Legs: Pheasant rump

Caddis Larva, Brown (Shane Stalcup)
Hook: TMC 200R, sizes 12-16
Thread: Brown, 6/0
Underbody: White flat floss, Pantone tan
Overbody: Clear Liqua Lace, Pantone top gray
Legs: Heavy brown thread, lacquered

Caddis Larva, Brown Olive (Gary LaFontaine)
Hook: TMC 200R, sizes 12-16, weighted
Thread: Dark olive, 6/0
Rib: Olive hackle stem
Abdomen: Olive Antron
Thorax: Medium brown Antron
Legs: Woodduck mallard

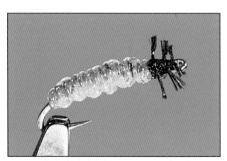

Caddis Larva, Olive (Shane Stalcup)
Hook: TMC 200R, sizes 12-16
Thread: Black, 6/0
Underbody: White flat floss, Pantone olive
Overbody: Clear Liqua Lace, woven, Pantone top green
Legs: Heavy black thread, lacquered

Caddis Pupa, Brown (Nori Tashiro)
Hook: TMC 3769, sizes 12-14
Thread: Brown, 6/0
Back: Dark turkey
Rib: Pearlescent tinsel
Abdomen: Tannish olive Antron
Thorax: Brown Superfine
Wingcase: Dark turkey
Legs: Brown partridge
Antennae: Woodduck mallard
Eyes: Black monofilament

Caddis Pupa, Green (Nori Tashiro)
Hook: TMC 3769, sizes 12-16
Thread: Black, 6/0
Rib: Mint Flashabou
Abdomen: Caddis green Antron
Thorax: Black Superfine
Wingcase: Dark turkey
Legs: Brown partridge
Antennae: Pheasant tail
Eyes: Black monofilament

Carrot Nymph *(Ed Schroeder)*
>   Hook: TMC 5263, sizes 12-16
>   Thread: Orange, 3/0
>   Tail: Pheasant tail
>   Back: Peacock
>   Rib: Fine gold wire
>   Abdomen: Orange thread, 3/0
> Wingcase: Pearl Flashabou
>   Hackle: Brown
>   Thorax: Peacock

CDC Caddis Emerger, Brown
>   Hook: TMC 100, sizes 14-20
>   Thread: Coffee, 6/0
>   Tail: Brown Z-Lon
>   Rib: Fine wire
>   Abdomen: Chocolate brown Antron or Z-Lon, twisted tightly
>   Legs: Partridge
>   Wing: Dun CDC over brown Z-Lon
> Antennae: Woodduck mallard flank
>   Head: Chocolate brown Antron

CDC Caddis Emerger, Cream
>   Hook: TMC 100, sizes 14-18
>   Thread: Brown, 6/0
>   Tail: Gold Z-lon
>   Rib: Fine gold wire
>   Abdomen: Gold Antron or Z-Lon, twisted tightly
>   Legs: Brown partridge
>   Wing: Cream CDC over cream Z-Lon
> Antennae: Woodduck mallard flank
>   Head: Brown Antron

CDC Caddis Emerger, Olive
>   Hook: TMC 100, sizes 14-20
>   Thread: Olive, 6/0
>   Tail: Olive Z-Lon
>   Rib: Fine copper wire
>   Abdomen: Olive Antron or Z-Lon, twisted tightly
>   Legs: Brown partridge
>   Wing: Dark dun CDC over dark dun Z-Lon
> Antennae: Woodduck mallard flank
>   Head: Dark brown Antron

CDC Caterpillar *(Gerhard Laible)*
>   Hook: TMC 5212, size 8
>   Thread: Black, 8/0
>   Rib: Peacock herl and natural gray CDC
>   Body: Yellow poly

CDC Emerging Nymph, Blue-Winged Olive
>   Hook: TMC 100, size 20
>   Thread: Olive, 6/0
>   Rib: Fine copper wire
>   Wing: Dun CDC
>   Tail: Dun hackle fibers
>   Body: Olive Superfine

CDC Floating Nymph/Emerger, Blue-Winged Olive
>   Hook: TMC 5230, sizes 16-20
>   Thread: Olive, 6/0
>   Tail: Teal flank fibers
>   Rib: Fine gold wire
>   Abdomen: Olive rabbit or Antron
>   Wing: Dark dun CDC, short, light gray Z-Lon, dark dun CDC, and light dun CDC
>   Thorax: Same as abdomen

CDC Floating Nymph/Emerger, Callibaetis
>   Hook: TMC 5230, sizes 14-16
>   Thread: Tan, 6/0
>   Tail: Woodduck mallard
>   Rib: Fine copper wire
>   Abdomen: Tan rabbit or Antron
>   Wing: Brown Z-Lon, brown partridge, and medium dun CDC
>   Thorax: Same as abdomen

CDC Floating Nymph/Emerger, Hendrickson
>   Hook: TMC 100, sizes 14-16
>   Thread: Brown, 6/0
>   Tail: Woodduck mallard
>   Rib: Fine copper wire
>   Abdomen: Rusty brown Superfine
>   Wing: Light dun Z-Lon, dark dun CDC, and light partridge

CDC Floating Nymph/Emerger, Pale Morning Dun
- Hook: TMC 100, sizes 16-20
- Thread: Light olive, 6/0
- Tail: Yellow mallard
- Rib: Fine gold wire
- Abdomen: Yellow-olive Superfine
- Wing: Yellow Z-Lon, dun CDC, and brown partridge
- Thorax: Same as abdomen

CDC Floating Nymph/Emerger, Trico
- Hook: TMC 100, sizes 20-22
- Thread: Black, 6/0
- Tail: Woodduck mallard
- Rib: Fine copper wire
- Abdomen: Olive Superfine
- Wing: Light dun Z-Lon, light partridge, and white CDC
- Thorax: Dark brown Superfine

CDC Green Drake Emerger (*Shane Stalcup*)
- Hook: TMC 2302, sizes 10-12
- Thread: Olive, 6/0
- Tail: Brown partridge
- Rib: Fine copper wire
- Abdomen: Olive turkey biot
- Thorax: Chartreuse Superfine
- Wing: Natural gray CDC
- Legs: Brown partridge
- Overwing: Dun Z-lon

CDC Loop Wing Emerger, Gray (*Shane Stalcup*)
- Hook: TMC 2487, sizes 18-22
- Thread: Gray, 6/0
- Tail: Dun hen saddle
- Abdomen: Gray goose biot
- Wingcase: Dun CDC
- Thorax: Adams gray Superfine
- Legs: Dun hen saddle

CDC Loop Wing Emerger, Olive (*Shane Stalcup*)
- Hook: TMC 2487, sizes 18-22
- Thread: Olive, 6/0
- Tail: Dun hen saddle
- Abdomen: Olive goose biot
- Wingcase: Dun CDC
- Thorax: Gray-olive Superfine
- Legs: Dun hen saddle

Chironomid Pupa, Black (*Randall Kaufmann*)
- Hook: TMC 900BL, sizes 14-20
- Thread: Black, 6/0
- Tail: Clear Antron fibers tied short
- Antennae: Clear Antron fibers, short
- Rib: White silk thread
- Abdomen: Black, olive, browns, etc. Superfine; bodies must be slender
- Thorax: Peacock
- Wings: Grizzly hen hackle tips tied one-third body length

Chironomid Pupa, Olive (*Randall Kaufmann*)
- Hook: TMC 900BL, sizes 14-20
- Thread: Black, 6/0
- Tail: White Z-Lon or clear Antron fibers
- Antennae: Same as tail
- Rib: White thread
- Abdomen: Olive dubbing
- Thorax: Peacock herl
- Wing: Grizzly hen hackle tips

Cranefly (*John Barr*)
- Hook: TMC 200R, sizes 6-10, weighted
- Head: Gold bead
- Thread: Olive, 6/0
- Tail: Grizzly marabou from base of hackle
- Back: Clear heavy mil plastic
- Abdomen: Sooty olive Scintilla dubbing
- Thorax: Gray ostrich

Cranefly Larva, Olive
- Hook: TMC 9395, size 4, weighted
- Thread: Black, 6/0
- Tail: Dun gray brown hackle fluff
- Rib: Olive Swannundaze
- Abdomen: Olive Paxton's dubbing
- Head: Black Paxton's dubbing

Cranefly Larva, Tan
Hook:	TMC 9395, size 4, weighted
Thread:	Tan, 6/0
Tail:	Mottled tan hen saddle fibers
Rib:	Clear Swannundaze
Abdomen:	Cream Paxton's dubbing
Head:	Pale hare's ear

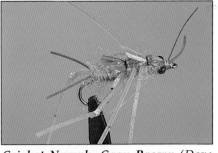

Cricket Nymph, Gray-Brown (Dave Whitlock)
Hook:	TMC 5212, sizes 8-12
Thread:	Brown, 6/0
Antennae:	Gray rubber
Eyes:	Monofilament nymph eyes
Abdomen:	Tan Haretron
Tail:	Black and fire orange rubber
Legs:	Tan Sili-Legs
Wingcase:	Brown Swiss Straw with pearl Flashabou
Thorax:	Same as abdomen

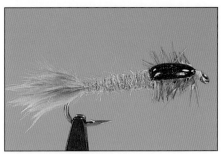

Damsel (Hal Janssen)
Hook:	TMC 5263, sizes 8-10
Thread:	Olive, 6/0
Tail:	Brownish-olive marabou
Rib:	Olive thread
Abdomen:	Bleached beaver (40%) and olive rabbit (60%)
Wingcase:	Mottled turkey wing quill, lacquered
Hackle:	Ginger hackle, clipped top and bottom, trimmed on sides
Thorax:	Light olive chenille

Damsel, Brown (Dave Whitlock)
Hook:	TMC 5262, sizes 8-10
Thread:	Brown, 6/0
Eyes:	Monofilament
Tail:	Brown marabou
Rib:	Gold oval tinsel
Abdomen:	Brown Antron
Wingcase:	Brown raffia
Legs:	Mottled dark brown hen saddle
Thorax:	Same as abdomen

Damsel, Olive (John Barr)
Hook:	TMC 200R, size 8
Thread:	Olive, 6/0
Eyes:	Extra small monofilament nymph eyes
Tail:	Olive grizzly hackle fluff
Rib:	Clear 4X monofilament
Back:	Clear plastic, across entire top of fly
Abdomen:	Olive brown Scintilla
Legs:	Soft olive grizzly hackle fibers
Thorax:	Same as abdomen

Damsel, Olive (Andy Burk)
Hook:	TMC 9300, size 10
Thread:	Olive, 6/0
Eyes:	Extra small monofilament nymph eyes
Tail:	Olive marabou tied onto end of abdomen
Abdomen:	Olive Ultra Chenille or Vernille
Wingcase:	Dark turkey tail
Thorax:	Brown olive Paxton's Buggy Nymph

Damsel, Olive (Dave Whitlock)
Hook:	TMC 5263, sizes 8-10
Thread:	Olive, 6/0
Eyes:	Monofilament nymph eyes
Tail:	Olive marabou
Rib:	Fine gold wire
Abdomen:	Olive Antron
Wingcase:	Olive Swiss Straw
Legs:	Olive grouse or hen
Thorax:	Olive Antron
Head:	Olive Swiss Straw

Damsel, Tan (Andy Burk)
Hook:	TMC 9300, size 10
Thread:	Coffee, 6/0
Eyes:	Extra small monofilament nymph eyes
Tail:	Buff marabou tied onto end of abdomen
Abdomen:	Tan Ultra Chenille or Vernille
Wingcase:	Dark turkey tail
Thorax:	Cinnamon Paxton's Buggy Nymph

Danger Baby, Chocolate (Theo Bakelaar)
Hook:	TMC 3769, sizes 10-14
Head:	Gold bead
Thread:	Black, 6/0
Tag:	Chartreuse Flexibody
Abdomen:	Peacock
Wing:	Chocolate Antron yarn or Z-Lon
Thorax:	Peacock

Danger Baby, Copper *(Theo Bakelaar)*
Hook: TMC 3769, sizes 10-14
Head: Gold bead
Thread: Black, 6/0
Tag: Chartreuse Flexibody
Abdomen: Peacock
Wing: Copper Antron yarn or Z-Lon
Thorax: Peacock

Danger Baby, Olive *(Theo Bakelaar)*
Hook: TMC 3769, sizes 10-14
Head: Gold bead
Thread: Black, 6/0
Tag: Chartreuse Flexibody
Abdomen: Peacock
Wing: Olive Antron yarn or Z-Lon
Thorax: Peacock

Deep Sparkle Pupa, Ginger *(Gary LaFontaine)*
Hook: TMC 100, sizes 12-14
Thread: Cream, 6/0
Abdomen/Veil: Cream Antron yarn
Abdomen: Cream Antron
Wing: Woodduck mallard
Head: Same as abdomen

Deep Sparkle Pupa, Gray *(Gary LaFontaine)*
Hook: TMC 100, sizes 12-16
Thread: Gray, 6/0
Abdomen Veil: Gray Antron yarn
Abdomen: Gray Antron
Wing: Woodduck mallard
Head: Same as abdomen

Deep Sparkle Pupa, Green *(Gary LaFontaine)*
Hook: TMC 100, sizes 14-16
Thread: Brown, 6/0
Abdomen Veil: Green Antron yarn
Abdomen: Green Antron
Wing: Brown partridge
Head: Brown Superfine

Deep Sparkle Pupa, Tan *(Gary LaFontaine)*
Hook: TMC 100, sizes 12-16
Thread: Brown, 6/0
Abdomen/Veil: Tan Antron yarn
Abdomen: Tan Antron
Wing: Woodduck mallard
Head: Brown Superfine

Dinky Stone *(Mike Mercer)*
Hook: TMC 100, sizes 16-18
Thread: Brown, 6/0
Antennae: Brown turkey or goose biot
Head: Copper bead
Tail: Same as antennae
Abdomen: Golden Antron overwrapped with golden tan turkey biot, Panton brown on top
Wingcase: Brown hen
Thorax: Golden Antron
Legs: Same as wingcase

Disco Midge, Light Olive *(Bill Fitzsimmons)*
Hook: TMC 200R, size 20
Thread: Light Olive, 8/0
Abdomen: Light olive Accent Flash
Head: Peacock herl

Disco Midge, Pearl *(Bill Fitzsimmons)*
Hook: TMC 200R, size 20
Thread: Cream, 8/0
Abdomen: Pearl Accent Flash
Head: Peacock herl

Disco Midge, Pink *(Bill Fitzsimmons)*
Hook: TMC 200R, size 20
Thread: Cream, 8/0
Abdomen: Pink Accent Flash
Head: Peacock herl

Disco Midge, Red *(Bill Fitzsimmons)*
Hook: TMC 200R, sizes 18-22
Thread: Red, 8/0
Abdomen: Red Accent Flash
Head: Peacock herl

Diving Caddis, Green *(Gary LaFontaine)*
Hook: TMC 9300, sizes 12-16
Thread: Black, 6/0
Body: Green Antron
Wing: Brown partridge over clear Antron fibers
Hackle: Brown

Diving Caddis, Tan *(Gary LaFontaine)*
Hook: TMC 9300, sizes 14-16
Thread: Black, 6/0
Body: Tan Antron
Wing: Brown partridge over clear Antron fibers
Hackle: Brown

Dragon *(John Gierach)*
Hook: TMC 200R, sizes 8-12, weighted
Thread: Black, 6/0
Eyes: Monofilament nymph eyes
Rib: Fine flat gold tinsel
Abdomen: Hare's ear dubbing
Underwing: Dark brown deer
Wing: Dark turkey
Legs: Ringneck pheasant or brown partridge
Head: Hare's ear
Notes: Tied with the hook pointed up.

Dragon *(John Barr)*
Hook: TMC 200R, size 4
Thread: Brown, 6/0
Eyes: Small monofilament nymph eyes
Tail: Black marabou
Back: Clear plastic; mark with brown and black Pantone pen
Rib: 3X monofilament
Abdomen: Brown-olive Scintilla or Paxton's Buggy Nymph
Legs: Black hen hackle or soft rooster hackle

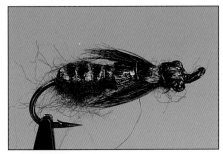

Dragon, Black *(Dave Whitlock)*
Hook: TMC 7999, sizes 4, 8, wghtd.
Thread: Black, 6/0
Eyes: Monofilament nymph eyes
Back/Wingcase: Brown Swiss Straw; black Pantone highlights
Rib: Fine gold wire
Abdomen: Black and red Antron
Legs: Chocolate brown hackle fibers, soft
Thorax: Black Antron
Head: Black Antron

Dragon, Brown *(Dave Whitlock)*
Hook: TMC 7999, sizes 4 and 8
Thread: Brown, 6/0
Eyes: Monofilament nymph eyes
Back/Wingcase: Brown Swiss Straw; black Pantone highlights
Rib: Fine gold wire
Abdomen: Brown Antron
Legs: Brown hen saddle or brown grizzly, soft
Thorax: Brown Antron
Head: Brown Antron

Dragon, Olive *(Dave Whitlock)*
Hook: TMC 7999, sizes 4, 8, wghtd.
Thread: Olive, 6/0
Eyes: Monofilament nymph eyes
Back/Wingcase: Olive Swiss Straw; black Pantone highlights
Rib: Fine gold wire
Abdomen: Olive Antron
Legs: Olive grizzly hackle fibers, soft
Thorax: Olive Antron
Head: Olive Antron

Drifting Cased Caddis, Olive Green
   Hook: TMC 5262, sizes 12-16
   Thread: Black, 6/0
   Abdomen: Turkey tail
   Thorax: Green Antron
   Head: Black Antron
   Legs: Black hackle fibers, stiff and clipped

Dutch CDC (Theo Bakelaar)
   Hook: TMC 3761, sizes 10-14
   Head: Gold bead
   Thread: Brown, 6/0
   Tail: Dyed brown pheasant tail fibers
   Rib: Fine copper wire
   Abdomen: Same as tail
   Legs: Natural gray CDC
   Thorax: Peacock

Egg Leech, Black and Orange
   Hook: TMC 5263, sizes 2-6
   Thread: Black 6/0
   Eyes: Nickel plated steel
   Tail: Black rabbit strip
   Body: Black cross-cut rabbit strip
   Thorax: Black rabbit dubbing
   Head: Fluorescent hot pink chenille

Egg Leech, Black and Red
   Hook: TMC 5263, sizes 2-6
   Thread: Black 6/0
   Eyes: Nickel plated steel
   Tail: Black rabbit strip
   Body: Black cross-cut rabbit strip
   Thorax: Black rabbit dubbing
   Head: Fluorescent red chenille

Electric Caddis, Cream (Mike Lawson)
   Hook: TMC 3761, sizes 14-16
   Thread: Cream, 6/0
   Rib: Fine copper wire
   Back: Pearlescent flat tinsel
   Abdomen: Cream Paxton's dubbing
   Head: Dark brown Paxton's dubbing

Electric Caddis, Olive (Mike Lawson)
   Hook: TMC 3761, sizes 14-16
   Thread: Olive, 6/0
   Rib: Fine copper wire
   Back: Pearlescent flat tinsel
   Abdomen: Olive Paxton's dubbing
   Head: Dark brown Paxton's dubbing

Emergent Sparkle Pupa, Bright Green
(Gary LaFontaine)
   Hook: TMC 100, sizes 12-18
   Thread: Black, 6/0
   Shuck: Bright green Antron yarn
   Abdmn. Veil: Bright green Antron yarn
   Abdomen: Bright green Antron
   Wing: Natural deer
   Head: Dark brown Superfine

Emergent Sparkle Pupa, Brown and Yellow (Gary LaFontaine)
   Hook: TMC 100, sizes 12-18
   Thread: Black, 6/0
   Shuck: Tan Antron yarn
   Abdmn. Veil: Tan Antron yarn
   Abdomen: Tan Antron
   Wing: Natural tan deer
   Head: Dark brown Superfine

Emergent Sparkle Pupa, Dark Gray
(Gary LaFontaine)
   Hook: TMC 100, sizes 12-18
   Thread: Gray, 6/0
   Shuck: Dark gray Antron yarn
   Abdmn. Veil: Dark gray Antron yarn
   Abdomen: Dark gray Antron
   Wing: Natural gray deer
   Head: Same as abdomen

Emergent Sparkle Pupa, Ginger *(Gary LaFontaine)*

Hook:	TMC 100, sizes 12-18
Thread:	Cream, 6/0
Shuck:	Cream Antron yarn
Abdomen Veil:	Cream Antron yarn
Abdomen:	Cream Antron
Wing:	Light deer
Head:	Same as abdomen

Emerger, Dry, Blue-Winged Olive *(John Barr)*

Hook:	TMC 101, sizes 16-22
Thread:	Gray, 8/0
Tail:	Brown hackle fibers (stiff)
Abdomen:	Olive-brown Scintilla
Wingcase:	Dun hackle fibers (stiff)
Thorax:	Blue dun Superfine
Legs:	Dun hackle fibers (stiff)

Emerger, Dry, Pale Morning Dun *(John Barr)*

Hook:	TMC 101 sizes 16-22
Thread:	Light olive, 8/0
Tail:	Brown hackle fibers (stiff)
Abdomen:	Olive-brown Scintilla
Wingcase:	Pale olive hackle fibers (stiff)
Thorax:	Pale olive Superfine
Legs:	Pale olive hackle fibers (stiff)

Emerger, Pale Morning Dun *(Mike Lawson)*

Hook:	TMC 100 or TMC 5210, sizes 16-18
Thread:	Pale olive, 6/0
Tail:	Woodduck mallard
Rib:	Light olive Monocord
Body:	Pale yellow olive hare's ear
Hackle:	Medium gray hen

Emerger, Wet, Blue-Winged Olive *(John Barr)*

Hook:	TMC 2457, sizes 14-18; TMC 2487, sizes 20-22
Thread:	Gray, 8/0
Tail:	Brown hackle fibers (stiff)
Abdomen:	Olive brown Superfine
Wingcase:	Dun hackle fibers (stiff)
Thorax:	Blue dun Superfine
Legs:	Dun hackle fibers (stiff)

Emerger, Wet, Pale Morning Dun *(John Barr)*

Hook:	TMC 2457, sizes 14-18; TMC 2487, sizes 20-22
Thread:	Light olive, 8/0
Tail:	Brown hackle fibers (stiff)
Abdomen:	Olive brown Superfine
Wingcase:	Pale olive hackle fibers (stiff)
Thorax:	Pale olive Superfine
Legs:	Pale olive hackle fibers (stiff)

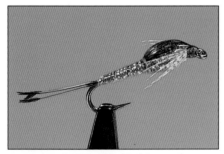

Emerging Callibaetis *(Hal Janssen)*

Hook:	TMC 5262, sizes 14-16
Thread:	Gray, 6/0
Tail:	Dyed gray Amherst pheasant tippets
Abdomen:	Gray rabbit dubbing, over-wrapped with clear plastic
Wingcase:	Dark duck quill, epoxied
Thorax:	Same as abdomen
Legs:	Woodduck mallard

Epoxy Scud, Amber *(Brad Befus)*

Hook:	TMC 200R, sizes 12-18
Thread:	Orange, 6/0
Tail:	Woodduck or mallard dyed woodduck
Back:	Hot orange Krystal Flash, coated with epoxy
Body:	No. 46 Ligas dubbing
Eyes:	Black Pantone

Epoxy Scud, Olive *(Brad Befus)*

Hook:	TMC 200R, sizes 12-18
Thread:	Olive, 6/0
Tail:	Woodduck or mallard dyed woodduck
Back:	Pearl Krystal Flash coated with epoxy
Body:	Gray-olive Ligas Dubbing
Eyes:	Black Pantone

Feather Duster
  Hook: TMC 5262, sizes 10-16
  Thread: Brown, 6/0
  Tail: Brown partridge
  Rib: Fine gold wire
  Abdomen: Natural brown ostrich
  Wingcase: Brown partridge
  Thorax: Same as abdomen
  Legs: Brown partridge

Flash Gun (Theo Bakelaar)
  Hook: TMC 2312, sizes 10-14
  Head: Gold bead
  Thread: Black, 6/0
  Tail: Black hackle fibers
  Abdomen: Pearl Flashabou
  Wingcase: Same as abdomen
  Thorax: Black Paxton's Buggy Nymph

Flashabou (Ed Schroeder)
  Hook: TMC 5263, sizes 10-14,
            weighted
  Thread: Black, 3/0
  Tail: Pheasant tail fibers
  Rib: Fine gold wire
  Abdomen: Pearl Flashabou
  Wingcase: Pearl Flashabou
  Thorax: Black Antron, picked out

Flash-A-Bugger, Black and Black
  Hook: TMC 300, sizes 2-10, weighted
  Thread: Black, 3/0
  Tail: Black marabou with pearl
            Flashabou
  Rib: Fine copper wire
  Body: Black chenille with pearl
            Flashabou
  Hackle: Black

Flash-A-Bugger, Black and Olive
  Hook: TMC 300, sizes 2-10, weighted
  Thread: Black 3/0
  Tail: Black marabou with olive
            Flashabou
  Rib: Fine copper wire
  Body: Dark olive chenille with olive
            Flashabou
  Hackle: Black

Flash-A-Bugger, Black and Orange
  Hook: TMC 300, sizes 2-10, weighted
  Thread: Black, 3/0
  Tail: Black marabou with pearl
            Flashabou
  Rib: Fine copper wire
  Body: Orange chenille with pearl
            Flashabou
  Hackle: Black

Flashback, Black
  Hook: TMC 700, sizes 4-6, weighted
  Thread: Black, 3/0
  Rib: Pearl Flashabou
  Tail: Black hackle fibers and pearl
            Flashabou
  Abdomen: Coarse black dubbing; try
            Angora goat and rabbit
  Wingcase: Dark turkey or dyed black
            goose
  Legs: Black hen hackle and pearl
            Flashabou

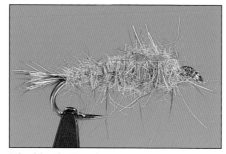

Flashback, Hare's Ear
  Hook: TMC 3761, sizes 8-20
  Thread: Tan, 6/0
  Tail: Brown partridge
  Rib: Fine oval gold tinsel
  Abdomen: Hare's ear dubbing
  Wingcase: Pearl Flashabou
  Thorax: Hare's ear dubbing
  Legs: Fur picked out from the
            abdomen

Flashback, Pheasant Tail
  Hook: TMC 3761 or 200R, sizes 12-
            22
  Thread: Brown, 6/0
  Tail: Ringneck pheasant tail
  Rib: Fine copper wire
  Abdomen: Ringneck pheasant tail
  Wingcase: Pearl Flashabou
  Head: Copper wire

Floating Nymph, Blue-Winged Olive
(Mike Lawson)
        Hook: TMC 100, sizes 20-22
      Thread: Olive, 8/0
          Tail: Light blue dun hackle fibers
          Rib: Olive thread, 6/0
  Abdomen: Blue-winged olive Superfine
        Wing: Light gray ball of poly dubbing
    Thorax: Same as abdomen
        Legs: Same as tail

Floating Nymph, Pale Morning Dun
(Mike Lawson)
        Hook: TMC 100, sizes 16-18
      Thread: Brown, 8/0
          Tail: Light blue dun hackle fibers
  Abdomen: Pale morning dun Superfine
        Wing: Light gray ball of poly dubbing
    Thorax: Same as abdomen
        Legs: Same as tail

Floating Nymph, Slate Tan (Mike Lawson)
        Hook: TMC 100, sizes 16-18
      Thread: Tan, 8/0
          Tail: Dark blue dun hackle fibers
  Abdomen: Tan Superfine
        Wing: Dark gray ball of poly dubbing
    Thorax: Same as abdomen
        Legs: Same as tail

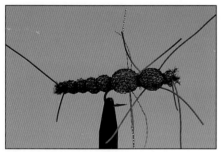

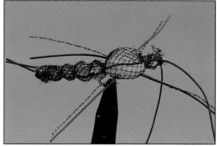

Foam Nymph, Dark Stone (Sandy Pittendrigh)
        Hook: TMC 3769, sizes 12-14
      Thread: Black, 3/0
        Body: Gray open cell foam with dyed brown spawn sack covering
        Legs: Fine gray rubber with pearl Krystal Flash
          Rib: Black thread
          Tail: Fine gray rubber
  Antennae: Same as tail

Foam Nymph, Light Stone (Sandy Pittendrigh)
        Hook: TMC 3769, size 14
      Thread: Tan, 6/0
        Body: Natural white open cell foam with dyed brown spawn sack material covering
        Legs: Fine gray rubber with Krystal Flash
          Rib: Brown tying thread
          Tail: Fine gray rubber
  Antennae: Fine gray rubber

Freshwater Shrimp, Gray (Dave Whitlock)
        Hook: TMC 3761, sizes 10-14, weighted
      Thread: Gray, 6/0
        Eyes: Monofilament nymph eyes
  Antennae: Gray Kevlar thread
  Abdomen: Gray spectrumized dubbing
        Legs: Natural grizzly hackle
        Back: Clear plastic
          Rib: Fine gold wire

Freshwater Shrimp, Olive (Dave Whitlock)
        Hook: TMC 3761, sizes 10-14, weighted
      Thread: Olive, 6/0
        Eyes: Monofilament nymph eyes
  Antennae: Gray Kevlar thread
  Abdomen: Olive spectrumized dubbing
        Legs: Natural grizzly hackle
        Back: Clear plastic
          Rib: Fine gold wire

Giant Caddis Pupa (Nori Tashiro)
        Hook: TMC 700, size 8
      Thread: Tan, 6/0
  Abdomen: Cream Antron
    Thorax: Brown Antron
        Legs: Woodduck mallard
        Wing: Dark turkey
        Eyes: Monofilament nymph eyes
  Antennae: Woodduck mallard

Girdle Bug
        Hook: TMC 5263, sizes 4-8, weighted
      Thread: Black, 6/0
          Tail: White rubber
        Body: Black chenille
        Legs: White rubber
  Antennae: White rubber

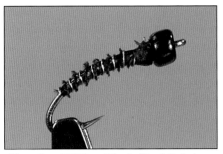

Glass Bead Midge, Black *(Brad Befus)*
Hook: TMC 200R, sizes 18, 20
Head: Black glass bead
Thread: Black, 6/0
Rib: Fine gold wire
Body: Black turkey biot

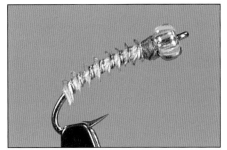

Glass Bead Midge, Olive *(Brad Befus)*
Hook: TMC 200R, sizes 18, 20
Head: Olive glass bead
Thread: Olive, 6/0
Rib: Fine gold wire
Body: Olive turkey biot

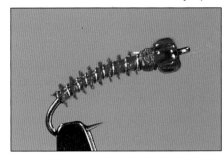

Glass Bead Midge, Red *(Brad Befus)*
Hook: TMC 200R, sizes 18, 20
Head: Red glass bead
Thread: Red, 6/0
Rib: Fine gold wire
Body: Red turkey biot

Glass Bead Midge, White *(Brad Befus)*
Hook: TMC 200R, sizes 18, 20
Head: Pearl glass bead
Thread: White, 6/0
Rib: Fine gold wire
Body: White turkey biot

Gold-Ribbed Hare's Ear
Hook: TMC 3761, sizes 8-20, weighted
Thread: Black, 6/0
Tail: Hare's mask guard hairs
Rib: Fine oval gold tinsel
Abdomen: Hare's ear dubbing
Wingcase: Mottled turkey quill
Thorax: Hare's ear dubbing

Golden Stone, Revised *(Dave Whitlock)*
Hook: TMC 9395, sizes 6-8, weighted
Thread: Golden olive or pale yellow, 6/0
Eyes: Gold lead or steel
Antennae: Tan Wag's Life Flex, Pantone
Abdomen: Golden yellow Antron and Partridge SLF, blend 50/50
Tail: Same as antennae
Rib: Gold wire
Back: Gold Swiss Straw, Pantone black
Thorax: Same as abdomen
Wingcase: Gold Swiss Straw, Pantone black
Legs: Same as antennae, 3 sets

Green Drake *(Mike Lawson)*
Hook: TMC 3761, sizes 10-12
Thread: Olive, 3/0
Tail: Dark mottled partridge or grouse fibers
Rib: Fine gold wire
Abdomen: Dark olive-brown Antron; pick out both sides for gills
Wingcase: Dark gray goose quill segment
Thorax: Same as abdomen
Legs: Mottled brown partridge or grouse

Green Drake *(Roy Palm)*
Hook: TMC 3769, size 12, weighted
Thread: Olive, 6/0
Tail: Turkey tail fibers
Rib: Fine copper wire
Abdomen: Dark olive rabbit
Wingcase: Dark turkey
Thorax: Same as abdomen

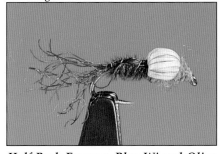

Half Back Emerger, Blue-Winged Olive *(Mike Lawson)*
Hook: TMC 100, size 18-20
Thread: Olive, 6/0
Shuck: Brown Z-Lon
Rib: Fine red copper wire
Abdomen: Pheasant tail
Wingcase: Medium gray deer
Thorax: Olive Superfine

Half Back Emerger, Pale Morning Dun
(Mike Lawson)
- Hook: TMC 100, sizes 16-18
- Thread: Pale yellow, 6/0
- Shuck: Brown Z-Lon
- Rib: Fine red copper wire
- Abdomen: Pheasant tail
- Wingcase: Light gray natural deer
- Thorax: Pale morning dun Superfine

Halo Emerger, Olive (Gary Lafontaine)
- Hook: TMC 100, size 16
- Thread: Olive, 6/0
- Antennae: Orange deer
- Tag: Clear Antron
- Tail: Olive-brown marabou
- Halo: Closed cell foam
- Body: Olive angora goat

Hare's Ear, Black (Randall Kaufmann)
- Hook: TMC 3761, sizes 12-16, weighted
- Thread: Black, 6/0
- Tail: Black hare's mask guard hair
- Rib: Medium copper wire
- Abdomen: Black hare's ear
- Wingcase: Peacock
- Thorax: Same as abdomen

Hare's Ear, Olive (Randall Kaufmann)
- Hook: TMC 3761, sizes 12-16, weighted
- Thread: Olive, 6/0
- Tail: Olive hare's mask guard hair
- Rib: Medium copper wire
- Abdomen: Olive hare's ear
- Wingcase: Peacock
- Thorax: Same as abdomen

Hellgrammite (Harry Murray)
- Hook: TMC 5262, sizes 8-10
- Thread: Black, 6/0
- Tail: Black ostrich herl
- Rib: Black thread or fine copper wire
- Abdomen: Black chenille
- Hackle: Very soft dark dun, palmered
- Antennae: Black rubber

Hellgrammite (Dave Whitlock)
- Hook: TMC 9395, bent to ride upside down, sizes 4-8, weighted
- Thread: Brown, 6/0
- Tail: Brown goose biot
- Antennae: Same as tail
- Rib: Medium copper wire
- Back: Brown Swiss Straw; same piece covers thorax area
- Abdomen: Gray-brown dubbing
- Thorax: Same as abdomen
- Legs: Mottled golden-brown hen saddle

Hexagenia (Andy Burk)
- Hook: TMC 200R, sizes 4-6, weighted
- Thread: Primrose or yellow, 6/0
- Tail: Natural gray marabou
- Back: Dark turkey quill
- Gills: Gray pheasant filoplume
- Rib: Copper wire
- Abdomen: Pale yellow rabbit or Paxton's Buggy Nymph
- Wingcase: Dark turkey tail
- Thorax: Same as abdomen
- Legs: Mottled brown hen saddle

Hunchback Infrequens (Andy Burk)
- Hook: TMC 2487, sizes 14-18, weighted
- Thread: Orange, 6/0
- Tail: Woodduck mallard
- Rib: Orange thread
- Abdomen: Rusty brown rabbit with trace of orange and olive
- Wingcase: Dark brown turkey tail
- Thorax: Same as abdomen
- Legs: Woodduck mallard

Kaufmann Stone, Black (Randall Kaufmann)
- Hook: TMC 300, sizes 2-10, weighted
- Thread: Black, 6/0
- Antennae: Black turkey biot
- Tail: Black turkey biot
- Rib: Black transparent Swannundaze
- Abdomen: Black Haretron, 50%, and claret, red, orange, rust, black, brown, blue, and purple goat
- Wingcase: Dark turkey tail, three sections
- Thorax, Head: Same as abdomen

Kaufmann Stone Rubber Legs, Black
(Randall Kaufmann)
Hook:	TMC 300 or 5263, sizes 4-12
Thread:	Black, 6/0
Antennae:	Black turkey biot
Tail:	Black turkey biot
Rib:	Black Swannundaze, size to fit
Abdomen:	Black Kaufmann Stone mix
Wingcase:	Three sections lacquered dark turkey tail, clipped to shape.
Legs:	Black rubber
Thorax:	Same as abdomen
Head:	Same as abdomen

Kaufmann Stone, Brown (Randall Kaufmann)
Hook:	TMC 300, sizes 2-10, weighted
Thread:	Brown, 6/0
Antennae:	Brown goose biot
Tail:	Brown turkey biot
Rib:	Brown transparent Swannundaze
Abdomen:	Brown Haretron, 50%, and claret, amber, orange, rust, black, brown, blue, purple, and ginger Angora goat, 50%
Wingcase:	Dark turkey tail, three sections
Thorax, Head:	Same as abdomen

Kaufmann Stone, Golden (Randall Kaufmann)
Hook:	TMC 300, sizes 8-12, weighted
Thread:	Brown, 6/0
Antennae:	Ginger goose biot
Tail:	Ginger goose biot
Rib:	Amber Swannundaze
Abdomen:	Golden brown Haretron, 50%, and claret, amber, orange, rust, black, brown, blue, purple, and ginger Angora goat, 50%
Wingcase:	Mottled turkey quil
Thorax, Head:	Same as abdomen

Krystal Bugger, Black
Hook:	TMC 5263, size 4
Thread:	Black 3/0
Eyes:	Nickel plated lead
Tail:	Black marabou with black Accent Flash
Rib:	Black thread or fine silver wire
Body:	Black Crystal Chenille
Hackle:	Black

Krystal Bugger, Motor Oil
Hook:	TMC 5263, size 4, weighted
Thread:	Black, 3/0
Eyes:	Nickel plated lead
Tail:	Black marabou with olive Accent Flash
Body:	Olive Crystal Chenille
Hackle:	Black

Krystal Bugger, Purple
Hook:	TMC 5263, size 4, weighted
Thread:	Black, 3/0
Eyes:	Nickel plated lead
Tail:	Black marabou with purple Accent Flash
Rib:	Fine silver wire
Body:	Purple Crystal Chenille
Hackle:	Black

Lake Dragon, Olive (Randall Kaufmann)
Hook:	TMC 5263, sizes 6-10, weighted
Thread:	Olive, 6/0
Eyes:	Monofilament nymph eyes
Tail:	Olive grizzly marabou, short
Rib:	Fine copper wire
Abdomen:	Olive rabbit, 50%; and blue, purple, green, amber, olive, rust, and brown Angora goat
Legs:	Olive ringneck rump
Wingcase:	Brown turkey tail
Thorax:	Same as abdomen

Lectric Leech, Black (Dave Whitlock)
Hook:	TMC 7999, sizes 1/0, 4, and 8, weighted
Thread:	Black, 6/0
Tail:	Black marabou, peacock, and blue Flashabou; continue peacock and Flashabou along each side of body
Body:	Black angora goat and black rabbit, 50/50 blend
Hackle:	Black saddle, long, webby, soft
Head:	Black, trimmed w/blue Flashabou

Lectric Leech, White (Dave Whitlock)
Hook:	TMC 7999, sizes 1/0, 4, and 8, weighted
Thread:	White, 6/0
Tail:	White marabou, peacock, and pearl Flashabou; continue peacock and Flashabou along each side of body
Body:	White angora goat and white rabbit, 50/50 blend
Hackle:	White saddle, long, webby, soft
Head:	White, trimmed with pearl Flashabou

Leech, Black (Larry Dahlberg)
Hook: TMC 800B, size 4
Thread: Black, 3/0
Eyes: Nickel plated steel
Snag Guard: Stainless wire
Tail: Black latex cut into a spiral shape
Body: Black cross-cut rabbit strip

Leech, Purple (Larry Dahlberg)
Hook: TMC 800B, size 4
Thread: Black, 3/0
Snag Guard: Stainless wire
Eyes: Nickel plated steel
Tail: Purple latex cut into a spiral shape
Body: Purple cross-cut rabbit strip

Leg, Hare's Ear (Andy Burk)
Hook: TMC 947BL, sizes 12-20
Thread: Cream or brown, 6/0
Tail: Mottled brown hen saddle
Rib: Gold wire
Abdomen: Hare's ear
Thorax: Hare's ear
Legs: Dark mottled hen saddle, Flexament into position
Wingcase: Dark turkey tail feather

Marabou Damsel, Olive (Randall Kaufmann)
Hook: TMC 200R, sizes 10-12
Thread: Olive, 6/0
Tail: Olive marabou, short
Rib: Fine copper wire
Body: Olive marabou, wrapped
Wing: Olive marabou, short; leftover tips from body; tear to length

Marabou Leech, Black (Hal Janssen)
Hook: TMC 300, sizes 4-8
Thread: Black 6/0
Tail: Black marabou
Body: Black thread, 6/0
Wing: Black marabou, staggered across top of body, with 6 strands black Accent Flash

Marabou Leech, Brown (Hal Janssen)
Hook: TMC 300, sizes 4-8
Thread: Brown, 6/0
Tail: Brown marabou
Body: Brown thread, 6/0
Wing: Brown marabou, staggered across top of body, with 6 strands brown Accent Flash

Marabou Leech, Olive (Hal Janssen)
Hook: TMC 300, sizes 4-8
Thread: Olive, 6/0
Tail: Olive marabou
Body: Olive thread, 6/0
Wing: Olive marabou, staggered across top of body, with 6 strands olive Accent Flash

Marabou Midge Larva, Olive (Bill Fitzsimmons)
Hook: TMC 200R, sizes 18-22
Thread: Olive, 8/0
Rib: Olive Accent Flash
Body: Olive marabou

Marabou Midge Larva, Red (Bill Fitzsimmons)
Hook: TMC 200R, sizes 18-22
Thread: Red, 8/0
Rib: Red Accent Flash
Body: Red marabou

Marabou Midge Larva, White (Bill Fitzsimmons)
Hook: TMC 200R, sizes 18-22
Thread: White, 8/0
Rib: Pearl Accent Flash
Body: White marabou

March Brown
Hook: TMC 3761, sizes 10-16, weighted
Thread: Brown, 6/0
Tail: Dark moose
Rib: Stripped peacock herl
Abdomen: Brown floss
Wingcase: Natural gray duck
Hackle: Brown
Thorax: Peacock

March Brown (Bob Jacklin)
Hook: TMC 5263, sizes 10-14, weighted
Thread: Brown, 6/0
Tail: Two ringneck tail fibers
Rib: Dark brown floss
Abdomen: Medium brown dubbing
Wingcase: Dark brown turkey
Legs: Dark mottled brown hen saddle, pulled flat over thorax
Thorax: Same as abdomen

Matt's Fur
Hook: TMC 5263, sizes 8-10, weighted
Thread: Brown, 6/0
Tail: Woodduck mallard
Rib: Fine oval gold tinsel
Abdomen: Cream Angora goat, 50% and otter, 50%
Wingcase: Woodduck mallard; tips form legs
Thorax: Same as abdomen

Mayfly (Ed Schroeder)
Hook: TMC 5263, sizes 12-16
Thread: Brown, 6/0
Tail: Woodduck mallard
Rib: Fine gold wire
Abdomen: Dark turkey
Legs: Woodduck mallard
Thorax: Dark gray ostrich

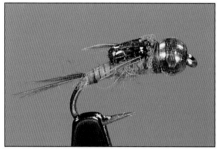

Micro Mayfly (Mike Mercer)
Hook: TMC 921, sizes 16-18
Head: Copper bead
Thread: Chartreuse, 6/0
Tail: Olive pheasant tail, 3 fibers, splayed
Abdomen: Olive stripped peacock herl
Wingcase: Pearl Flashabou over dark mottled turkey, epoxied
Legs: Olive pheasant tail fibers
Collar: Olive Superfine

Midge Biot, Black (Bill Fitzsimmons)
Hook: TMC 101, sizes 18-22
Thread: Black, 8/0
Body: Black goose or turkey biot
Thorax: Peacock
Hackle: Dark grizzly, soft

Midge Biot, Gray (Bill Fitzsimmons)
Hook: TMC 101, sizes 18-22
Thread: Gray, 8/0
Body: Gray goose or turkey biot
Thorax: Gray Superfine
Hackle: Dun hackle, soft

Midge Biot, Reddish Brown (Bill Fitzsimmons)
Hook: TMC 101, sizes 18-22
Thread: Reddish brown, 8/0
Body: Reddish brown goose or turkey biot
Thorax: Reddish brown Superfine
Hackle: Reddish brown, soft

Midge Emerger *(Craig Mathews)*
Hook: TMC 100, sizes 20-22
Thread: Black, 8/0
Shuck: White Z-Lon
Rib: Gray or white thread, 6/0
Abdomen: Black Superfine
Wing: White Z-Lon
Head: Black Superfine

Midge Emerger, Dun *(John Betts)*
Hook: TMC 101, sizes 20-24
Thread: Black, 8/0
Back: White Z-Lon (also forms tail)
Legs: Dun Z-Lon
Body: Black tying thread, 8/0

Midge Pupa
Hook: TMC 100, sizes 18-20
Thread: Black, 6/0
Rib: White thread
Body: Black Superfine
Thorax: Black Superfine

Mini Leech, Black *(Randall Kaufmann)*
Hook: TMC 200R, size 10
Thread: Black, 6/0
Tail: Black marabou, with 4 strands of black and red Krystal Flash
Body: Red and black Krystal Flash, 3-5 strands, and black angora goat

Mini Leech, Burgundy *(Randall Kaufmann)*
Hook: TMC 200R, size 10
Thread: Claret, 6/0
Tail: Burgundy hackle fluff or marabou with wine and pearl Krystal Flash
Body: Wine and pearl Krystal Flash and maroon angora goat
Note: Form dubbing loop for body, which should be sparse.

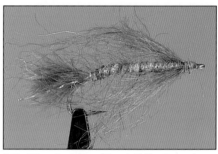

Mini Leech, Olive *(Randall Kaufmann)*
Hook: TMC 200R, size 10
Thread: Olive, 6/0
Tail: Olive marabou, with 4 strands olive Krystal Flash
Body: Olive Krystal Flash, 3-5 strands, olive angora goat

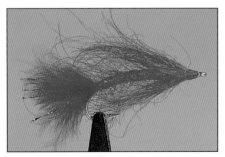

Mini Leech, Red *(Randall Kaufmann)*
Hook: TMC 200R, size 10
Thread: Red, 6/0
Tail: Red marabou, with 4 strands of red and pearl Krystal Flash
Body: Red and pearl Krystal Flash, 3-5 strands, and red angora goat

Montana Stone
Hook: TMC 5263, sizes 4-10, weighted
Thread: Black, 6/0
Tail: Black hackle fibers
Abdomen: Black chenille
Wingcase: Black chenille
Hackle: Black
Thorax: Yellow chenille

Morristone, Dark *(Skip Morris)*
Hook: TMC 200R, sizes 4-10, weighted
Thread: Black, 6/0
Tail: Mottled hen saddle
Rib: Brown V-Rib
Abdomen: Black sparkle blends
Wingcase: Dyed brown pheasant
Legs: Mottled hen saddle
Thorax: Same as abdomen
Head: Same as abdomen

Mosquito Larva
Hook: TMC 100, sizes 12-14
Thread: Black, 6/0
Tail: Grizzly hackle fibers
Body: Stripped peacock quill
Thorax: Peacock
Antennae: Grizzly hackle fibers

Muskrat
Hook: TMC 5263, sizes 10-12, weighted
Thread: Gray, 6/0
Tail: Gray squirrel or grizzly hackle fibers
Abdomen: Muskrat
Hackle: Grizzly

Mysis Shrimp (Bill Fitzsimmons)
Hook: TMC 200R, sizes 16-20
Thread: White, 6/0
Eyes: Black monofilament
Tail: White hackle, cut short, with a slightly longer strand of pearl Flashabou on top
Rib: Pearl Flashabou
Legs: White ostrich herl, palmered over the abdomen
Abdomen: White dubbing

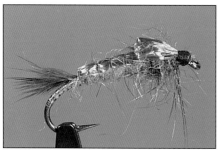

Near Nuff Caddis, Green (Dave Whitlock)
Hook: TMC 2302, sizes 12-14, weighted
Thread: Black, 6/0
Tag: Olive Krystal Flash
Tail: Light gray filoplume
Rib: Olive Krystal Flash
Back: Olive Swiss Straw
Abdomen: Green Antron and green rabbit, blend 50/50
Wingcase: Olive Swiss Straw
Thorax: Olive squirrel and dun gray Antron, 50/50

Near Nuff Caddis, Tan (Dave Whitlock)
Hook: TMC 2302, sizes 12-14, weighted
Thread: Black, 6/0
Tag: Orange Krystal Flash
Tail: Light gray filoplume
Rib: Orange Krystal Flash
Back: Brown Swiss Straw
Abdomen: Cream and light tan Antron and tan rabbit, equal parts
Wingcase: Brown Swiss Straw
Thorax: Natural squirrel and gray Antron, 50/50 blend

Net Builder, Amber (John Barr)
Hook: TMC 2457, sizes 8-14
Thread: Brown, 6/0
Tail: Gray ostrich
Back: Plastic from Zip-Lock bag
Rib: Clear 4X monofilament
Abdomen: Squirrel belly Umpqua sparkle blend
Thorax: Dark ostrich (represents legs); color top of plastic with brown Pantone

Net Builder, Cream (John Barr)
Hook: TMC 2457, sizes 8-14
Thread: Brown, 6/0
Tail: Gray ostrich
Back: Plastic from Zip-Lock bag
Rib: Clear 4X monofilament
Abdomen: Cream Scintilla
Thorax: Dark ostrich herl; color top of plastic with brown Pantone

Net Builder, Olive (John Barr)
Hook: TMC 2457, sizes 8-14, weighted
Thread: Brown, 6/0
Tail: Gray ostrich
Back: Plastic from Zip-Lock bag
Rib: Clear 4X monofilament
Abdomen: Olive Scintilla
Thorax: Dark ostrich herl; color top of plastic with brown Pantone

October Caddis Pupa (Mike Mercer)
Hook: TMC 200R, sizes 6-8
Thread: Orange, 6/0
Rib: Pearl flat tinsel
Abdomen: Orange Antron
Wing: Natural gray marabou, one clump on each side
Head: Natural dark brown ostrich or marabou
Hackle: Brown grouse or golden brown hen back feather

Palomino Cased Caddis, Black (Brett Smith)

Hook:	*TMC 2457, sizes 14-18*
Thread:	*Black, 6/0*
Abdomen:	*Olive Ultra Chenille, sizes 14 and 16; Olive Micro Chenille, size 18*
Tuft:	*Black Salmo-Web*
Abdmn. Taper:	*Black Superfine*
Legs:	*Black hen hackle*
Head:	*Black pheasant*

Palomino Cased Caddis, Olive (Brett Smith)

Hook:	*TMC 2457, sizes 14-18*
Thread:	*Olive, 6/0*
Abdomen:	*Olive Ultra Chenille for sizes 14 and 16; olive Micro Chenille for size 18*
Tuft:	*Dark olive Salmo-Web*
Abdmn. Taper:	*Caddis green Superfine*
Legs:	*Brown partridge*
Head:	*Olive pheasant*

Palomino Cased Caddis, Tan (Brett Smith)

Hook:	*TMC 2457, sizes 14-18*
Thread:	*Brown, 6/0*
Abdomen:	*Tan Ultra Chenille, sizes 14 and 16; tan Micro Chenille, size 18*
Tuft:	*Brown Salmo-Web*
Abdmn. Taper:	*Lava brown Paxton's Buggy Nymph*
Legs:	*Brown partridge*
Head:	*Natural pheasant*

Palomino Deep Caddis Pupa, Black (Brett Smith)

Hook:	*TMC 2457, sizes 14-18*
Thread:	*Black, 6/0*
Abdomen:	*Olive Ultra Chenille, size 14; olive Micro Chenille, size 16; green New Dub, size 18*
Thorax:	*Charcoal gray Paxton's Buggy Nymph*
Wing:	*Blue dun Salmo-Web*
Legs:	*Black hen hackle*
Head:	*Black Superfine*

Palomino Deep Caddis Pupa, Olive (Brett Smith)

Hook:	*TMC 2457, sizes 14-18*
Thread:	*Olive, 6/0*
Abdomen:	*Olive Ultra Chenille, size 14; olive Micro Chenille, size 16; green New Dub, size 18*
Thorax:	*Olive Paxton's Buggy Nymph*
Wing:	*Medium olive Salmo-Web; represents air bubble*
Legs:	*Brown partridge*
Head:	*Caddis green Superfine*

Palomino Deep Caddis Pupa, Tan (Brett Smith)

Hook:	*TMC 2457, sizes 14-18*
Thread:	*Olive, 6/0*
Abdomen:	*Tan Ultra Chenille, size 14; buckskin Micro Chenille, size 16; cream New Dub, size 18*
Thorax:	*Red fox squirrel belly fur*
Wing:	*Yellow Salmo-Web; represents air bubble*
Legs:	*Brown partridge*
Head:	*Light hare's ear Paxton's Buggy Nymph*

Palomino Emergent/Diving Caddis, Black (Brett Smith)

Hook:	*TMC 2457, sizes 14-18*
Thread:	*Black, 6/0*
Abdomen:	*Black Ultra Chenille (size 14); black Micro Chenille (size 16); black New Dub (size 18)*
Abdmn. Taper:	*Charcoal gray Superfine*
Wing:	*Black deer mixed with black Salmo-web*
Head:	*Black Superfine*

Palomino Emergent/Diving Caddis, Olive (Brett Smith)

Hook:	*TMC 2457, sizes 14-18*
Thread:	*Olive, 6/0*
Abdomen:	*Olive Ultra Chenille (size 14); olive Micro Chenille (size 16); green New Dub (size 18)*
Abdmn. Taper:	*Olive Paxton's Buggy Nymph*
Wing:	*Dyed dun deer mixed with blue dun Salmo-web*
Head:	*Caddis green Superfine*

Palomino Emergent/Diving Caddis, Tan (Brett Smith)

Hook:	*TMC 2457, sizes 14-18*
Thread:	*Olive, 6/0*
Abdomen:	*Tan Ultra Chenille (size 14); tan Micro Chenille (size 16); cream New Dub (size 18)*
Abdmn. Taper:	*Red fox belly*
Wing:	*Bleached deer mixed with yellow Salmo-web*
Head:	*Light hare's ear Paxton's Buggy Nymph*

Palomino Midge, Black (*Brett Smith*)
Hook: TMC 2487, sizes 18-22
Thread: Black, 8/0
Abdomen: Black New Dub
Wingcase: White Z-Lon; ends form anten-
            nae
Thorax: Black rabbit

Palomino Midge, Brown (*Brett Smith*)
Hook: TMC 2487, sizes 18-22
Thread: Brown, 6/0
Abdomen: Brown New Dub
Wingcase: White Z-Lon; ends form anten-
            nae
Thorax: Brown rabbit

Palomino Midge, Dark Olive (*Brett Smith*)
Hook: TMC 2487, sizes 18-22
Thread: Olive, 6/0
Abdomen: Olive New Dub
Wingcase: Dun Z-Lon; ends form anten-
            nae
Thorax: Olive rabbit

Palomino Midge, Gray (*Brett Smith*)
Hook: TMC 2487, sizes 18-22
Thread: Gray, 6/0
Abdomen: Dun New Dub
Wingcase: Dun Z-Lon; ends form anten-
            nae
Thorax: Gray rabbit

Palomino Midge, Red (*Brett Smith*)
Hook: TMC 2487, sizes 18-22
Thread: Tan, 6/0
Abdomen: Red New Dub
Wingcase: Dun Z-Lon; ends form anten-
            nae
Thorax: Tan rabbit

Peeking Caddis, Cream (*George Anderson*)
Hook: TMC 5262, sizes 10-16, weighted
Thread: Black, 6/0
Rib: Medium gold wire
Abdomen: Dark hare's ear and mask
Thorax: Cream rabbit
Legs: Brown partridge
Head: Black ostrich

Peeking Caddis, Green (*George Anderson*)
Hook: TMC 5262, sizes 10-16, weighted
Thread: Black, 6/0
Rib: Medium gold wire
Abdomen: Dark hare's ear and mask
Thorax: Olive or bright green rabbit
Legs: Brown partridge
Head: Black ostrich

Pheasant Tail
Hook: TMC 3761, sizes 10-20, weighted
Thread: Brown, 6/0
Tail: Ringneck pheasant tail
Rib: Fine copper wire
Abdomen: Ringneck pheasant tail
Wingcase: Ringneck pheasant tail fibers;
            tips form legs
Thorax: Peacock

Possie, Dark (*Dennis Black*)
Hook: TMC 3769, sizes 8-16, weighted
Thread: Black, 6/0
Tail: Light Australian opossum
Rib: Medium copper wire
Abdomen: Light Australian opossum
Thorax: Dark Australian opossum, left
            coarse

Possie, Light *(Dennis Black)*

Hook:	TMC 3769, sizes 8-16, weighted
Thread:	Black, 6/0
Tail:	Light Australian opossum
Rib:	Medium copper wire
Abdomen:	Light Australian opossum
Thorax:	Light Australian opossum, left coarse

Poxyback, Baetis *(Mike Mercer)*

Hook:	TMC 200R, sizes 18-20
Thread:	Chartreuse, 6/0
Tail:	Three pheasant tail fibers
Rib:	Chartreuse thread, 6/0
Abdomen:	Rusty olive Antron
Gills:	Light tan marabou clumps
Wingcase:	Dark mottled turkey tail, epoxied
Thorax:	Rusty olive Antron
Legs:	Woodduck or mallard
Head:	Chocolate brown Antron

Poxyback, Biot Golden Stone *(Mike Mercer)*

Hook:	TMC 2302, sizes 10-14, weighted
Thread:	Coffee, 6/0
Ant./Tail:	Callibaetis turkey biot; highlight with brown Pantone
Overbody:	Sulphur orange turkey biot
Underbody:	Golden superfine
Legs:	Golden hen saddle
Wingcase:	Pearl Flashabou over dark mottled turkey, epoxied
Thorax:	Golden stone Buggy Nymph
Collar:	Same as thorax, Pantone top br.

Poxyback, Callibaetis *(Mike Mercer)*

Hook:	TMC 200R, sizes 16-18
Thread:	Chartreuse, 6/0
Tail:	Natural gray ostrich herls
Rib:	Single strand pearl Flashabou
Abdomen:	Light tan-olive Antron
Gills:	Light gray tufts of marabou
Wingcase:	Dark brown mottled turkey tail, epoxied
Thorax:	Light tan-olive Antron
Legs:	Woodduck mallard
Head:	Light tan-olive Antron

Poxyback, Green Drake *(Mike Mercer)*

Hook:	TMC 200R, sizes 10-12, weighted
Thread:	Olive, 6/0
Tail:	Grouse or hen saddle fibers
Back:	Dark mottled turkey tail
Rib:	Fine copper wire
Gills:	Dark olive filoplume
Abdomen:	Dark olive-brown Antron
Wingcase:	Dark mottled turkey, epoxied
Legs:	Dark grouse, flat over thorax
Thorax:	Dark olive brown Antron
Head:	Dark olive brown Antron

Poxyback, Pale Morning Dun *(Mike Mercer)*

Hook:	TMC 200R, sizes 16-18
Thread:	Orange, 6/0
Tail:	Natural pheasant tail fibers
Back:	Dark mottled turkey tail
Rib:	One strand of pearl Flashabou
Abdomen:	Rusty orangish brown Antron
Gills:	Light tan tufts of marabou
Wingcase:	Same as back, epoxied
Thorax:	Same as abdomen
Legs:	Dark brown mottled grouse
Head:	Same as abdomen

Poxyback, Trico *(Mike Mercer)*

Hook:	TMC 900, sizes 20-24
Thread:	Black, 6/0
Tail:	Three splayed mottled hen saddle fibers
Back:	Dark mottled turkey tail
Rib:	Fine copper wire
Abdomen:	Dark chocolate brown ostrich
Wingcase:	Dark mottled turkey tail, epoxied
Thorax:	Dark chocolate brown Antron
Legs:	Brown partridge
Head:	Dark chocolate brown Antron

Poxy Biot Nymph, Black *(Mike Mercer)*

Hook:	TMC 200R, sizes 14-18
Thread:	Black, 6/0
Tail:	Black pheasant tail fibers, three
Back:	Pearl Flashabou, single strand
Abdomen:	Black turkey biot
Wing Pad:	Dun Z-Lon
Wingcase:	Mottled brown turkey tail, epoxied
Thorax:	Black Antron
Legs:	Same as tail
Head:	Same as thorax

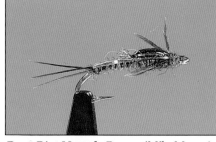

Poxy Biot Nymph, Brown *(Mike Mercer)*

Hook:	TMC 200R, sizes 14-18
Thread:	Tobacco brown, 6/0
Tail:	Natural pheasant tail fibers
Back:	Pearl Flashabou, single strand
Abdomen:	Black turkey biot
Wing Pad:	Brown Z-Lon
Wingcase:	Mottled turkey tail, epoxied
Thorax:	Antron dubbing to match abdomen
Legs:	Same as tail
Head:	Same as thorax

Poxy Biot Nymph, Olive (*Mike Mercer*)
- Hook: TMC 200R, sizes 14-18
- Thread: Olive, 6/0
- Tail: Yellow pheasant tail fibers
- Back: Pearl Flashabou, single strand
- Abdomen: Blue-winged olive turkey biot
- Wing Pad: Olive-brown Z-Lon
- Wingcase: Mottled turkey tail, epoxied
- Thorax: Antron dubbing to match abdomen
- Legs: Same as tail
- Head: Same as thorax

Prince
- Hook: TMC 5263, sizes 6-18, weighted
- Thread: Black, 6/0
- Tail: Brown goose or turkey biot
- Rib: Fine flat gold tinsel
- Body: Peacock
- Legs: Brown or furnace hackle
- Wing: White goose or turkey biot

Red Fox Squirrel (*Dave Whitlock*)
- Hook: TMC 5262, sizes 4-16, weighted
- Thread: Orange or black, 6/0
- Tail: Hair from red fox squirrel back
- Rib: Oval gold tinsel
- Abdomen: Red fox squirrel belly mixed 50/50 with fox tan Antron
- Thorax: Red fox squirrel back mixed 50/50 with charcoal Antron
- Legs: Mottled golden-brown hen saddle or brown partridge (smaller sizes)

Rough Squirrel Caddis, Dun (*Dave Whitlock*)
- Hook: TMC 2302, sizes 12-18
- Head: Gold bead
- Thread: Black, 6/0
- Tag: Pearl Krystal Flash
- Rib: Same as tag
- Abdomen: Muskrat and natural squirrel, 50/50 blend
- Legs: Mottled dark hen or partridge
- Collar: Same as abdomen

Rough Squirrel Caddis, Olive (*Dave Whitlock*)
- Hook: TMC 2302, sizes 12-18
- Head: Gold bead
- Thread: Olive, 6/0
- Tag: Light Olive Krystal Flash
- Rib: Same as tag
- Abdomen: Olive muskrat and olive squirrel, 50/50 blend
- Legs: Mottled dark hen or partridge
- Collar: Same as abdomen

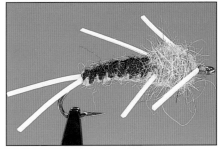

Rubber Legs Stone (*George Anderson*)
- Hook: TMC 5263, sizes 4-10, weighted
- Thread: Dark brown, 3/0
- Tail: White round rubber
- Abdomen: Cream (on bottom—to match hare's ear thorax) and medium brown (on top) woven synthetic fuzzy yarn
- Thorax: Medium brown hare's ear and mask dubbing, shaggy
- Legs: White round rubber (2 sets)

San Juan Worm, Fire Orange
- Hook: TMC 2457, sizes 6-10
- Thread: Orange, 6/0
- Body: Orange Vernille or Ultra Chenille, singed with a flame on both ends

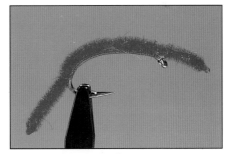

San Juan Worm, Red
- Hook: TMC 2457, sizes 6-10
- Thread: Red, 6/0
- Body: Red Vernille or Ultra Chenille, singed with a flame on both ends

San Juan Worm, Wine
- Hook: TMC 2457, sizes 6-10
- Thread: Maroon, 6/0
- Body: Maroon Vernille or Ultra Chenille, singed with a flame on both ends

Scintillator, Black (Kenn Ligas)
Hook: TMC 101, sizes 14-16
Thread: Black, 6/0
Abdomen: Black Scintilla
Bubble: Pearlescent plastic bead
Legs: Soft black hackle fibers
Antennae: Woodduck mallard
Head: Dark gray ostrich

Scintillator, Brown (Kenn Ligas)
Hook: TMC 101, sizes 14-16
Thread: Brown, 6/0
Abdomen: Sepia Scintilla
Bubble: Pearlescent plastic bead
Legs: Soft partridge
Antennae: Woodduck mallard
Head: Dark gray ostrich

Scintillator, Olive (Kenn Ligas)
Hook: TMC 101, sizes 14-16
Thread: Gray, 6/0
Abdomen: Bright lime Scintilla
Bubble: Pearlescent plastic bead
Legs: Partridge
Antennae: Woodduck mallard
Head: Gray ostrich

Scintillator, Pale Olive (Kenn Ligas)
Hook: TMC 101, sizes 14-16
Thread: Light olive, 6/0
Abdomen: Pale olive green (No. 03) Scintilla
Bubble: Pearlescent plastic bead
Legs: Woodduck mallard
Antennae: Same as legs
Head: Light brown ostrich

Scud, Brown Olive (Randall Kaufmann)
Hook: TMC 2457, sizes 10-18, weighted
Thread: Olive, 6/0
Tail: Brown olive marabou or hackle fibers
Antennae: Same as tail
Back: Heavy mil clear plastic with pearl Flashabou or pearl Holographic tinsel underneath
Rib: Clear monofilament
Abdomen: Brown olive blend of Angora goat and Hare-Tron

Scud, Gray Olive (Randall Kaufmann)
Hook: TMC 2457, sizes 10-18, weighted
Thread: Olive, 6/0
Tail: Olive marabou or hackle fibers
Antennae: Same as tail
Back: Heavy mil clear plastic with pearl Flashabou or pearl Holographic tinsel underneath
Rib: Clear monofilament
Abdomen: Gray olive blend of Angora goat and Hare-Tron, or use Kaufmann Gray-Olive blend

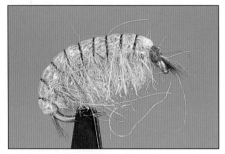

Scud, Tan (Randall Kaufmann)
Hook: TMC 2457, sizes 10-18, weighted
Thread: Tan, 6/0
Tail: Tan marabou or hackle fibers
Antennae: Same as tail
Back: Heavy mil clear plastic with pearl Flashabou or pearl Holographic tinsel underneath
Rib: Clear monofilament
Abdomen: Tan blend of Angora goat and Hare-Tron

Serendipity, Brown (Craig Mathews)
Hook: TMC 2487, sizes 14-22
Thread: Brown, 8/0
Body: PMD brown Z-Lon, twisted
Wingcase: Trimmed deer

Serendipity, Dark Green (Craig Mathews)
Hook: TMC 2487, sizes 14-22
Thread: Dark green, 8/0
Body: Dark green Z-Lon, twisted
Wingcase: Trimmed deer

Serendipity, Gray *(Craig Mathews)*
Hook: TMC 2487, sizes 14-22
Thread: Gray, 8/0
Body: Gray Z-Lon, twisted
Wingcase: Trimmed deer

Serendipity, Light Green *(Craig Mathews)*
Hook: TMC 2487, sizes 14-22
Thread: Light green, 8/0
Body: Light green Z-Lon, twisted
Wingcase: Trimmed deer

Serendipity, Red *(Craig Mathews)*
Hook: TMC 2487, sizes 14-22
Thread: Red, 8/0
Body: Red Z-Lon, twisted
Wingcase: Trimmed deer

Simple Winged *(Theo Bakelaar)*
Hook: TMC 3769, sizes 12-16
Head: Gold bead
Thread: Brown, 6/0
Abdomen: Pheasant tail fibers
Wing: Pearl or white Antron

Simulator, Peacock *(Randall Kaufmann)*
Hook: TMC 5263, sizes 4-12, weighted
Thread: Maroon, 6/0
Tail: Brown turkey biot
Rib: Medium to fine copper wire
Body: Peacock
Hackle: Furnace, palmered through body and clipped at an angle
Note: Other colors to suit.

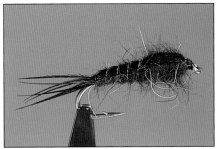

Skip's, Black *(Skip Morris)*
Hook: TMC 3761, sizes 10-20, weighted
Thread: Black, 6/0
Tail: Black hackle fibers
Rib: Fine copper wire
Back: Moose
Abdomen: Dark chocolate rabbit
Wingcase: Moose
Thorax: Same as abdomen

Skip's, Brown *(Skip Morris)*
Hook: TMC 3761, sizes 10-20, weighted
Thread: Brown, 6/0
Tail: Pheasant tail fibers
Rib: Fine copper wire
Back: Pheasant tail fibers
Abdomen: Medium brown hare's ear
Wingcase: Pheasant tail fibers
Thorax: Same as abdomen

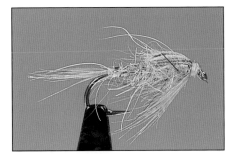

Soft Hackle Hare's Ear, Amber
Hook: TMC 3761, sizes 12-18
Thread: Yellow, 6/0
Tail: Amber or tan hen hackle fibers
Abdomen: Amber hare's mask and ear
Rib: Fine flat gold tinsel
Thorax: Same as abdomen
Legs: Amber hen hackle
Wingcase: Amber goose or turkey wing quill

Soft Hackle Hare's Ear, Black
Hook: TMC 3761, sizes 12-18
Thread: Black, 6/0
Tail: Black hen hackle fibers
Abdomen: Black hare's mask and ear
Rib: Fine flat gold tinsel
Thorax: Same as abdomen
Legs: Black hen hackle
Wingcase: Black goose or turkey wing quill

Soft Hackle Hare's Ear, Natural
- Hook: TMC 3761, sizes 12-18
- Thread: Brown, 6/0
- Tail: Brown hen hackle fibers
- Abdomen: Brown hare's mask and ear
- Rib: Fine flat gold tinsel
- Thorax: Same as abdomen
- Legs: Brown hen hackle
- Wingcase: Dyed brown goose or turkey wing quill

Soft Hackle Hare's Ear, Olive
- Hook: TMC 3761, sizes 12-18
- Thread: Olive, 6/0
- Tail: Olive hen hackle fibers
- Abdomen: Olive hare's mask and ear
- Rib: Fine flat gold tinsel
- Thorax: Same as abdomen
- Legs: Olive hen hackle
- Wingcase: Olive goose or turkey wing quill

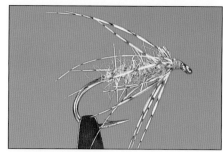

Soft Hackle, March Brown Spider
(Sylvester Nemes)
- Hook: TMC 3769, sizes 12-16
- Thread: Orange, 6/0
- Rib: Fine flat silver tinsel
- Body: Hare's mask
- Hackle: Brown partridge

Soft Hackle, Partridge and Green
(Sylvester Nemes)
- Hook: TMC 3769, sizes 12-14
- Thread: Green, 6/0
- Body: Green floss
- Thorax: Hare's ear
- Hackle: Gray partridge

Soft Hackle, Partridge and Herl
(Sylvester Nemes)
- Hook: TMC 3769, sizes 12-16
- Thread: Black, 6/0
- Body: Peacock
- Hackle: Brown partridge

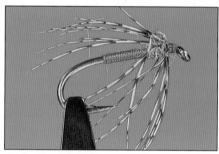

Soft Hackle, Partridge and Orange
(Sylvester Nemes)
- Hook: TMC 3769, sizes 12-14
- Thread: Orange, 6/0
- Body: Orange floss
- Thorax: Hare's ear
- Hackle: Gray partridge

Soft Hackle, Partridge and Yellow
(Sylvester Nemes)
- Hook: TMC 3769, sizes 12-14
- Thread: Yellow, 6/0
- Body: Yellow floss
- Thorax: Hare's ear
- Hackle: Brown partridge

Soft Hackle, Pheasant Tail *(Sylvester Nemes)*
- Hook: TMC 3769, sizes 12-16
- Thread: Olive, 6/0
- Rib: Fine copper wire
- Body: Pheasant tail fibers
- Hackle: Brown partridge

Sowbug
- Hook: TMC 2457, sizes 14-18
- Thread: Gray, 6/0
- Back: Plastic
- Abdomen: Paxton's Buggy Nymph; abdomen is bulky and trimmed flat on bottom, even on sides; begin dubbing before tail is tied in so plastic back comes over top and between tails
- Legs: Gray goose biot
- Rib: Gray thread

Stone, Dark *(John Barr)*
    Hook: TMC 200F, sizes 4-6, weighted
    Thread: Brown, 6/0
    Tail: Brown turkey biot
    Back: Plastic cut from Zip-Lock bag; also covers thorax area
    Rib: Dark brown thread, 3/0
    Abdomen: Rust Scintilla
    Thorax: Same as abdomen
    Legs: Black hen or rooster hackle, palmered
Note: The dorsal (top) surface of the nymph is colored with brown and black Pantone.

Stone, Light *(John Barr)*
    Hook: TMC 200R, sizes 8-10, weighted
    Thread: Tan, 6/0
    Tail: Ginger turkey biot
    Back: Plastic cut from Zip-Lock bag
    Rib: Cream thread, 3/0
    Abdomen: Cream Scintilla
    Thorax: Same as abdomen
    Legs: Ginger hen or rooster hackle, palmered

Stonefly, Black *(John Betts)*
    Hook: TMC 200R, sizes 4-6, weighted
    Thread: Black, 6/0
    Underbody: Furry foam over lead wire
    Wingcase: Black Tyvek paper, in layers
    Antennae: Black 12 lb. braided dacron
    Eyes: Black glass beads or mono
    Tail: Black 12 lb. braided dacron
    Abdomen: Black latex, wrapped
    Thorax: Brown Furry Foam
    Legs: Black 30 lb. braided dacron

Stonefly, Brown *(John Betts)*
    Hook: TMC 200R, sizes 4-8, weighted
    Thread: Brown, 6/0
    Underbody: Furry Foam over lead wire
    Wingcase: White Tyvek paper; 3 sections
    Antennae: Brown 12-lb. braided dacron
    Eyes: Brown glass beads or mono
    Tail: Brown 12-lb. braided dacron
    Abdomen: Brown latex
    Thorax: Brown Furry Foam or Z-Lon
    Legs: Same as tail, only 30 lb.
Note: All materials are white, then colored with Pantone pens.

Strymph, Black *(Harry Murray)*
    Hook: TMC 5262, sizes 2-10, weighted
    Thread: Black, 6/0
    Tail: Black ostrich
    Body: Black chenille
    Hackle: Mottled brown hen saddle

Strymph, Olive *(Harry Murray)*
    Hook: TMC 5262, sizes 2-10, weighted
    Thread: Olive, 6/0
    Tail: Olive ostrich
    Body: Olive rabbit
    Hackle: Mottled brown hen saddle

Surface Emerger, Brown-Olive
    Hook: TMC 100, sizes 14-20
    Thread: Olive 6/0
    Tail: Woodduck mallard
    Rib: Fine copper wire
    Abdomen: Brown-olive Superfine
    Wingcase: Turkey tail
    Legs: Brown partridge

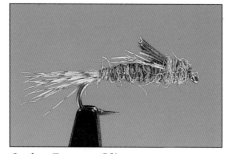

Surface Emerger, Olive
    Hook: TMC 100, sizes 16-20
    Thread: Olive, 6/0
    Tail: Woodduck mallard
    Rib: Fine copper wire
    Abdomen: Olive Superfine
    Wingcase: Turkey tail
    Legs: Brown partridge
    Head: Same as abdomen

Surface Emerger, Rusty
    Hook: TMC 100, sizes 16-20
    Thread: Brown, 6/0
    Tail: Woodduck mallard
    Rib: Brown thread, 6/0
    Abdomen: Rust rabbit or Superfine
    Wingcase: Rusty brown duck quill
    Legs: Light brown hackle fibers
    Head: Rust rabbit or Superfine

Swimming Caddis Larva, Cream (Nori Tashiro)
Hook:	TMC 400T, sizes 12-14
Thread:	Black, 6/0
Tail:	Brown partridge
Tag:	Mint green Antron
Back:	Dark turkey
Rib:	Yellow thread
Abdomen:	Light yellow olive Antron
Wingcase:	Moose
Legs:	Brown partridge
Head:	Chocolate dubbing

Swimming Caddis Larva, Mint (Nori Tashiro)
Hook:	TMC 400T, sizes 12-14
Thread:	Brown, 6/0
Tail:	Brown partridge
Body:	Mint green Antron
Back:	Pearl Accent Flash
Rib:	Mint green thread
Legs:	Brown partridge

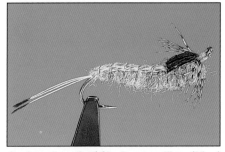

Swimming Caddis Larva, Tan (Nori Tashiro)
Hook:	TMC 400T, sizes 12-14
Thread:	Light olive , 6/0
Tail:	Amherst pheasant tippet
Back:	Pheasant tail fibers
Rib:	Yellow thread
Abdomen:	Olive-tan sparkle dubbing
Wingcase:	Dark turkey
Thorax:	Same as abdomen
Legs:	Brown partridge

Swimming Damsel, Brown (A.K. Best)
Hook:	TMC 400T, size 8
Thread:	Brown, 6/0
Eyes:	Monofilament
Tail:	Brown ostrich herl or marabou
Rib:	Fine gold wire
Abdomen:	Brown Antron
Wingcase:	Brown Swiss Straw
Legs:	Brown partridge

Swimming Damsel, Olive (A. K. Best)
Hook:	TMC 400T, size 8
Thread:	Olive, 6/0
Eyes:	Monofilament
Tail:	Olive ostrich herl or marabou
Rib:	Fine gold wire
Abdomen:	Olive green Antron
Wingcase:	Olive Swiss Straw
Legs:	Olive partridge

Swimming Nymph (Harrison R. Steeves III)
Hook:	TMC 400T, size 10
Thread:	Olive brown, 6/0
Tail:	Moose
Body:	Bronze and pale yellow Kreinik, medium braid
Thorax:	Natural fox squirrel dubbing
Wingcase:	Mottled dark turkey tail, lacquered
Legs:	Golden ginger hackle, palmered and trimmed

Swimming Nymph, Blonde (Bob Clouser)
Hook:	TMC 3761, sizes 8-10, weighted
Thread:	Tan, 6/0
Tail:	Tan rabbit and brown Flashabou
Abdomen:	Yellowish tan rabbit
Wingcase:	Peacock
Legs:	Mottled golden brown hen saddle, palmered
Thorax:	Same as abdomen

Swimming Nymph, Gold (Bob Clouser)
Hook:	TMC 3761, sizes 8-10, weighted
Thread:	Gray or tan, 6/0
Tail:	Golden brown rabbit and bronze Flashabou
Abdomen:	Golden brown Antron
Wingcase:	Peacock
Legs:	Mottled brown hen saddle, palmered through thorax
Thorax:	Golden brown Antron

Swimming Nymph, Rusty (Bob Clouser)
Hook:	TMC 3761, sizes 8-10, weighted
Thread:	Fluorescent fire orange, 6/0
Tail:	Brown rabbit and copper Flashabou
Abdomen:	Rusty claret Antron
Wingcase:	Peacock
Legs:	Mottled dark brown hen saddle, palmered
Thorax:	Same as abdomen

Telico
- Hook: TMC 3761, sizes 10-14
- Thread: Black, 6/0
- Tail: Guinea
- Back: Ringneck pheasant tail fibers or peacock
- Rib: Peacock
- Abdomen: Yellow floss
- Hackle: Furnace

Timberline Emerger, Gray (Randall Kaufmann)
- Hook: TMC 3761, sizes 12-16, weighted
- Thread: Gray, 6/0
- Tail: Natural gray ringneck fluff, short and heavy
- Rib: Fine copper wire
- Abdomen: Gray Angora goat and gray Haretron, blended
- Legs: Brown hackle
- Wing: Grizzly hen hackle tips

Ugly Bug (Brad Jackson)
- Hook: TMC 300, sizes 2-8, heavily weighted
- Thread: Black, 3/0
- Tail: Black rubber
- Legs: Black rubber
- Antennae: Black rubber
- Body: Black chenille

Water Boatman (Andy Burk)
- Hook: TMC 200R, sizes 14 and 16 and 16, weighted
- Thread: Olive, 6/0
- Tail: Pearl Accent Flash
- Back: Pearl Flashabou with strand of Zing
- Legs: Black fine round rubber
- Body: Peacock herl

Water Boatman, Bubble (Kenn Ligas)
- Hook: TMC 101, sizes 14 and 16
- Thread: Tan, 6/0
- Abdomen: Pearl plastic bead (Scintillator bubble)
- Tail: Brown foam; cover tie down with brown Antron
- Legs: Brown turkey biot and soft tan hen hackle fibers, or partridge
- Head: Brown Antron

Western Coachman
- Hook: TMC 3761, sizes 8-16
- Thread: Black, 6/0
- Tail: Golden pheasant tippet
- Rib: Fine gold wire
- Body: Peacock
- Hackle: Brown
- Wing: White calftail

Whitlock's Stone, Black (Dave Whitlock)
- Hook: TMC 7999, sizes 4-8, wghtd.
- Thread: Black, 6/0
- Antennae: Black Amnesia
- Back/Wngcse: Black Swiss Straw
- Butt: Rusty Antron
- Tail: Black Amnesia
- Rib: Medium copper wire
- Abdomen: Black Antron
- Legs: Mottled dark hen saddle
- Thorax: Same as butt
- Head: Same as abdomen

Whitlock's Stone, Brown (Dave Whitlock)
- Hook: TMC 7999, sizes 4-8, wghtd.
- Thread: Brown, 6/0
- Antennae: Golden or brown Amnesia
- Back/Wngcse: Brown Swiss Straw
- Butt: Golden Antron
- Tail: Golden or brown Amnesia
- Rib: Medium copper wire
- Abdomen: Rusty brown Antron
- Legs: Mottled dark hen saddle
- Thorax: Same as butt
- Head: Same as abdomen

Whitlock's Stone, Gold (Dave Whitlock)
- Hook: TMC 7999, sizes 4-8, wghtd.
- Thread: Yellow, 6/0
- Antennae: Yellow Amnesia
- Back/Wngcse: Light mottled turkey
- Butt: Cream Antron
- Tail: Yellow Amnesia
- Rib: Yellow single strand flat floss
- Abdomen: Gold Antron
- Legs: Mottled light hen saddle
- Thorax: Same as butt
- Head: Same as abdomen

Woolly Bugger, Black
Hook: TMC 300, sizes 2-10, weighted
Thread: Black, 6/0
Tail: Black marabou
Rib: Fine silver wire
Body: Black chenille
Hackle: Black, palmered

Woolly Bugger, Brown
Hook: TMC 5263, sizes 4-10, weighted
Thread: Brown, 6/0
Tail: Brown marabou
Rib: Fine copper wire
Body: Brown chenille
Hackle: Brown, palmered

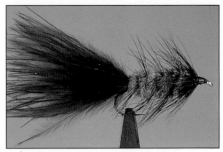

Woolly Bugger, Brown and Black
Hook: TMC 300, sizes 2-10, weighted
Thread: Black, 6/0
Tail: Black marabou
Rib: Fine copper wire
Body: Dark brown wool
Hackle: Black, palmered

Woolly Bugger, Olive
Hook: TMC 5263, sizes 4-10, weighted
Thread: Olive, 6/0
Tail: Olive marabou
Rib: Fine gold wire
Body: Olive chenille
Hackle: Olive, palmered

Woolly Bugger, Olive and Black
Hook: TMC 300, sizes 2-10, weighted
Thread: Black, 6/0
Tail: Olive marabou
Rib: Fine copper wire
Body: Olive chenille
Hackle: Black, palmered

Woolly Worm, Black and Grizzly
Hook: TMC 5262, sizes 6-10, weighted
Thread: Black, 6/0
Rib: Fine gold wire
Tail: Red yarn
Body: Black chenille
Hackle: Grizzly

Woolly Worm, Brown and Grizzly
Hook: TMC 5262, sizes 6-10, weighted
Thread: Black, 6/0
Tail: Red yarn
Rib: Fine copper wire
Body: Brown chenille
Hackle: Grizzly

Woolly Worm, Olive and Grizzly
Hook: TMC 5262, sizes 6-10, weighted
Thread: Black, 6/0
Tail: Red yarn
Rib: Fine gold wire
Body: Dark olive chenille
Hackle: Grizzly

Woolly Worm, Peacock and Grizzly
Hook: TMC 5262, sizes 6-10, weighted
Thread: Black, 6/0
Tail: Red yarn
Rib: Fine gold or copper wire
Body: Peacock
Hackle: Grizzly

Woolly Worm, Yellow and Grizzly
Hook:	TMC 5263, sizes 6-10, weighted
Thread:	Black, 6/0
Tail:	Red yarn
Rib:	Fine gold wire
Body:	Yellow chenille
Hackle:	Grizzly

Woven Sparkle (Harrison R. Steeves III)
Hook:	TMC 5262, sizes 6-10, weighted
Thread:	Black, 6/0
Tail:	Brown turkey biot
Abdomen:	Green and black Kreinik medium round braid
Wingcase:	Dark mottled brown turkey
Legs:	Natural dark dun hackle
Thorax:	Peacock green Glo-Brite chenille

Yuk Bug
Hook:	TMC 300, sizes 4-8, weighted
Thread:	Black, 6/0
Tail:	Gray squirrel
Rib:	Black thread or fine gold wire
Body:	Black chenille
Legs:	White rubber, evenly spaced along side of body, slanting backward
Hackle:	Light badger, palmered

Z-Wing Caddis Pupa, Amber (Mike Mercer)
Hook:	TMC 2457, sizes 12-18, weight optional
Thread:	Tan, 6/0
Back:	Light brown marabou
Rib:	Fine to medium copper wire
Abdomen:	Golden brown Haretron, dubbing loop method
Wing:	Cream or ginger Z-Lon
Antennae:	Woodduck mallard; two fibers over top of each side of fly
Head:	Tan marabou; twist and wrap

Z-Wing Caddis Pupa, Cream (Mike Mercer)
Hook:	TMC 2457, sizes 12-18, weight optional (6-10 wraps, 0.15 to 0.25 lead wire)
Thread:	Cream or light tan, 6/0
Back:	Dark golden brown turkey, extending to middle of each side of fly
Rib:	Cream thread, 6/0
Abdomen:	Cream Antron
Wing:	Cream Z-Lon, 1/2 to 2/3 body
Head:	Light gray ostrich, twisted

Z-Wing Caddis Pupa, Green (Mike Mercer)
Hook:	TMC 2457, sizes 12-18
Thread:	Fluorescent green, 6/0
Back:	Dark golden brown turkey, extending to the middle of the fly
Rib:	Chartreuse thread
Abdomen:	Bright olive Antron
Wing:	Olive or green Z-Lon, 1/2 to 2/3 body length, tied along each side
Collar:	Chartreuse Antron
Head:	Peacock, twisted

Z-Wing Caddis Pupa, Olive (Mike Mercer)
Hook:	TMC 2457, sizes 12-18, weight optional
Thread:	Olive, 6/0
Back:	Dark golden brown turkey, extending to the middle of the fly
Rib:	Olive thread
Abdomen:	Dark olive Antron
Wing:	Ginger or cream Z-Lon, 1/2 to 2/3 body, tied along each side
Head:	Peacock, twisted

Z-Wing, Micro, Lime (Mike Mercer)
Hook:	TMC 921, sizes 16-18
Head:	Copper bead
Thread:	Chartreuse, 6/0
Back:	Dark mottled turkey tail
Rib:	Chartreuse thread, 6/0
Abdomen:	Fluorescent lime Antron
Wingpads:	Light olive Z-Lon or pearl Flashabou
Collar:	Same as abdomen
Head:	Peacock

Zug Bug
Hook:	TMC 3761, sizes 8-18, weighted
Thread:	Black, 6/0
Tail:	Peacock sword
Rib:	Flat silver mylar
Abdomen:	Peacock
Legs:	Brown hackle fibers
Wingcase:	Woodduck mallard, clipped short

Chapter 4

Streamers

Bob Clouser

My dad presented me with a fly tying kit as a Christmas gift when I was 14. Fascination with the various materials that could be applied to a hook and made to resemble various foods the fish would eat spurred my persistence. Although there are many fine fly patterns available to the fly angler, my quest for a fly pattern or patterns that would mimic many food forms and their movements was on-going. Another goal was to find consistently effective patterns that would reduce the number of fly patterns that had to be carried on any given fishing excursion.

Lefty Kreh is my mentor and the driving force behind my continued quest for knowledge. The thirst for satisfaction that pleases, teaches, and enhances another person's outdoor experience is my philosophy towards a successful career. Designing and tying fly patterns that have become standards in the fishing world has been the highlight of my tying career. Perhaps many ideas for the fly patterns I developed came from the need for client satisfaction while guiding for smallmouth bass on the Susquehanna River in Pennsylvania. Although the purpose of my fly patterns was to increase catch rates for smallmouth bass, I, along with many other anglers, have caught other species of fish (freshwater and saltwater) with these flies.

The Clouser Deep Minnow

A consistently effective smallmouth fly must sink as the fly is being dead drifted or between strip retrieves. Basically, the fly needs to mimic the darting movements of a baitfish being chased by a predator. In order to mimic this flight for safety, the fly must not stop and remain stationary while being fished. Smallmouth bass (or any other species), especially the older, larger, wiser fish, have never seen a baitfish stop, turn, and look at them during the chase. This deviation from the natural fleeing procedure of the baitfish warns the predator that something is amiss. With these thoughts in mind, I developed the Clouser Deep Minnow. It mimics the fleeing trait—the fly never stops.

Other functions were also considered. The eyes are attached to the top of the hook so the fly rides with the hook point up. Hair for the belly is attached in front of and in back of the eyes to hold the hair in the shape of a minnow's belly. The top, or back, hair of the fly is tied only in front of the eyes. This angles the front portion of the hair upward, leaving the thinner rear hair fibers bent down during the stripping retrieve, touching the rear portion of the belly hair. Bending together of the rear portion of the fly gives a thin rear profile with a deep front portion—the outline of a real minnow's body. This tying style also allows the hair to undulate in an up-and-down motion, somewhat like an injured minnow lying on its side. If tied sparsely with Krystal Flash or Flashabou in the center of the hair, the fly presents the illusion of transparent baitfish. If the Krystal Flash or Flashabou is tied longer (about an eighth inch) than the hair portion of the fly, it adds the look of a rocking motion to the fly, giving it another illusion of life. The metallic eyes cause the fly to dip and dart with an action and speed similar to a live baitfish fleeing from a predator.

The unique tying style of the Clouser Minnow has spurred many other effective patterns. Materials such as the guard hairs and tail fibers from many animal species and synthetic fibers make this style of fly versatile. For example, minnow imitations smaller than two inches can be made by using the guard hairs from fox, squirrel, calf, or others with similar hair consistency. Although small or short minnow imitations can be made with deer tail hair, the use of guard hair fibers will give the same movement to the shorter fly as does the deer tail hair on the longer ones. I have made styles of Clouser Minnows from one inch to over 12 inches in length. This is made possible by varying the materials. Materials such as long wool fibers and synthetic fibers like Ultra Hair, FisHair, and others allow the creation of long flies.

At this time there are seven important series of the Clouser Minnow: Deep (original), Ultra, Foxee, Mad Tom, Half and Half, B-P, and Maxi-Mini. Each of these series has an important application for different species and situations that may be encountered.

In recent years, Lefty has caught over 70 different species of fish with the Clouser Minnow. I will always remember his expression when I handed him the first flies. With an astonished look, Lefty asked, "Are these finished? Is this all there is to them?" I told him to try them as they were satisfying to my clients. Since that day, trout, bass, salmon, steelhead, snook, tarpon, bonefish, permit, barracuda, bluefish, and stripers, just to name a few, have fallen prey to the versatile Clouser Minnow. Just about any species in fresh or salt water can be taken on this fly.

In addition to varying the weight by using various sizes of metallic eyes, methods of presentation can be varied. Adjust the retrieve speed to accommodate or duplicate the quarry or its prey. For example, allowing the fly to dead drift in moving water can be very effective. In some instances a large fly with smaller, lighter eyes may be more effective than a heavier version. Anglers fishing shallow waters find that the lighter versions catch more fish in addition to being easier to cast. Some species, especially smallmouth bass, take flies as they slowly descend. It pays to carry various weights of the same color combinations.

Regardless of the species of fish or the technique used, the Clouser Minnow could just be the most effective underwater fly you have ever used.

Author's Note: Bob, his wife, Joan, and their son, Bob, Jr., operate the Clouser Fly Shop in Middletown, Pennsylvania, where they teach fly tying and fly fishing and guide smallmouth bass anglers. Bob is constantly working to protect and enhance smallmouth habitat and works with various state agencies. He also enjoys the lecture circuit. The Clouser Minnow is one of the world's most versatile and effective flies.

Bob Clouser
Middletown, Pennsylvania
June, 1994

Bird's Nest Muddler, Dark (Cal Bird)
  Hook: TMC 3761, sizes 8-12
Thread: Tan, 6/0
  Tail: Maple sugar color mallard or
           teal
  Body: Gold mylar tinsel
  Wing: Same as tail
  Legs: Same as tail
Thorax: Gray Australian opossum

Bird's Nest Muddler, Light (Cal Bird)
  Hook: TMC 3761, sizes 8-12
Thread: Cream, 6/0
  Tail: Woodduck mallard
  Body: Gold mylar tinsel
  Wing: Same as tail
  Legs: Same as tail
Thorax: Cream (light Cahill) Australian
           opossum

Black Ghost
  Hook: TMC 300, sizes 6-10
Thread: Black, 6/0
  Tail: Yellow hackle fibers
  Rib: Medium flat silver tinsel
  Body: Black floss
Hackle: Yellow
  Wing: Four white saddle hackles

Black-Nosed Dace
  Hook: TMC 300, sizes 6-10
Thread: Black, 6/0
  Tail: Red yarn
  Body: Flat silver tinsel
  Wing: Brown bucktail over black calf-
           tail over white bucktail

Bullet Head Streamer, Gold (Andy Burk)
     Hook: TMC 9395, size 6
   Thread: White, 3/0
     Body: Gold Flashabou
Underwing: Ginger Crinkle Z-Lon
     Wing: Copper brown Crystal Hair
    Gills: Red Flashabou
Gill Plates: Copper brown Crystal Hair
     Eyes: Yellow with black pupil plas-
              tic; epoxy head

Bullet Head Streamer, Silver (Andy Burk)
     Hook: TMC 9395, size 6
   Thread: White, 3/0
     Body: Silver Flashabou
Underwing: Light dun Crinkle Z-Lon
     Wing: Black and light olive Z-Lon,
              straight, with olive Flashabou
    Gills: Red Flashabou
Gill Plates: Peacock Accent Flash
     Eyes: Yellow with black pupil plas-
              tic; epoxy head

Clouser's Deep Minnow, Black (Bob
Clouser)
  Hook: TMC 811S, sizes 2/0, 2, and 6
           weighted
Thread: Black, 6/0
  Eyes: Lead, painted dark red with
           black pupils
  Tail: Black bucktail
  Body: Bucktail, tied down for tail;
           keep smooth and level
  Wing: Black bucktail with dark green
           Accent Flash

**Clouser's Deep Minnow, Chartreuse and
White** (Bob Clouser)
  Hook: TMC 811S, sizes 2/0, 2, and 6
           weighted
Thread: White, 6/0
  Eyes: Lead, painted dark red with
           black pupils
  Wing: White bucktail on top; char-
           treuse bucktail underside with
           pearlescent Krystal Flash over
           top

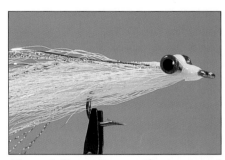

**Clouser's Deep Minnow, Chartreuse and
Yellow** (Bob Clouser)
  Hook: TMC 811S, sizes 2/0, 2, and 6
           weighted
Thread: Yellow, 6/0
  Eyes: Lead, painted dark red with
           black pupils
  Tail: Chartreuse bucktail
  Wing: Yellow bucktail with gold
           Accent Flash and gold
           Flashabou

Clouser's Deep Minnow, Foxee Dace
(Bob Clouser)
     Hook: TMC 200R, sizes 6-10
     Thread: Black, 6/0
     Eyes: Lead, painted dark red with
             black pupils
     Tail: White Arctic fox
     Body: Tie down area for tail; smooth
             and level
     Wing: Gray and black Arctic fox with
             silver Accent Flash

Clouser's Deep Minnow, Foxee Red (Bob
Clouser)
     Hook: TMC 200R, sizes 6-8
     Thread: Tan, 6/0
     Eyes: Lead, painted dark red with
             black pupils
     Wing: Red fox tail with tan guard
             hairs on top; red fox tail, black
             tipped guard hairs, gold
             Accent Flash and rust
             Flashabou underneath

Clouser's Deep Minnow, Golden Shiner
(Bob Clouser)
     Hook: TMC 811S, sizes 2/0, 2, and 6
     Thread: Tan, 6/0
     Eyes: Lead, painted dark red with
             black pupils
     Wing: White bucktail on top; tan
             bucktail with gold Krystal
             Flash underneath

Clouser's Deep Minnow, Red and White
(Bob Clouser)
     Hook: TMC 811S, sizes 2/0, 2, and 6
     Thread: Red, 6/0
     Eyes: Lead, painted dark red with
             black pupils
     Tail: White bucktail
     Body: Bucktail tied down for tail;
             keep smooth and level
     Wing: Red over white bucktail with
             gray ghost and pearl Accent
             Flash

Clouser's Deep Minnow, Red-Finned
(Bob Clouser)
     Hook: TMC 200R, sizes 6-10
     Thread: Light brown, 6/0
     Eyes: Mini lead, painted dark red
             with black pupils
     Wing: Dyed orange squirrel on top;
             gray squirrel with silver
             Accent Flash underneath

Clouser's Deep Minnow, Sculpin (Bob
Clouser)
     Hook: TMC 811S, sizes 2/0, 2, and 6
     Thread: Brown, 6/0
     Eyes: Lead, painted dark red with
             black pupils
     Wing: Pale orange bucktail on top;
             rusty brown bucktail with gold
             Accent Flash underneath

Clouser's Deep Minnow, Silver Shiner
(Bob Clouser)
     Hook: TMC 811S, sizes 2/0, 2, and 6
     Thread: Light gray, 6/0
     Eyes: Lead, painted dark red with
             black pupils
     Wing: White bucktail on top; light
             gray bucktail with rainbow
             Accent Flash underneath

Floating Smelt (Milt Jensen)
     Hook: TMC 300, sizes 2-6
     Thread: White, 3/0
 Underbody: Closed cell foam
     Tail: Gray marabou
     Body: Pearl minnow body; Pantone
             top greenish-gray
     Eyes: Yellow and black paint
     Gills: Red paint

Gray Ghost
     Hook: TMC 300, sizes 6-10
     Thread: Black, 6/0
     Tag: Fine flat silver tinsel
     Rib: Fine flat silver tinsel
     Body: Orange floss
     Wing: Gray dun saddle hackles, four,
             and peacock, four strands
     Throat: Golden pheasant crest
     Cheeks: Silver pheasant body feathers
             overlaid with jungle cock eyes

113

Hare Sculpin, Black (Dave Whitlock)
- Hook: TMC 700, sizes 2-6, weighted
- Thread: White single strand nylon floss
- Eyes: Lead, painted black
- Gills: Red hackle and dyed dark brown pheasant body
- Body: Mason monofilament foundation, white rabbit fur strip on top, black rabbit strip underneath; pull both strips over hook point and glue together

Hare Sculpin, Gold (Dave Whitlock)
- Hook: TMC 700, sizes 2-6, weighted
- Thread: White single strand nylon floss
- Eyes: Lead, painted black
- Gills: Red hackle and natural ringneck body
- Body: Mason monofilament foundation, white rabbit fur strip on top, golden-tan rabbit strip underneath; pull both strips over hook point and glue together

Hare Sculpin, Olive (Dave Whitlock)
- Hook: TMC 700, sizes 2-6, weighted
- Thread: White single strand nylon floss
- Eyes: Lead, painted black
- Gills: Red hackle and natural ringneck rump
- Body: Mason monofilament foundation, white rabbit fur strip on top, olive rabbit strip underneath; pull both strips over hook point and glue together

Hornberg
- Hook: TMC 5263, sizes 6-10
- Thread: Black, 6/0
- Body: Flat silver tinsel
- Wing: Gray mallard flank; yellow hackle or yellow calftail underwing
- Cheeks: Jungle cock or substitute
- Hackle: Grizzly

Janssen's Minnow, Brook (Hal Janssen)
- Hook: TMC 5263, sizes 4-10
- Thread: White, 3/0
- Tail: Olive marabou
- Underbody: Zonker tape, cut to shape and folded over hook
- Body: Gold Mylar tubing; paint to suit and cover with clear epoxy

Janssen's Minnow, Brown (Hal Janssen)
- Hook: TMC 5263, sizes 4-10
- Thread: White, 3/0
- Tail: Golden marabou
- Underbody: Zonker tape, cut to shape and folded over hook
- Body: Gold mylar tubing; paint to suit and cover with clear epoxy

Janssen's Minnow, Rainbow (Hal Janssen)
- Hook: TMC 5263, sizes 2-10
- Thread: White, 6/0
- Tail: Olive marabou
- Underbody: Zonker tape, cut to shape and fold over hook
- Body: Silver mylar piping; paint to suit and cover with clear epoxy

Janssen's Minnow, Shad (Hal Janssen)
- Hook: TMC 5263, sizes 2-10
- Thread: White, 6/0
- Tail: Gray marabou
- Underbody: Zonker tape, cut to shape and fold over hook
- Body: Silver mylar piping; paint to suit and cover with clear epoxy

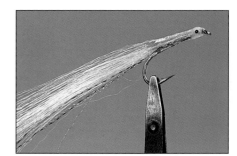

Lumi Smelt (Dennis Black)
- Hook: TMC 3769, sizes 6-8
- Thread: White, 6/0
- Wing: White super hair with phosphorescent Flashabou and red and pearl Accent Flash
- Body: Five-minute epoxy over wing
- Eyes: Painted black pupil

Marabou Muddler, Black
Hook:	TMC 5263, sizes 4-10, weighted.
Thread:	Black, 6/0
Tail:	Red hackle fibers
Body:	Silver Diamond Braid
Wing:	Black marabou over black calf
Collar:	Spun deer
Head:	Deer or caribou, spun and clipped

Marabou Muddler, Brown
Hook:	TMC 5263, sizes 6-8, weighted.
Thread:	Black, 3/0
Tail:	Red hackle fibers
Body:	Gold Diamond Braid
Wing:	Peacock over brown marabou over brown calf
Collar:	Deer
Head:	Deer or caribou, spun and clipped

Marabou Muddler, Olive
Hook:	TMC 5263, sizes 4-10, weighted.
Thread:	Black, 3/0
Tail:	Red hackle fibers
Body:	Gold Diamond Braid
Wing:	Peacock over olive marabou over olive calf
Collar:	Deer
Head:	Deer or caribou, spun and clipped

Marabou Muddler, White
Hook:	TMC 5263, sizes 4-10 weighted
Thread:	Black, 6/0
Tail:	Red hackle fibers
Body:	Silver Diamond Braid
Wing:	Peacock over white marabou over white calf
Collar:	Deer
Head:	Deer or caribou, spun and clipped

Marabou Muddler, Yellow
Hook:	TMC 5263, sizes 4-10, weighted.
Thread:	Black, 6/0
Tail:	Red hackle fibers
Body:	Silver Diamond Braid
Wing:	Peacock over yellow marabou over yellow calf
Collar:	Deer
Head:	Deer or caribou, spun and clipped

Match the Minnow, Black-Nosed Dace
(Dave Whitlock)
Hook:	TMC 300, size 2
Thread:	White, 3/0
Underbody:	Zonker tape, cut to shape, folded over hook shank
Body:	Pearlescent mylar tubing
Wing:	Furnace and golden badger hackles
Shoulder:	Ringneck pheasant body
Eyes:	Solid plastic
Head:	White or pearl, painted olive

Match the Minnow, Golden Shiner *(Dave Whitlock)*
Hook:	TMC 300, size 2
Thread:	White, 3/0
Underbody:	Zonker tape
Body:	Pearlescent mylar tubing
Wing:	Olive hackles (2-4), split around the hook point and cemented along top of body
Shoulder:	Ringneck pheasant feather
Eyes:	Solid plastic
Head:	White or pearl, painted brown

Match the Minnow, Threadfin Shad
(Dave Whitlock)
Hook:	TMC 300, size 2
Thread:	White, 3/0
Underbody:	Zonker tape
Body:	Pearlescent mylar tubing, painted fluorescent red
Wing:	Olive badger and silver badger hackles
Shoulder:	Mallard breast, paint black spot
Eyes:	Solid plastic
Head:	White or pearl, painted black

Match the Minnow, Trout-Salmon Parr
(Dave Whitlock)
Hook:	TMC 300, size 2
Thread:	White, 3/0
Underbody:	Zonker tape
Body:	Pearlescent mylar tubing, decorated with parr markings
Wing:	Grizzly variant, dyed gold olive
Shoulder:	Ringneck pheasant body
Eyes:	Solid plastic
Head:	White or pearl, painted olive on top (bottom in vise)

Match the Minnow, Yellow Perch (Dave Whitlock)
- Hook: TMC 300, size 2
- Thread: White, 3/0
- Tail: Hot orange rabbit
- Underbody: Zonker tape
- Body: Pearlescent mylar tubing
- Wing: Olive grizzly hackles (4)
- Shoulder: Ringneck pheasant body
- Eyes: Solid plastic
- Throat: Same as tail
- Head: Metallic copper, painted on top (bottom in vise); black bottom

Matuka, Black
- Hook: TMC 5263, sizes 4-8
- Thread: Black, 6/0
- Rib: Fine oval silver tinsel
- Body: Black chenille
- Gills: Red yarn or dubbing
- Wing: Four black hen saddle hackles, tied down over body with the rib
- Hackle: Black hen

Matuka, Dark Spruce
- Hook: TMC 5263, sizes 4-8
- Thread: Black, 6/0
- Rib: Fine oval gold tinsel or wire
- Body: Red floss and peacock
- Wing: Furnace hackle (4)
- Hackle: Furnace

Matuka, Olive
- Hook: TMC 5263, sizes 2-6
- Thread: Olive, 6/0
- Rib: Fine copper wire or oval gold tinsel
- Body: Olive chenille
- Gills: Red yarn or dubbing
- Wing: Olive hen grizzly saddle hackles, four
- Hackle: Dyed olive grizzly hackle
- Eyes: Painted, yellow with a black pupil; optional

Matuka Sculpin, Black (Dave Whitlock)
- Hook: TMC 9395, sizes 2-6, weighted
- Thread: Cream or yellow single strand floss,
- Rib: Medium brass wire
- Body: Cream Crystal Seal
- Wing: Furnace dyed coachman hackles, four
- Pectoral Fins: Dyed dark brown ringneck body
- Gills: Red Crystal Seal
- Collar, Head: Black and white deer
- Eyes: Orange and black plastic

Matuka Sculpin, Gold (Dave Whitlock)
- Hook: TMC 9395, sizes 2-6, weighted
- Thread: Cream or yellow SSNF
- Rib: Brass wire
- Body: Cream Crystal Seal
- Wing: Natural and dyed olive cree neck hackle, four of each
- Pectoral Fins: Ringneck rump
- Gills: Red Crystal Seal
- Collar, Head: Cream, natural gray, black, olive and gold mule or white-tail deer
- Eyes: Brown and black plastic

Matuka Sculpin, Olive (Dave Whitlock)
- Hook: TMC 9395, sizes 2-6, wghtd.
- Thread: Cream or yellow single strand floss
- Rib: Medium brass wire
- Body: Cream Crystal Seal
- Wing: Olive grizzly hackles, four
- Pect. Fins: Ringneck rump
- Gills: Red Crystal Seal
- Collar/Head: Black, dark brown, dark olive, and cream deer
- Eyes: Green and black plastic

Matuka, Spruce
- Hook: TMC 5263, sizes 6-8
- Thread: Black, 6/0
- Body: Red floss and peacock
- Rib: Fine oval gold tinsel or wire
- Wing: Badger hackle (4)
- Hackle: Badger

Mickey Finn
- Hook: TMC 300, sizes 4-10
- Thread: Black, 6/0
- Rib: Fine oval silver tinsel
- Body: Flat silver tinsel
- Wing: Yellow, red, and yellow bucktail, from bottom to top
- Note: A holdover from the golden days of streamer patterns.

Muddler Minnow

 Hook: TMC 5263, sizes 2-12, weight optional
 Thread: Black, 6/0
 Tail: Mottled turkey quill
 Body: Gold Diamond Braid or flat tinsel
Underwing: Gray squirrel tail
 Wing: Mottled turkey quill
 Collar: Natural deer, spun
 Head: Natural caribou or deer
Note: The most famous streamer, created by Don Gapen, in the 1950's.

Mylar Minnow *(Dennis Goddard)*

 Hook: TMC 811S, size 6
 Thread: Clear, fine monofilament
Overbody: Pearlescent mylar piping braid
Underbody: Pearlescent mylar piping braid
 Tail: Pearlescent mylar piping braid; tail is same piece from overbody or underbody
 Body: Five-Minute Epoxy, fill in space between mylar braid, shape flat along sides; Pantone blue top and thread tie downs
 Eyes: Silver/black prismatic stick-on

Pass Lake Special

 Hook: TMC 5262, sizes 6-10, weighted
 Thread: Black, 6/0
 Tail: Brown hackle fibers
 Body: Black chenille
 Wing: White calftail
 Hackle: Brown

Shad Fly, Green

 Hook: TMC 5263, size 6
 Thread: Fluorescent green single strand nylon floss
 Eyes: Silver bead chain
 Tail: Fluorescent green floss
 Body: Fluorescent green floss

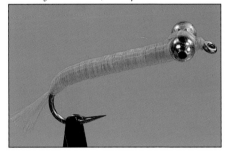

Shad Fly, Orange

 Hook: TMC 5263, size 6
 Thread: Fluorescent fire orange single strand nylon floss
 Eyes: Silver bead chain
 Tail: Fluorescent fire orange floss
 Body: Fluorescent fire orange floss

Spruce

 Hook: TMC 300, sizes 4-8
 Thread: Black, 6/0
 Tail: Peacock sword fibers
 Rib: Fine gold wire
 Body: Red yarn, rear half; peacock, front half
 Wing: Two badger hackles, flared
 Hackle: Badger

Ultra Smelt *(Dennis Black)*

 Hook: TMC 3769, sizes 6-8
 Thread: White, 6/0
 Wing: White super hair with red Accent Flash (2 strands)
 Body: Five-minute epoxy
 Eyes: Black pupils, painted

Wiggle Lemming *(Jonathan Olch)*

 Hook: TMC 8089, size 2, rear; front same, with bend and point removed
 Thread: Black, 3/0
 Tail: Muskrat fur strip
 Body: Cross-cut muskrat fur strip, wrapped
Head, Ears: Gray deer body hair, spun and trimmed to shape
 Eyes: Black paint
Whiskers: Black monofilament

Wiggletail, Orange *(Jonathan Olch)*

 Hook: TMC 7999, size 1/0, weighted
 Thread: Fluorescent fire orange single strand nylon floss
 Tail: Fluorescent orange marabou
 Rib: Flat gold mylar
 Body: Fluorescent orange chenille
 Collar: Gold braided mylar (use dubbing needle to de-braid)

Woolhead Sculpin, Black (Mike Lawson)
Hook:	TMC 300, size 4, weighted
Thread:	Black, 3/0
Tail:	Black 1/8 inch rabbit fur strip and black Accent Flash
Body:	Black 1/8 inch rabbit fur strip wound around hook and clipped on the bottom
Pect. Fins:	Black hen saddle
Head:	Black wool, spun and clipped to shape

Woolhead Sculpin, Olive (Mike Lawson)
Hook:	TMC 300, size 4, weighted
Thread:	Olive, 3/0
Tail:	Olive 1/8 inch rabbit fur strip
Body:	Olive 1/8 inch rabbit fur strip wound around hook and clipped on the bottom
Pect. Fins:	Olive hen saddle
Head:	Olive wool, spun and clipped to shape

Z-Smelt (Dennis Black)
Hook:	TMC 3769, sizes 6-8
Thread:	White, 6/0
Wing:	White Z-lon
Overwing:	Red and Pearl Accent Flash (2 strands each)
Body:	Five-minute epoxy
Eyes:	Painted black pupil

Zonker, Black (Dan Byford)
Hook:	TMC 300, sizes 2-8, weighted
Thread:	Black, 3/0
Underbody:	Lead wire, bent to shape
Body:	Black mylar piping
Wing:	Black rabbit strip; Pliobond to body
Overwing:	Pearl Accent Flash
Throat:	Red rabbit
Eyes:	Yellow and black, painted

Zonker, Natural and Copper (Dan Byford)
Hook:	TMC 300, sizes 2-8, weighted
Thread:	White, 3/0
Underbody:	Lead wire, bent to shape
Body:	Copper mylar piping
Wing:	Natural gray-chinchilla rabbit strip, Pliobond to body
Overwing:	Pearl Accent Flash
Throat:	Natural gray rabbit
Eyes:	Yellow and black, painted

Zonker, Natural and Pearl (Dan Byford)
Hook:	TMC 300, sizes 2-6
Thread:	White, 6/0
Underbody:	Wire, bent to shape
Body:	Pearl mylar piping
Wing:	Natural gray tan rabbit strip, Pliobond to body
Overwing:	Pearl Accent Flash
Throat:	Natural gray-tan rabbit
Eyes:	Yellow with black pupils, painted

Zonker, Olive (Dan Byford)
Hook:	TMC 300, sizes 2-6
Thread:	White, 6/0
Underbody:	Wire, bent to shape
Body:	Olive pearl mylar piping
Wing:	Dyed olive yellow rabbit strip, Pliobond to body
Overwing:	Pearl Accent Flash
Throat:	Olive yellow rabbit
Eyes:	Yellow with black pupils, painted

Zonker, Purple and Black (Dan Byford)
Hook:	TMC 300, sizes 2-8, weighted
Thread:	Black 3/0
Underbody:	Wire, bent to shape
Body:	Black mylar piping
Wing:	Purple rabbit strip; Pliobond to body
Overwing:	Pearl Accent Flash
Throat:	Purple or red rabbit
Eyes:	Yellow and black, painted

Zonker, White and Pearl (Dan Byford)
Hook:	TMC 300, sizes 2-8, weighted
Thread:	White, 3/0
Underbody:	Wire, bent to shape
Body:	Pearl mylar piping
Wing:	White rabbit strip; Pliobond to body
Overwing:	Pearl Accent Flash
Throat:	White rabbit
Eyes:	Yellow and black, painted

Chapter 5

Steelhead, Salmon

Randall Kaufmann

During the course of one's life there are chance meetings that radically change one's direction. The first person to have that impact on my life was my stepfather, Jack Moore. Jack tied flies and fly fished and was very good at both. I was 14 when Jack started me on the pathway to tying flies, fishing, backpacking, and adventuring. On family vacations, he introduced me to the mountains of the American West, revealing the freedom and wildness they represent. These revelations had a profound effect on me and overrode everything from that time onward in my life.

When I was 15, we would drive from Rialto, California to the High Sierra to fish. Soon I began selling flies to sporting goods stores in Bishop, Mammoth Lakes, and June Lake. Within six months I had saved enough money for backpacking gear and spent a week in the High Sierra Mountains exploring golden trout waters. Six months later I had enough money for a car, and all the famous trout waters of the West became my playground. During the next several years I tied flies all winter and fished and backpacked in the High Sierra and Rocky mountains all summer. During one of those summer trips, my brother, Lance, and I met Jack Dennis. He was tying flies at his father's sporting goods store near Lander, Wyoming. We hung around, tied some flies, and a week later the three of us backpacked into the Wind River Mountains, beginning a life-long friendship.

A couple of summers later, Jack Dennis and I were tying flies in the Rod & Reel Shop in Jackson, Wyoming, when Dennis Black wandered into the shop. This chance meeting proved to be another major turning point in my life. I was 19, and there were the usual expectations that I would knuckle down in school, get a "real job," and amount to something. I was close to abandoning commercial fly tying, but Dennis changed that notion when he ordered 600 dozen flies, or all I could tie in six weeks. The price was $1.80 per dozen, and I went into serious production. I tied them all and received a check for $1,000, which was a small fortune at the time. None of my friends could believe it. Forget the "real job"—I was getting into fly tying in a much bigger way.

Dennis and I developed a close friendship, and, between Dennis and my other commercial accounts, I was turning down orders. In 1968, Dennis moved from Fresno, California, to Winchester, Oregon, where he opened a mail order fly shop on the banks of the North Umpqua River. I visited Dennis the following year on my return from the Banff School of Fine Arts in Canada. I fell in love with Oregon and stayed. I was 21.

Dennis was probably the most versatile fly tyer in the country, and he tied flies at an incredible rate of speed. He shared his speed techniques with me, and together we devised more efficient ways of tying flies. Two dozen winged dry flies or three dozen nymphs per hour became our average production. Dennis made Lance and I aware that a fly fishing mail order and retail business was an obtainable goal—and I was another step further away from a "real job."

In 1971, Lance and I started Streamborn Flies with help, encouragement, and assistance from our parents, Jack and Oda Moore. We started the business in the family garage in Tigard, Oregon. We sent out 1,500 catalogs, intending to keep the business a mail order operation and on our terms. We outgrew the garage and soon had a store front, but we didn't keep regular hours. That didn't last long either, and, before we knew it, the 10:00-6:00 retail business was added to the mail order business.

Shortly after we started Streamborn Flies, we met Frank Amato, who published a regional fishing magazine and was established in the book publishing business. Frank took a chance and published my first book, *American Nymph Fly Tying Manual*, in 1975. This helped establish our business, and demands on our time increased. Our business would have curtailed my fishing education were it not for Lance, a genius at business management and organization, and my mother, Oda, an expert money manager, detail person and mediator. Their diligence and hard work allowed me time to expand my fishing horizons worldwide.

During the late 1970s we started running Deschutes River float trips and fishing schools and developed Kaufmann's Fly Fishing Expeditions, Inc., which specializes in exotic fly fishing destinations. Retail stores in Bellevue and Seattle, Washington, soon followed.

During the early 1980s I outfitted and guided group trips around the world and operated our fly fishing schools on the Deschutes River. This allowed me time to experiment with, develop, and refine several trout and steelhead patterns. It also gave me the needed perspective and understanding of how best to organize and present techniques to students. I transferred this teaching technique and my lake fishing experience into *Lake Fishing With A Fly*, published in 1984.

Bonefish became a passion, and I spent several winters fishing everywhere from Venezuela to Christmas Island, researching and gathering information for *Bonefishing With A Fly*, published by Western Fisherman's Press in 1992. Bonefishing is perhaps the most fun a light tackle fly angler can have. The warm tropical ambiance is soothing, and the visuals are unrivaled. Bonefish are unbelievably strong for their size, they attack a fly aggressively, and there are plenty of them. Bonefishing is stalking and sight fishing at its best.

During the past 30 years I have tied, studied, collected, dissected, designed, redesigned, ordered, sold, explained, demonstrated, and dreamed flies. This mania has always led to better, more efficient methods. I have always enjoyed sharing knowledge, teaching others, and making a sometimes confusing and traditional sport less so. This fact, more than anything else, led to *The Fly Tyers Nymph Manual, Tying Dry Flies, Tying Nymphs, Trying Dry Flies, Revised Edition*, and this book.

Steelhead flies are my favorite to tie, partly because their boundaries of creation are less defined than other, more traditional styles of flies, allowing creativity and imagination to flow freely. Steelhead flies can be tied in nearly any size, shape, or color with almost any material. For me, the color spectrum (visuals) and animation possibilities are their main attraction. Steelhead flies allow one to experiment and create much like a painter does on canvas. In my imagination I can mix colors and movement that may stir the steelhead's memory of past saltwater feeding frenzies, stimulate a response to currently available foods, or simply arouse their curiosity.

I can also create off-the-wall attractor flies that may or may not resemble anything within nature's realm. All steelhead flies can be fished with some degree of confidence because, at one time or another, steelhead have attacked just about everything. Standard steelhead flies consist of a tail, rib, body, wing, and hackle. If you can tie one, you can tie many. The basic tying style remains the same; only the colors and materials change. I like to tie and fish sparse steelhead flies that are well animated. My favorite materials include sparkly dubbings, marabou, long flowing hackle, and reflective materials, especially holographic tinsels.

Without oversimplifying matters, Pacific Coast steelheading is relatively straightforward. It is a numbers game. The more steelhead that see your fly (or flies), the better your chances of success. The greased line, dead drift, and quarter-downstream-and-across are the most popular presentation techniques. There are variations of these and other methods. Anglers should keep an open mind and be versatile. A technique that works on one river may not work on another.

Of the three most popular techniques, the quarter-downstream-and-across is the simplest and most popular method. I like to fish the water close to the bank, work out a comfortable length of line, and then wade to a comfortable depth. Take a step, make a cast, and continue through the run, covering the water in a systematic manner. Remember, steelhead cannot hit your fly when it is in the air. Lift your line and get it back into the water as quickly as possible. Control the fly line so the fly is "fishing" in an effective manner as much as possible.

When I was instructing and guiding anglers, I would observe their fishing technique from a high bank. Using a stopwatch, I would time the minutes the fly was swimming or drifting in an effective manner. Usually, anglers clocked between three and seven minutes of effective angling per hour! When you fish effectively for 30 to 40 minutes per hour, it only stands to reason that you should hook several times the number of fish! My point is, just because you are "fishing" doesn't mean you have maximized your chances of success. Like any endeavor, if you do it best, the reward is great.

I like to fish two flies: a large and small, bright and dark (or transition color), surface and subsurface, nymph and skater, or any other combination. A steelhead that may not be responsive to one size, color, or swimming depth of fly, may be excited about another. Fishing two flies is another way to appeal to more fish in half the angling time. Fish through a run, change flies and/or presentation technique, and fish through again. Usually only a small percentage of fish will be in an aggressive mood. Keep fishing and covering water until you find one. Eventually, a steelhead will attack your offering, usually when you least expect it, and jolt you into steelhead la-la land. Anglers wishing to learn more about steelhead flies and fly fishing should read Trey Combs' books, *Steelhead Fly Fishing and Flies* and *Steelhead Fly Fishing.*

Successful steelhead anglers should consider releasing all fish. They are not numerous enough to end up on the barbecue. Every fish that is removed from the river deprives other anglers of the chance to enjoy what you did. Land your fish quickly, handle and release them carefully, and keep fishing!

Randall Kaufmann
Tigard, Oregon
February, 1995

Air BC *(Bill McMillan)*
    Hook: TMC 7989, sizes 4-6
  Thread: Orange, 3/0
     Tail: White calftail
    Wing: White calftail
    Body: Orange deer or elk, spun and
               clipped to shape
Side Wings: Unclipped tufts of orange body
               hair

Babine Special
    Hook: TMC 7999, sizes 2-6, weighted
  Thread: Black, 6/0
     Tail: White marabou
    Body: Fluorescent orange chenille
               tied in two balls, divided by
               red hackle
  Hackle: White

Black Bear, Green Butt
    Hook: TMC 7999, sizes 6-8
  Thread: Black, 6/0
    Wing: Black bear or calf
      Tag: Fine flat silver tinsel
     Butt: Fluorescent green wool or floss
     Tail: Black hackle fibers
      Rib: Oval silver tinsel
    Body: Black wool
  Hackle: Black hen
Note: Atlantic Salmon Favorite

Blue Charm
    Hook: TMC 7999, sizes 6-8
  Thread: Black, 6/0
    Wing: Gray squirrel tail
      Tag: Fine flat silver tinsel
     Butt: Yellow floss
     Tail: Golden pheasant crest
      Rib: Oval silver tinsel
    Body: Black floss
   Throat: Silver doctor blue hackle
Note: Atlantic Salmon Favorite

Bomber
    Hook: TMC 7989, sizes 4-6
  Thread: Black, 3/0
     Tail: White calftail
    Wing: White calftail
  Hackle: Grizzly, palmered through
               body
    Body: Deer, spun and clipped

Bomber, Brown and Orange
    Hook: TMC 300, size 6
  Thread: Black, 6/0
     Tail: Elk hair
    Wing: Elk hair
  Hackle: Orange saddle
    Body: Deer
Note: Atlantic Salmon Favorite

Bomber, Green
    Hook: TMC 300, size 6
  Thread: Black, 3/0
     Tail: Green calftail
    Wing: Green calftail
  Hackle: Brown
    Body: Green deer
Note: Atlantic Salmon Favorite

Boss
    Hook: TMC 7999, sizes 2-8
  Thread: Black, 6/0
    Eyes: Silver bead chain
     Tail: Black bucktail at least as long
               as the hook shank
      Rib: Silver flat tinsel
    Body: Black chenille
  Hackle: Hot orange

Brindle Bug
    Hook: TMC 7999, sizes 6-8
  Thread: Black, 6/0
     Tail: Brown hackle tips
      Rib: Gold oval tinsel
    Body: Variegated black and yellow
               chenille
    Wing: Brown hackle tips
  Hackle: Brown

Brite Pink (Mike Mercer)
Hook: TMC 800S, sizes 4-8
Thread: Fluorescent fire orange, 6/0, coated with epoxy
Tail: Pearl Flashabou
Body: Fire orange flat waxed nylon, coated with epoxy
Hackle: Hot orange
Underwing: Fire orange Accent Flash
Overwing: Cerise Accent Flash

Coal Car (Randall Kaufmann)
Hook: TMC 7999, sizes 2-6
Thread: Black, 6/0
Wing: Black calf with black Krystal Flash over top
Tail: Black hackle fibers
Rib: Oval silver tinsel
Body: Fluorescent fire orange fuzzy wool, fluorescent red fuzzy wool, and black chenille
Hackle: Black

Coal Car Spey (Randall Kaufmann)
Hook: Partridge CS10/1, sizes 3/0 and 1/0
Thread: Black, 6/0
Tag: Silver flat tinsel
Rib: Silver oval tinsel
Body: Fluorescent fire orange and fluorescent red floss, with black Crystal Chenille
Hackle: Black marabou, palmered through black Crystal Chenille
Wing: Black hackle tips, four

Double Egg Sperm Fly, Orange (Dave Whitlock)
Hook: TMC 7999, sizes 4-6 weighted
Thread: Fluorescent fire orange, 6/0
Tag: Gold tinsel, flat
Tail: Yellow hackle fibers
Body: Hot orange chenille, flat gold tinsel, and hot orange chenille
Hackle: Hot orange
Wing: White marabou and pearl Accent Flash

Double Egg Sperm Fly, Pink (Dave Whitlock)
Hook: TMC 7999, sizes 4-6 weighted
Thread: Fluorescent fire orange, 6/0
Tag: Silver tinsel, flat
Tail: Yellow hackle fibers
Body: Fluorescent red chenille, flat silver tinsel, and fluorescent red chenille
Hackle: Fluorescent red
Wing: White marabou and pearl Accent Flash

Dredger, Fluorescent Green (Randall Kaufmann)
Hook: TMC 700, sizes 4-6
Thread: Fluorescent green single strand flat floss
Eyes: Non-toxic, painted black, white, fluorescent green, and black
Tail: Fluorescent green and black marabou with fluorescent green and black Krystal Flash
Rib: Gold wire
Body: Fluorescent green thread or floss
Hackle: Black

Dredger, Fluorescent Orange (Randall Kaufmann)
Hook: TMC 700, sizes 4-6
Thread: Fl. fire orange single strand flat floss
Eyes: Non-toxic, painted black, white, fl. orange, and black
Tail: Fl. orange and black marabou w/fl. orange, black, and pearl KF
Rib: Gold wire
Body: Fluorescent fire orange SSNF
Hackle: Black

Dredger, Purple (Randall Kaufmann)
Hook: TMC 700, sizes 4-6
Thread: Fl. red single strand flat floss
Eyes: Non-toxic, painted black, white, fl. red, and black; epoxy over top
Tail: Purple marabou with pearl, purple, and wine Krystal Flash
Rib: Gold wire
Body: Fluorescent red SSNF
Hackle: Purple

Ferry Canyon (Randall Kaufmann)
Hook: TMC 7999, sizes 2-6, weighted
Thread: Black, 6/0
Tail: Purple hackle fibers
Rib: Fine silver oval tinsel
Body: Fluorescent fire orange fuzzy wool, rear quarter; purple chenille, front three quarters
Wing: Strands of red, blue, wine and pearl Krystal Flash and purple marabou
Hackle: Purple

Freight Train (Randall Kaufmann)
Hook: TMC 7999, sizes 2-6
Thread: Black, 6/0
Wing: White calftail, and pearl Krystal Flash
Tail: Purple hackle fibers
Rib: Fine silver oval tinsel
Body: Fluorescent fire orange fuzzy wool, fluorescent red fuzzy wool, and black chenille
Hackle: Purple

Freight Train, Krystal Flash (Randall Kaufmann)
Hook: TMC 7999, sizes 2-6
Thread: Black, 6/0
Wing: Pearl, blue, and purple Krystal Flash
Tail: Purple hackle fibers
Rib: Fine silver oval tinsel
Body: Fluorescent fire orange fuzzy wool, fluorescent red fuzzy wool, and black chenille
Hackle: Purple

Freight Train Spey (Randall Kaufmann)
Hook: Partridge CS10/1, sizes 3/0 and 1/0
Thread: Black, 6/0
Tag: Silver flat tinsel
Rib: Silver oval tinsel
Body: Fluorescent fire orange and fluorescent red floss, with black Crystal Chenille
Hackle: Purple marabou, palmered through black Crystal Chenille
Wing: White hackle tips, four

Irresistible, Moosetail
Hook: TMC 7989, sizes 6-8
Thread: Black, 3/0
Wing: White calftail
Tail: Moose
Body: Natural deer or caribou, spun and clipped to shape
Hackle: Brown

Krystal Egg, Chartreuse (Ted Leeson)
Hook: TMC 800B, sizes 4-8
Thread: Fluorescent fire orange, 6/0
Body: Chartreuse Accent Flash
Hackle: White

Krystal Egg, Orange (Ted Leeson)
Hook: TMC 800B, sizes 4-8
Thread: Fluorescent fire orange, 6/0
Body: Orange Accent Flash
Hackle: White

Krystal Egg, Pink (Ted Leeson)
Hook: TMC 800B, sizes 4-8
Thread: Fluorescent fire orange, 6/0
Body: Pink Accent Flash
Hackle: White

Krystal Egg, Red (Ted Leeson)
Hook: TMC 800B, sizes 4-8
Thread: Fluorescent fire orange, 6/0
Body: Red Accent Flash
Hackle: White

Laser Fly, Blue and Purple (Ed Bordas)
Hook: TMC 7999, size 6
Thread: Red, 3/0
Tail: White Laser
Body: Blue and purple Laser yarn

Laser Fly, Fluorescent Green and Fluorescent Yellow *(Ed Bordas)*
- Hook: TMC 7999, size 6
- Thread: Red, 3/0
- Tail: White Laser
- Body: Fluorescent green and fluorescent yellow Laser yarn

Laser Fly, Fluorescent Pink *(Ed Bordas)*
- Hook: TMC 7999, size 6
- Thread: Red, 3/0
- Tail: White Laser
- Body: Fluorescent pink Laser yarn

Laser Fly, Fluorescent Yellow and Fire Orange *(Ed Bordas)*
- Hook: TMC 7999, size 6
- Thread: Red, 3/0
- Tail: White Laser
- Body: Fluorescent yellow and fluorescent fire orange Laser yarn

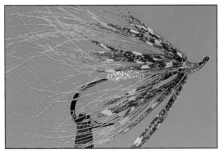

Laser Fly, Pink, Brown and Tan *(Ed Bordas)*
- Hook: TMC 7999, size 6
- Thread: Red, 3/0
- Tail: White Laser
- Body: Pink, brown, and tan Laser yarn

Max Canyon
- Hook: TMC 7999, sizes 4-6
- Thread: Black, 6/0
- Wing: White over orange calftail
- Tail: Orange and white hackle fibers
- Rib: Medium silver oval tinsel
- Body: Hot orange yarn, rear third; black yarn, front two thirds
- Hackle: Black

Muddler Minnow
- Hook: TMC 7999, sizes 2-12
- Thread: Brown, 6/0
- Tail: Brown turkey quill or tail
- Body: Flat gold tinsel or gold Diamond Braid
- Wing: Brown turkey quill over gray squirrel tail or brown calftail
- Head: Natural brown deer, spun and clipped to shape; tips form collar

Orange Spey *(Deke Meyer)*
- Hook: TMC 7999, sizes 2-4
- Thread: Fluorescent fire orange, 6/0
- Body: Gold Polyflash and black sparkle yarn, with hot orange Spey or schlappen palmered through front half
- Rib: Small gold oval tinsel through front half
- Wing: Black hackles, two, facing each other
- Hackle: Orange guinea

Pixies' Revenge *(George Cook)*
- Hook: TMC 7999, size 1/0
- Thread: Fluorescent fire orange, 6/0
- Wing: White, fluorescent orange, and fluorescent pink or cerise marabou with highlights of pearl and fluorescent orange Krystal Flash and gold Flashabou

Polar Shrimp
- Hook: TMC 7999, sizes 2-8
- Thread: White, 6/0
- Wing: White calftail
- Tail: Fluorescent orange hackle fibers
- Body: Fluorescent orange chenille
- Hackle: Fluorescent orange

Popsicle *(George Cook)*
Hook: *TMC 7999, size 1/0*
Thread: *Fluorescent fire orange, 6/0*
Wing: *Fluorescent or hot orange, fluorescent red (cherry) marabou, and bright or dark purple schlappen, with highlights of purple and gold Flashabou and orange, pearl, and purple Krystal Flash*

PreFontaine *(Lee Wulff)*
Hook: *TMC 7989, size 8*
Thread: *Black 6/0*
Tail: *Two badger hackle tips*
Wing: *White calftail, spun and flared*
Hackle: *Badger, palmered*
Note: *Atlantic Salmon Favorite*

Purple Peril
Hook: *TMC 7999, sizes 2-6*
Thread: *Black, 6/0*
Wing: *Red fox squirrel*
Tail: *Purple hackle fibers*
Rib: *Fine silver oval tinsel*
Body: *Purple chenille*
Hackle: *Purple*

Purple Spey *(Deke Meyer)*
Hook: *TMC 7999, sizes 2-4*
Thread: *Black, 6/0*
Body: *Purple poly flash, black sparkle yarn; purple Spey or schlappen palmered through front half*
Rib: *Small silver oval tinsel through front half*
Body, Front: *Sparkle yarn, black (use only 2 of 4 plies)*
Wing: *Black hackles, two, facing each other*
Hackle: *Dark guinea*

Roe Bug, Chartreuse
Hook: *TMC 2457, sizes 6 and 10*
Thread: *White, 3/0*
Body: *Chartreuse egg yarn*

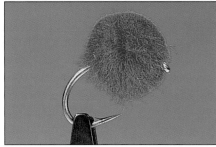

Roe Bug, Fire Orange
Hook: *TMC 2457, sizes 6 and 10*
Thread: *White, 3/0*
Body: *Fluorescent fire orange egg yarn*

Roe Bug, Peach
Hook: *TMC 2457, sizes 6 and 10*
Thread: *White, 3/0*
Body: *Peach egg yarn*

Roe Bug, Pink
Hook: *TMC 2457, sizes 6 and 10*
Thread: *White, 3/0*
Body: *Pink egg yarn*

Royal Wulff
Hook: *TMC 7989, sizes 4-6*
Thread: *Black, 6/0*
Wing: *White calftail*
Tail: *Moose*
Rib: *Fine gold wire, counter-wrapped*
Body: *Peacock, red floss, peacock (equal thirds)*
Hackle: *Brown*

Rusty Rat
Hook: TMC 7999, sizes 6-8
Thread: Red, 6/0
Wing: Gray fox guard hair
Tag: Fine oval gold tinsel
Tail: Peacock sword fibers, short
Rib: Oval gold tinsel
Body: Rear half, orange floss; front half, peacock
Veiling: Yellow floss, at body joint
Hackle: Grizzly, collar style
Note: Atlantic Salmon Favorite

Salmon Skater, Brown (Lee Wulff)
Hook: TMC 7989, size 8
Thread: Black, 6/0
Tail: Brown hackle tips
Hackle: Brown
Face: White deer
Note: Atlantic Salmon Favorite

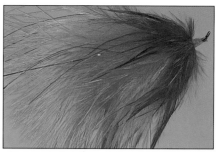

Showgirl (George Cook)
Hook: TMC 7999, size 1/0
Thread: Fluorescent fire orange, 6/0
Wing: Pink or cerise marabou and bright or dark purple schlappen, highlighted with purple and pearl Flashabou and Krystal Flash

Signal Light (Randall Kaufmann)
Hook: TMC 7999, sizes 2/0-6
Thread: Black, 6/0
Wing: Blue, pearl, lime, wine, and red Krystal Flash and black marabou
Tail: Dark purple hackle
Rib: Fine silver oval tinsel
Body: Fluorescent fire orange fuzzy wool, fluorescent green fuzzy wool, and black chenille
Hackle: Dark purple

Signal Light Spey (Randall Kaufmann)
Hook: Partridge CS10/1, sizes 3/0, 1/0
Thread: Black, 6/0
Tag: Silver flat tinsel
Rib: Silver oval tinsel
Body: Fluorescent fire orange and fluorescent green floss, with black Crystal Chenille
Hackle: Purple marabou, palmered through black Crystal Chenille with black marabou at front
Wing: Black hackle tips, four

Silver Hilton
Hook: TMC 7999, sizes 4-8
Thread: Black, 6/0
Tail: Grizzly hackle fibers or mallard flank
Rib: Flat silver tinsel
Body: Black chenille
Wing: Grizzly hackle tips, flared
Hackle: Grizzly

Silver Rat
Hook: TMC 7999, sizes 6-8
Thread: Fluorescent fire orange or red, 6/0
Wing: Gray fox guard hairs
Tail: Golden pheasant crest
Rib: Oval gold tinsel; use to form tag
Body: Flat silver tinsel or mylar
Hackle: Grizzly
Note: Atlantic Salmon Favorite

Skunk
Hook: TMC 7999, sizes 2-6
Thread: Black, 6/0
Wing: White calftail
Tail: Red hackle fibers
Rib: Flat silver tinsel
Body: Black chenille
Hackle: Black

Skunk, Green Butt
Hook: TMC 7999, sizes 1/0-8
Thread: Black, 6/0
Wing: White calftail
Tail: Red hackle fibers
Butt: Fluorescent green chenille
Rib: Fine silver oval tinsel
Body: Black chenille
Hackle: Black

Skunk, Red Butt
Hook: TMC 7999, sizes 4-6
Thread: Black, 6/0
Wing: White calftail
Tail: Red hackle fibers
Butt: Fluorescent red chenille
Rib: Flat silver tinsel
Body: Black chenille
Hackle: Black

Skykomish Sunrise
Hook: TMC 7999, sizes 2-6
Thread: Red, 6/0
Wing: White calftail
Tail: Red and yellow hackle fibers
Rib: Fine silver oval tinsel
Body: Red chenille
Hackle: Red and yellow

Steelhead Caddis (Bill McMillan)
Hook: TMC 7989, sizes 6-8
Thread: Brown, 6/0
Body: Hare's mask fur, orangish
          shade from base of ear
Wing: Light mottled turkey quill
Head: Deer, spun and clipped sparse-
          ly; tips form collar

Umpqua Special
Hook: TMC 7999, sizes 4-6
Thread: Red, 6/0
Wing: White calftail
Tail: White hackle fibers
Rib: Fine silver oval tinsel
Body: Yellow and red yarn
Hackle: Brown

Undertaker
Hook: TMC 7999, sizes 6-8
Thread: Black, 6/0
Wing: Black bear
Rib: Gold oval tinsel
Tag: Gold oval tinsel
Butt: Fluorescent green and fluores-
          cent fire orange floss
Body: Peacock
Hackle: Black

Waller Waker, Bumblebee (Lani Waller)
Hook: TMC 7999, sizes 2-6
Thread: Black, 3/0
Wing: Natural dark elk hair
Tail: Moose
Body: Rusty brown and black deer,
          spun and clipped to shape
Throat: Moose

Waller Waker, Standard (Lani Waller)
Hook: TMC 7999, sizes 2-6
Thread: Black, 3/0
Wing: White calftail
Tail: Moose
Body: Black and natural gray deer,
          spun and clipped to shape
Throat: Moose

Winter's Hope (Bill McMillan)
Hook: TMC 7999, size 2/0
Thread: Maroon, 6/0
Body: Flat silver tinsel
Wing: Two yellow hackle tips
          enclosed by two orange hackle
          tips, topped with golden-olive
          calftail, sparse
Hackle: Silver doctor blue and purple,
          long and soft

Yellow Humpy
Hook: TMC 7989, sizes 4-6
Thread: Yellow, 3/0
Wing: Same as tail
Tail: Light deer or elk; form back
          with butt ends
Body: Yellow thread or single strand
          nylon floss
Hackle: Brown and grizzly

Chapter 6

Bass Flies

Dave Whitlock

I was born in Muskogee, Oklahoma, without a fly rod in my hand or in my family, on November 11, 1934. In spite of that, I have been fly fishing for over 50 years, since I was nine years old. At the time Oklahoma was a virtual desert for fly fishermen. I had never seen fly fishing done nor did I know anyone who did it. I was fascinated reading about it and the fact that you could imitate small insects and small minnow forms that I had seen other fish feeding on regularly. I was just hamstrung to be able to catch them on what we had for artificial lures in those days.

At that point I urged my dad to get me a fly rod. He located a 9-foot bamboo fly rod with two broken tips and an old rusty reel with a section of rotten level silk line on it. There was no leader. It was a pretty crude outfit, even for those days. Without any instruction or much understanding of the sport, I struggled for quite a few years, catching some panfish and bass in local waters.

I had read some articles in *Field and Stream* about fly tying and fly fishing. I cut a page out of a *Mechanix Illustrated* on how to tie a wet fly. I didn't have a vise or any materials, so I used my mother's cotton sewing thread and a few feathers from hunting trips. I used long-shanked bait hooks because it was easy for me to hold them while I wrapped the thread and feathers by hand. Later I learned about fly tying vises. My flies were crude, but I caught a few bass and sunfish on them and was pleased.

I really got into fly tying at age 12, when my grandmother bought me a small fly tying kit. It contained an inexpensive pot metal vise that broke after a couple of days. My dad welded it so that it would work. The kit also contained a few colored feathers, hair, hooks, and threads. Looking back almost 50 years, it must have been very crude.

Nevertheless, I really enjoyed fly tying and fly fishing and felt good about being able to fashion imitations of fish foods with my own hands. My isolation from the sport allowed (forced) me to become more innovative and creative. I made up my own guidelines. This was a blessing in disguise because it allowed me to think for myself. That has stuck with me over the years. Although I am not reluctant to adapt other people's ideas to my tying, I feel that my ideas are just as important.

A friend, Tom Green, had learned about Polly Rosborough's nymphs and tying philosophies from Polly's first book. Tom Green and Polly Rosborough were the people who got me started tying nymphs.

Joe Brooks also had a lot of influence on me, and I followed everything he wrote. I especially liked those wonderful stories about Montana, fishing Muddler Minnows, Woolly Worms, lacquered ants, and Joe's Hoppers in the Big Hole and the Yellowstone. I was just on fire to try that water. I had my first opportunity when I was 17.

In my early twenties, once I was out of school, I met other fly tyers and was able to return to Montana. Dan Bailey's fly shop and his fly tyers were my first "live" exposure to professional fly tying. At about that time I got quite interested in ordering fly tying materials. Tom Green recommended that I order materials from Buz Buszek in California. Up until that time I had been ordering most of my materials from Herter's, which was a wonderful catalog with a lot of incredible materials. When I began to order from Buszek's, I understood the meaning of good materials and high-quality flies. After Buz died, his wife, Virginia, became a special person in my life, the person who most influenced me in becoming a professional fly tyer. She supplied me with the best possible materials.

My real break came when I converted my hobby into a business. I was fishing every late summer and fall at Yellowstone and would hang around Bud Lilly's Trout Shop in West Yellowstone. Bud was intrigued because I was successfully hooking some nice trout using some unique flies. These were flies that I had designed in the 50s and 60s for western fishing and included the Whit Stone Nymph series, Sculpin, Dave's Hopper, and Multi-Colored Marabou. Bud asked me if I might be interested in tying a few for the shop, and I did. This was my introduction to the importance of attaching one's name to a fly and marketing it as their product.

As the demand grew, I eventually had 18 tyers producing Dave Whitlock flies. I required them to tie a hundred dozen flies a year, furnished all the materials, and paid them a fair price.

Fly tying is the other half of fly fishing. It is a complement as a hobby or as a part-time or full-time income for many people. I try to design a fly that really works and that has eye appeal, one that answers a need to imitate a food form that a particular fish readily eats. It should fish well, perform, and endure. Flies may require a weed guard or snag guard, a number of swimming actions, or special materials that resist the rigors of hard casting. It should withstand being beaten on the gravel and being mauled, chewed, and removed from the fish's mouth.

One of the things that allows flies to be used most successfully is the acceptance of barbless hooks. Randall Kaufmann has been a pioneer in insisting on barbless hooks for flies. The barbless hook allows a fly to hook a fish much easier. It also allows a hook to be removed from both fish and anglers! A barbless hook is key to producing a high-quality fly that fishes well and does not self-destruct when you take it out of the fish's mouth.

I like to choose materials that are easily available and functional. Deer hair interests me because I feel it is the most versatile for trout, bass, and some saltwater flies. I like synthetic materials. One of my favorites is Swiss Straw, or rayon raffia. The availability of synthetics, such as Flashabou and Crystal Hair, has added another dimension to fly tying.

I have designed Whitlock flies for trout, bass, and saltwater, but I am most recognized for my bass flies. I approach bass fly design with two things in mind: what bass eat on a day-to-day basis, including insects, amphibians, fish, and invertebrates; and what bass hit—attractors, intimidators, exciters, and aggravators. A lot of my fly designs have been gleaned from successful bass lures.

I work to imitate everything a bass will eat on the surface, below the surface, and on the bottom on a year around basis. All my bass flies have weed guard protection. My weed guard flies have helped change people's thinking about bass fishing and where bass live.

With the same thought in mind, I have developed functional trout flies that represent natural food forms—leeches, stonefly nymphs, and grasshoppers. Many of these are relatively large and are designed to attract larger trout.

I regularly contribute art and writing on fly fishing to many publications, such as *Fly Fisherman, American Angler, Trout, In-Fisherman,* and *Field & Stream.* My books include *Dave Whitlock's Guide to Aquatic Trout Foods,* the *L. L. Bean Flyfishing Handbook,* the *L. L. Bean Bass Fly Fishing Handbook,* and *Imitating and Fishing Natural Fish Foods* for Lefty's Little Library.

I have also co-authored or contributed to many books, including *The Fly Tyer's Almanac, Second Fly Tyer's Almanac, Art Flick's Master Fly Tying Guide, McClane's Fishing Encyclopedia, Migel's Stream Conservation Book, Masters On The Nymph,* and others. I have illustrated over 20 books, including President Carter's *Outdoor Journal.* I also demonstrate fly fishing in four videos, through guest appearances on televised fly fishing programs, and in a movie made especially for 3M/Scientific Anglers, *The Flyfisher's Aquatic Insects.* In my spare time I lecture on fly fishing and conservation throughout the world and have produced many slide shows. Over the years I have been employed on a consulting basis by L. L. Bean, Bass Pro, Sage, and Gander Mountain.

One of my most satisfying contributions to wild trout management and preservation is the Whitlock-Vibert Box System—a unique and efficient instream salmonoid egg incubator and nursery device. Today, under the sponsorship of the Federation of Fly Fishers (FFF), this program is used throughout the world for introduction or enhancement of wild trout, char, and salmon stocks.

Fly fishing and fly tying is the greatest sport for any person from eight to 80, or nine to 90, that we could possibly have. It has become a lifestyle for many of us and is certainly an important part of recreation for other people. I really appreciate the special opportunities the sport has allowed me.

Author's Note: Dave has been a recipient of many awards, including the Max Ander Wild Trout Award in 1976 for his work on propagation of wild trout and the FFF's Conservation Man of the Year Award in 1981. He was presented the FFF James E. Henshall Award for his work in warmwater fishing and conservation and the FFF's Ambassador Award for national and international promotion of fly fishing and conservation. Dave also received the Buz Buszek Fly Tyer's Award, which is the highest honor in the fly tying world. In 1987 he was inducted into the National Fresh Water Hall of Fame. Dave Whitlock is a man totally devoted to the world of fly fishing and conservation.

Dave Whitlock
Mountain Home, Arkansas
January, 1995

Larry Dahlberg

Some of my earliest and fondest memories as a kid revolve around fishing. My grandfather was a "fishaholic" who fished live bait for sturgeon and catfish. My father fished exclusively with artificial lures, mostly for muskies. When I was three or four, my father took me fly fishing for spring panfish. He had an ice fishing stick too long to fit in the ice house, and that became my fly rod. For many years we fished together almost every evening. It was a hunter-gatherer thing, a way of life.

I wanted to catch a muskie, but my father would not let me go until I could place a lure on target. He made a deal with my mother. When I could place eight out of 10 casts under the swing set and into a box, I could go muskie fishing. When I was six, I could do it, and I got to go along to the St. Croix River for muskies. This is when I learned to row a boat.

While guiding I learned to cast a long line by watching a gentleman named Philip Pillsbury. To this day he is the best caster I have ever seen. He could throw 90 feet of sticky, gooey silk line with his Pinky Gillum 9-foot rod so quickly it would tear the feather off a popper. I watched him cast for hours and studied every subtle movement.

Chuck Walton, former fly rod world record holder for permit, was probably the greatest influence on my fly fishing ideas and techniques. It was Chuck who taught me to separate the important fishing ideas from the unimportant. He was the first client who showed any interest in the unconventional flies I'd been tying. I was in my mid-teens.

Dad tied mostly muskie bucktails, bass poppers, and Black Gnats for sunfish. As a youngster, I devastated his materials. I had no lessons or books to learn from—there was not much available—and for years I thought I had invented the Muddler. I feel there were some advantages to not having been exposed to literature or "how to" books. My techniques and ideas evolved from observation.

At 11, I became a guide for a private smallmouth bass fly fishing club, which included many "fat cats" of international industry. I guided almost every day until 4:30 p.m., when their cocktail hour began. I'd meet my dad at the landing and fish for muskies until dark almost every day of the season and all day Saturday and Sunday. My guiding put me through college; I graduated with a degree in English and a minor in political science. After college, Burger Brothers Sporting Goods in Minneapolis hired me, and I helped develop the tackle and fly fishing department. After four years I tired of that so I started my own rep business selling fly fishing equipment and resumed guiding on the St. Croix for smallmouth bass.

All told, I guided for 23 years, until I began working for *In Fisherman*, a media company in Brainerd, Minnesota that had a television, magazine, and radio business. After I hosted several programs, they offered me a job producing the show. I had no production experience, but my background in creative writing helped. That was in the mid 1980s. New challenges arose, and I left *In Fisherman* in 1992 and went on my own again. I really wanted to promote fishing for the sake of fishing and soon ended up producing *The Hunt For Big Fish* on ESPN. In 28 episodes I have released at least 30 line-class world record fish. I figure that all anglers like exciting fishing, even if they may never have the opportunity to do it for themselves. I go about producing a show that is entertaining and fun.

I am not a purist fly fisherman. I do a lot of fishing using other methods. By using live bait I have learned a thousand times more about catching fish on flies than I have from all the fly fishermen I have met. The knowledge just required transposing. I am probably a better plug fisherman than a fly fisherman because I grew up plugging. I have learned more about designing flies by studying the attracting and triggering attributes of artificial lures than I have from all the fly tying and fishing articles I have read. I like fly fishing best. It is more pleasurable than spinning, bait casting, or trolling. I fish to experience the fish. When I fly fish, I almost always choose a situation in which I can see the fish—sometimes before they take. If possible, I want to make the fish come up and blast the surface so I can see them open their mouths and show their teeth. When I am connected, I like the feeling of "who's gotten whom." I think fly fishing accomplishes these things best.

As a youngster, while helping to trim the Christmas tree, I dropped a piece of tinsel and watched in amazement as it fluttered, sparkling, to the floor. I stashed some and tied it onto a neutrally-buoyant wooden body. On the first cast it attracted a big bass. For years I kept the idea for a few clients and myself. This idea led to Flashabou, which is now used worldwide.

My Dahlberg Diver pattern is simply an underwater delivery system for Flashabou. The shaped deer hair head on the Diver creates a turbulent flow, which in turn creates a wild animation, bringing the fly to life. Like all productive and innovative patterns, the Diver has been modified over the years to represent anything from a frog to a sculpin. To this day the Diver is my best fly for fish who eat other fish—baramundi to brown trout. My angling strategy involves much more than fishing: hunting, spotting, stalking, and interactive observations are all integral to consistent success, especially when you are fishing for the "big boys." The most important consideration in the design of larger flies is to create the illusion of considerable size but with minimum weight, wind resistance, and bulk.

My approach to fishing is practical and pragmatic. Anglers either fish for fish that eat insects or for fish that eat other fish (of course, there is some crossover). The number one problem in terms of tactics for bug eaters is executing a drag-free presentation—that is, one that does not appear to be attached to a line but, rather, is controlled by the environment. Imitation and size are important, but I like to incorporate these ideas into nondescript buggy imitations that seem alive.

When fishing for large predators who eat each other, I do not imitate specific food sources. Instead, I appeal to the instinct of natural selection. I believe that when a fish sees something out of the ordinary or that does not belong there and appears to be reacting to the fish's presence, trying to get away, success is close at hand. I like to begin covering the water or fishing to specific fish with something bright and flashy. If that does not work, I change to something dark. I have always looked at lures that are effective and attempted to ascertain what it is that attracts or triggers fish into attacking them. I imitate this or incorporate similar traits into my fly patterns. I have been able to fish for many of the world's game fish in exotic locations, both near home and far away. I never made a conscious decision to pursue a career in fishing; I grew up fishing, and it just happened as a natural progression.

Author's Note: Larry is one of America's premier adventure anglers and is equally at home fishing brookies in local streams or billfish off the African coast. His first love is angling for big fish. Larry's latest television series, ESPN's *The Hunt For Big Fish* which airs Saturday mornings, has excited and enlightened anglers around the world. Larry lives in Brainerd, Minnesota.

Larry Dahlberg
Brainerd, Minnesota
May, 1994

Bass Popper, Frog
Hook:	TMC 8089, sizes 6 and 10
Thread:	Black, 3/0
Snag Guard:	Clear monofilament
Tail:	White, yellow, and green saddles, two each
Body:	Wapsi foam body, painted yellow, green with black spots
Collar:	White, yellow, and green saddles, two each
Eyes:	Yellow with black pupil

Bass Popper, Red and White
Hook:	TMC 8089, sizes 6 and 10
Thread:	Black, 3/0
Snag Guard:	Clear monofilament
Tail:	Red, white, and black saddles, two each
Body:	Wapsi foam body, painted white, black, and red
Collar:	Red white, and black saddles, two each
Eyes:	White with black pupil

Bouface, Black *(John Barr)*
Hook:	TMC 811S, sizes 2 and 6
Thread:	Black, 3/0
Tail:	Black rabbit strip with pearl Flashabou and black Accent Flash
Collar:	Black marabou
Comments:	Incorporate snag guard as needed.

Bouface, Chartreuse *(John Barr)*
Hook:	TMC 811S, sizes 2 and 6
Thread:	Black, 3/0
Tail:	Chartreuse rabbit strip with pearl Flashabou and black Accent Flash
Collar:	Chartreuse marabou

Bouface, Red and White *(John Barr)*
Hook:	TMC 811S, sizes 2 and 6
Thread:	White, 3/0
Tail:	White rabbit strip with pearl and red Flashabou or Accent Flash
Collar:	Red marabou

Bouface, Yellow and Black *(John Barr)*
Hook:	TMC 811S, sizes 2 and 6
Thread:	Black, 3/0
Tail:	Black rabbit strip with pearl flashabou and black Accent Flash
Collar:	Yellow marabou top; black marabou bottom

Brass Hare, Black *(Tim England)*
Hook:	Eagle Claw 214, size 2
Head:	Quarter-inch solid brass bead
Thread:	Black single strand nylon floss
Tail:	Black rabbit strip (1/8 inch wide), 1-1/2 inches long
Body:	Black rabbit strip, 1/8 inch wide, wrapped around hook
Collar:	Black rubber; 4 strands fine, 4 strands medium

Brass Hare, Chartreuse *(Tim England)*
Hook:	Eagle Claw 214, size 2
Head:	Quarter-inch solid brass bead
Thread:	Chartreuse single strand nylon floss
Tail:	Chartreuse rabbit strip (1/8 inch wide), 1-1/2 inches long
Body:	Chartreuse rabbit strip, 1/8 inch wide, wrapped around hook
Collar:	Forest green rubber, 4 strands fine, 4 strands medium; green Accent Flash, 6 strands

Brass Wonder, Olive *(Tim England)*
Hook:	Eagle Claw 214, size 6
Head:	3/16 inch brass bead
Thread:	Olive, 6/0
Tail:	Olive rabbit
Rib:	Clear 4-lb. monofilament
Body:	Olive rabbit dubbing with green Accent Flash

Brass Wonder, Silver Minnow *(Tim England)*

Hook:	*Eagle Claw 214, size 6*
Head:	*3/16-inch nickel plated brass bead*
Thread:	*Red, 6/0 or 8/0*
Tail:	*Pearl Accent Flash, 6 strands*
Overwing:	*Gray and white marabou*
Underwing:	*Gray marabou and peacock herl*

Bull-It Head, Black *(John Betts)*

Hook:	*Mustad 33903, size 2*
Weight:	*.025 lead wire*
Thread:	*White, 3/0*
Diving Lip:	*Clear .010 mylar*
Tail:	*Black marabou*
Body:	*Closed-cell foam (Evazote); Pantone with black marker*
Eyes:	*Steel or brass plated black-headed stainless steel dressmaker pins pushed through body*

Bull-It Head, Frog *(John Betts)*

Hook:	*Mustad 33903, size 2*
Weight:	*.025 lead wire*
Thread:	*Pale yellow, white, or olive, 3/0*
Diving Lip:	*Clear .010 mylar*
Tail:	*Grizzly saddle hackles splayed out with olive marabou*
Body:	*Closed-cell foam (Evazote); Pantone with black, yellow, and olive markers*
Eyes:	*Steel or brass plated black-headed stainless steel dressmaker pins pushed through body*

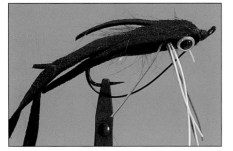

Chamois Lizard *(Dave Whitlock)*

Hook:	*TMC 7999, size 2*
Thread:	*Black single strand nylon floss*
Snag guard:	*Hard Mason nylon*
Eyes:	*Yellow and black solid plastic*
Underbody:	*Black dubbing*
Legs:	*Black and white rubber*
Belly, Back:	*Black chamois; cut hole in center, slip over hook eye, secure flat over top and under body; secure at back of body (top and underside) with Zap-A-Gap*

Crayfish, Dark Brown Turkey *(Bob Clouser)*

Hook:	*TMC 5263, sizes 6-10, weighted*
Thread:	*Olive, 6/0*
Antennae:	*Ringneck pheasant tail*
Nose (tail):	*Natural hen mallard fibers*
Back:	*Dark mottled turkey quill*
Body:	*Pale gray yarn or dubbing*
Claws:	*Same as nose*
Rib:	*Gray thread, 6/0*
Legs:	*Ginger, grizzly, or olive grizzly hackle*

Crayfish, Olive *(Larry Dahlberg)*

Hook:	*Mustad 91751, size 4, weighted*
Thread:	*White single strand nylon floss*
Eyes:	*Burned monofilament*
Antennae:	*Black Flashabou*
Underbody:	*White rabbit hide, trimmed to shape*
Overbody, Claws:	*Olive rabbit hide, trimmed to shape and glued (Zap-A-Gap) to underside of body*

Crayfish, Olive-Green *(Bob Clouser)*

Hook:	*TMC 5263, sizes 6-10, weighted*
Thread:	*Olive, 6/0*
Antennae:	*Ringneck pheasant tail*
Nose (tail):	*Natural hen mallard fibers*
Back:	*Olive Furry Foam*
Body:	*Pale gray yarn or dubbing*
Claws:	*Same as nose*
Rib:	*Gray thread, 6/0*
Legs:	*Ginger, grizzly, or olive grizzly hackle*

Crayfish, Tan Turkey *(Bob Clouser)*

Hook:	*TMC 5263, sizes 6-10, weighted*
Thread:	*Olive, 6/0*
Antennae:	*Ringneck pheasant tail*
Nose (tail):	*Natural hen mallard fibers*
Back:	*Light mottled turkey quill*
Body:	*Pale gray yarn or dubbing*
Claws:	*Same as nose*
Rib:	*Gray thread, 6/0*
Legs:	*Ginger, grizzly, or olive grizzly hackle*

Crystal Damsel Dragon, Blue *(Dave Whitlock)*

Hook:	*TMC 8089, sizes 6 and 10*
Thread:	*Fluorescent green SSNF*
Underbody:	*Closed-cell foam*
Abdomen:	*Blue (bottom), black (top) elk rump; one strand of wide pearlescent mylar each side*
Snag Guard:	*Mason hard nylon, 20 lb.*
Legs:	*Blue-speckled rubber, 3 each side*
Wing:	*2 bunches of pearl Accent Flash; black Pantone markings*
Eyes:	*Amber and black prismatic*

135

Dancing Frog, Green Yellow *(Jim Stewart)*
Hook: TMC 8089, size 2
Thread: Fluorescent green SSNF
Snag Guard: Mason hard nylon, 20 lb., double
Tail: 18 strands (9 tied at mid point and folded in half) yellow and fluorescent yellow rubber
Body: Bright green and dark green deer body hair stacked over yellow belly with double stacked spots of olive with black centers
Eyes: Orange and black plastic

Dancing Frog, Red and White *(Jim Stewart)*
Hook: TMC 8089, size 2
Thread: White, 3/0
Snag Guard: Mason hard nylon, 20 lb., double
Tail: White rubber
Body: White, gray, and red deer body hair
Eyes: White, 6 mm solid plastic

Deer Hair Bass Bug, Black Ann Blue *(Dave Whitlock)*
Hook: TMC 8089, sizes 2-10
Thread: Black, 3/0
Snag Guard: Mason hard nylon, 20 lb.
Tail: Blue and black rubber, 2 furnace neck hackles, 2 black hen hackles
Hackle: Black
Body: Black, white, blue, white, black, and white deer
Legs: Black rubber
Eyes: Blue and black plastic

Deer Hair Bass Bug, Black Ann Red *(Dave Whitlock)*
Hook: TMC 8089, sizes 2-10
Thread: Black, 3/0
Snag Guard: Mason hard nylon, 20 lb.
Tail: Two furnace saddle hackles, black and red rubber with a black hen hackle on each side
Hackle: Black saddle hackle
Body: Black, red, orange, and white deer, spun and clipped
Legs: Black rubber
Eyes: Red audible plastic eyes

Deer Hair Bass Bug, Black Ann Yellow *(Dave Whitlock)*
Hook: TMC 8089, sizes 2-10
Thread: Black, 3/0
Snag Guard: Mason hard nylon, 20 lb.
Tail: Black and yellow rubber, 2 furnace neck hackles, 2 black hen hackles
Hackle: Black
Body: Black, white, yellow, white, black, and white deer
Legs: Black rubber
Eyes: Gold and black plastic

Deer Hair Bass Bug, Black Peacock *(Dave Whitlock)*
Hook: TMC 8089, sizes 2-10
Thread: Black, 3/0
Snag Guard: Mason hard nylon, 20 lb.
Tail: White rubber; 4 black neck hackles
Hackle: Black, peacock sword
Body: Black and white deer
Legs: White rubber
Eyes: White and black plastic

Deer Hair Bass Bug, Frog *(Dave Whitlock)*
Hook: TMC 8089, sizes 2-10
Thread: White, 3/0
Snag Guard: Mason hard nylon, 20 lb.
Tail: Pearl Krystal Flash; white, fl. yellow, and olive grizzly hackle
Collar: White and fl. yellow deer, topped w/black and olive deer, pearl Krystal Flash
Body: Same as collar
Legs: Black, white, fl. green, yellow rubber
Eyes: Yellow and black plastic

Deer Hair Bass Bug, Fruit Cocktail *(Dave Whitlock)*
Hook: TMC 8089, sizes 2-10
Thread: Red, 3/0
Tail: Fl. orange, yellow, green round rubber; orange Krystal Flash; orange, yellow, and green hackle
Body: Fl. yellow, green, black, red, and fl. orange deer
Legs: Fl. yellow, fl. orange, fl. green, and green rubber
Eyes: Yellow and black plastic

Deer Hair Bass Bug, Porkey's Pet *(Dave Whitlock)*
Hook: TMC 8089, sizes 2-10
Thread: White, 3/0
Snag Guard: Mason hard nylon, 20 lb.
Tail: White rubber; black, red, and white hackle
Hackle: Guinea
Body: White, black, and red deer
Legs: White rubber
Eyes: White and black plastic

Deer Hair Bass Bug, Yellow Canary
(Dave Whitlock)
       Hook: TMC 8089, sizes 2-10
     Thread: White, 3/0
Snag Guard: Mason hard nylon, 20 lb.
        Tail: White, yellow, and grizzly
                 neck hackle, 2 each
     Hackle: White
       Body: Pale yellow, bright yellow, and
                 white deer
        Legs: Yellow rubber
        Eyes: White and black plastic

Dilg-Slider, Black (Larry Dahlberg)
       Hook: TMC 811S, size 2
     Thread: Black single strand nylon floss
Snag Guard: Mason hard nylon, 20 lb.
        Tail: Red Flashabou
       Wing: Black rabbit hide; grizzly neck
                 hackle
 Underwing: Black rabbit
      Collar: Black deer
       Head: Same as collar
        Eyes: Yellow and black plastic

Dilg-Slider, Chartreuse (Larry Dahlberg)
       Hook: TMC 811S, size 2
     Thread: Fluorescent green single
                 strand nylon floss
Snag Guard: Mason hard nylon, 20 lb.
        Tail: Red Flashabou
       Wing: Fluorescent green rabbit hide;
                 grizzly neck hackle
 Underwing: Fluorescent green rabbit
      Collar: Fluorescent green deer
       Head: Same as collar
        Eyes: Yellow and black plastic

Dilg-Slider, White (Larry Dahlberg)
       Hook: TMC 811S, size 2
     Thread: White single strand nylon floss
Snag Guard: Mason hard nylon, 20 lb.
        Tail: Red Flashabou
       Wing: White rabbit hide; grizzly neck
                 hackle
 Underwing: White rabbit
      Collar: White deer
       Head: Same as collar
        Eyes: Yellow and black plastic

Diving Bug, Black Grizzly (Larry
Dahlberg)
       Hook: TMC 8089, size 2
     Thread: Black, 3/0
Snag Guard: Mason hard nylon, 20 lb.
       Wing: Black marabou, pearl Flasha-
                 bou, peacock herl; black and
                 grizzly hackle along each side
      Collar: Black deer
       Head: Black deer

Diving Bug, Brown Grizzly (Larry
Dahlberg)
       Hook: TMC 8089, size 2
     Thread: Brown, 3/0
Snag Guard: Mason hard nylon, 20 lb.
       Wing: Brown marabou, gold and cop-
                 per Flashabou; brown and
                 grizzly hackle along each side
      Collar: Brown deer (underside), black
                 deer (top)
       Head: Brown deer

Diving Bug, Bubble Bee (Larry Dahlberg)
       Hook: TMC 8089, size 2
     Thread: White, 3/0
Snag Guard: Mason hard nylon, 20 lb.
       Wing: Yellow marabou, gold Flash-
                 abou, with 2 brown hackles
                 along each side
      Collar: Brown deer
       Head: Black deer (top rear), balance
                 yellow deer

Diving Bug, Frog (Larry Dahlberg)
       Hook: TMC 8089, size 2
     Thread: White, 3/0
Snag Guard: Mason hard nylon, 20 lb.
       Wing: Pale yellow marabou, gold
                 Flashabou, with yellow grizzly
                 and olive grizzly hackle along
                 each side
      Collar: Yellow grizzly and olive grizzly
                 hackle; pale yellow deer with
                 golden olive and black deer on top
       Head: Pale yellow deer

Diving Bug, Purple Blue (Larry Dahlberg)
       Hook: TMC 8089, size 2
     Thread: White, 3/0
Snag Guard: Mason hard nylon, 20 lb.
       Wing: Light blue marabou, peacock
                 herl, gold Flashabou, with pur-
                 ple grizzly and blue grizzly
                 hackle along each side
      Collar: Purple natural deer overlaid
                 with blue and black on top
       Head: Purple natural deer

Diving Bug, Yellow Grizzly (*Larry Dahlberg*)
- Hook: TMC 8089, size 2
- Thread: White, 3/0
- Snag Guard: Mason hard nylon, 20 lb.
- Wing: Yellow marabou, gold Flashabou, with yellow and yellow grizzly hackle along each side
- Collar: Yellow deer overlaid with black on top
- Head: Yellow deer (rear) and light yellow deer (front)

Diving Minnow, Black (*Larry Dahlberg*)
- Hook: TMC 9394, sizes 2-4
- Thread: Red single strand nylon floss
- Snag Guard: Mason hard nylon, 20 lb.
- Body: Silver diamond braid
- Wing: Pearl Flashabou, black marabou, black Flashabou, grizzly hackle, peacock herl
- Throat: Pearl and black Flashabou
- Collar: Black deer
- Head: Black deer

Diving Minnow, Darter (*Larry Dahlberg*)
- Hook: TMC 9394, sizes 2-4
- Thread: Red single strand nylon floss
- Snag Guard: Mason hard nylon, 20 lb.
- Body: Silver Diamond Braid
- Wing: Pearl Flashabou, pale yellow marabou, olive Flashabou, olive marabou, light badger hackle
- Throat: Pearl and red Flashabou
- Collar: Pale yellow deer body overlaid with olive, natural, and black deer
- Head: Pale yellow deer

Diving Minnow, Golden (*Larry Dahlberg*)
- Hook: TMC 9394, sizes 2-4
- Thread: Red single strand nylon floss
- Snag Guard: Mason hard nylon, 20 lb.
- Body: Gold Diamond Braid
- Wing: Pearl Flashabou, gold marabou, gold Flashabou, peacock herl, golden brown grizzly hackle
- Throat: Pearl and red Flashabou
- Collar: Golden brown deer, overlaid with black deer on top
- Head: Golden brown deer

Diving Minnow, Perch (*Larry Dahlberg*)
- Hook: TMC 9394, sizes 2-4
- Thread: Red single strand nylon floss
- Snag Guard: Mason hard nylon, 20 lb.
- Body: Gold Diamond Braid
- Wing: Green Flashabou, golden olive marabou, light olive grizzly hackle, red and gold Flashabou, peacock herl
- Throat: Red, green, and gold Flashabou
- Collar: Olive deer, black on top
- Head: Olive deer

Diving Minnow, Silver (*Larry Dahlberg*)
- Hook: TMC 9394, sizes 2-4
- Thread: Red single strand nylon floss
- Snag Guard: Mason hard nylon, 20 lb.
- Body: Silver Diamond Braid
- Wing: Pearl Flashabou, white marabou, grizzly hackle, silver Flashabou
- Throat: Pearl and red Flashabou
- Collar: White deer, overlaid on top with natural gray and black deer
- Head: White deer

Dragon Moth, Blue (*Jim Stewart*)
- Hook: TMC 8089, size 2
- Thread: Blue, 3/0
- Tail: Blue goose wing, left and right, Flexament together; black moose
- Body: Silver Crystal Chenille
- Wing: Silver Krystal Flash, black deer (top) and blue deer (bottom)
- Head: Blue and black deer; paint red spot on top
- Eyes: Half round black plastic beads

Dragon Moth, Olive (*Jim Stewart*)
- Hook: TMC 8089, size 2
- Thread: Olive, 3/0
- Tail: Olive goose wing, left and right, Flexament together; black moose
- Body: Olive Crystal Chenille
- Wing: Olive Krystal Flash, olive deer (top), natural gray deer (bottom)
- Head: Olive deer; paint red spot on top
- Eyes: Half round black plastic beads

Dragon Moth, White (*Jim Stewart*)
- Hook: TMC 8089, size 2
- Thread: White single strand nylon floss or 3/0
- Tail: Blue goose wing, left and right, Flexament together; black moose
- Body: Silver Crystal Chenille
- Wing: Red Krystal Flash, white deer
- Head: White deer; paint red spot on top
- Eyes: Half round black plastic beads

Eelworm Streamer, Black (Dave Whitlock)
Hook: TMC 7999, sizes 1/0 and 4
Thread: Red single strand nylon floss
Snag guard: Clear monofilament
Eyes: Chromed lead or silver bead chain
Tail: Black saddle hackle, 4, splayed, 3-4" long and 2 black soft hackles tied short
Rib: Black thread
Body: Black dubbing or yarn
Hackle: Black saddle, palmered
Head: Same as body

Eelworm Streamer, Purple (Dave Whitlock)
Hook: TMC 7999, sizes 1/0 and 4
Thread: Red single strand nylon floss
Snag guard: Clear monofilament
Eyes: Chromed lead or silver bead
Tail: White dyed purple and grizzly dyed purple saddle hackle, 2 each, splayed, 3-4" long and 2 additional purple grizzly tied short
Rib: Purple thread
Body: Purple dubbing or yarn
Hackle: Purple grizzly
Head: Same as body

Flashabou Floating Muddler, Black (Dave Whitlock)
Hook: TMC 300, size 4
Thread: Red single strand nylon floss
Snag Guard: Mason hard nylon, 20 lb.
Body: Silver tinsel piping
Wing: Pearl Flashabou, black marabou, peacock herl
Throat: Pearl and red Flashabou
Collar: Black deer
Head: Same as collar
Eyes: White and black audible plastic

Flashabou Floating Muddler, Silver (Dave Whitlock)
Hook: TMC 300, size 4
Thread: Red single strand nylon floss
Snag Guard: Mason hard nylon, 20 lb.
Body: Silver tinsel piping
Wing: Pearl Flashabou, white marabou, peacock herl
Collar: White (bottom), natural gray and black (top) deer
Head: Same as collar
Eyes: White and black audible plastic

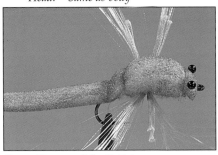

Foam Dragon (John Betts)
Hook: TMC 8089, size 10
Thread: Blue, 3/0
Tail: White closed cell foam color (Evazote) with blue Pantone marker
Underbody: Blue chenille
Legs: White 50 lb. braided dacron colored with blue Pantone marker
Wing: Clear nylon saltwater jig hair
Overbody: Same as tail
Eyes: Stainless steel dressmaker pins with black heads

Fuzzabou Shad (Jimmy Nix)
Hook: TMC 811S, sizes 1/0 and 4
Thread: White single strand nylon floss
Snag Guard: Mason hard nylon, 20 lb.
Eyes: Lead, painted white with black pupils
Wing: White marabou plumes with the stems removed, 4 to 6, with silver Accent Flash on top and grizzly hackle on the sides
Collar: Soft grizzly hackle
Head: Gray lamb's wool, spun and trimmed to shape

Gerbubble Bug, Black (Dave Whitlock)
Hook: TMC 8089, sizes 2-6
Thread: Black (rear) and white (front), 3/0
Snag Guard: Mason hard nylon, 20 lb.
Tail: Grizzly and black neck hackles
Skirt: Grizzly hackles, soft
Body: Black and brown bands of deer
Wing: (Whiskerwings) Grizzly and black neck hackles, soft, two on each side
Face: White deer body

Hare Grub, Black (Dave Whitlock)
Hook: TMC 8089, size 2
Thread: Black single strand nylon floss
Snag Guard: Mason hard nylon, 20 lb., one loop along each side of hook point
Eyes: Lead, painted black, white, red
Legs: Black rubber, 3 pair, with red and pearl Accent Flash
Tail, Body: Black rabbit, slit hide, slide over hook eye, secure in front, align along top and bottom; Zap-A-Gap at back

Hare Grub, Chartreuse (Dave Whitlock)
Hook: TMC 8089, size 2
Thread: Chartreuse or fluorescent green single strand nylon floss
Snag Guard: Mason hard nylon, 20 lb.
Eyes: Lead, painted fluorescent yellow with white and red centers
Legs: Green, fluorescent yellow and white rubber, fluorescent yellow and red Accent Flash
Tail, Body: Chartreuse rabbit hide, 1/4" x 5" long; Zap-A-Gap together

Hare Grub, Motor Oil (Dave Whitlock)
Hook: TMC 8089, size 2
Thread: Olive or yellow single strand nylon floss
Snag Guard: Mason hard nylon, 20 lb.
Eyes: Lead, painted green with yellow and black centers
Legs: Green, fluorescent yellow, and gray rubber; olive and fluorescent yellow Accent Flash
Tail, Body: Natural gray rabbit dyed olive; slide over hook eye, Zap-A-Gap

Hare Grub, Purple (Dave Whitlock)
Hook: TMC 8089, size 2
Thread: Red single strand nylon floss
Snag Guard: Mason hard nylon, 20 lb.
Eyes: Lead, painted lavender with yellow and fine orange centers
Legs: Purple, white, and red rubber; lavender and red Accent Flash
Tail, Body: Purple rabbit hide, 1/4" wide, 5" long; slit, slide over hook eye, secure in front; Zap-A-Gap together at back of body

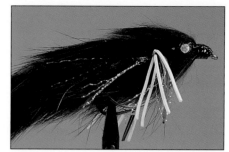

Hare Jig, Black and Chartreuse (Dave Whitlock)
Hook: TMC 8089, size 6
Thread: Black single strand nylon floss
Snag guard: Mason hard nylon, 20 lb.
Eyes: Lead, painted black with fl. yellow and fl. green centers
Legs: Fluorescent green, gray, and yellow rubber, with fluorescent yellow, green, and pearl Accent Flash
Tail, Body: Black rabbit hide (1/4" x 5") with 1/2" section of fluorescent green rabbit hide glued onto tail end

Hare Jig, Black and Fluorescent Red (Dave Whitlock)
Hook: TMC 8089, size 6
Thread: Black single strand nylon floss
Snag guard: Mason hard nylon, 20 lb.
Eyes: Lead, painted black with white and fluorescent fire orange centers
Legs: Red, white, and gray rubber; pearl and red Accent Flash
Tail, Body: Black rabbit hide (1/4"x5") with 1/2" section of fluorescent red rabbit hide glued onto tail end

Hare Jig, White (Dave Whitlock)
Hook: TMC 8089, size 6
Thread: White single strand nylon floss
Snag guard: Mason hard nylon, 20 lb.
Eyes: Lead, painted white with fluorescent yellow, fluorescent orange, and black centers
Legs: Red and white rubber, 3 pair each, with pearl and red Accent Flash
Tail, Body: White rabbit hide (1/4" wide, 5" long); cut slit in hide

Hare Waterpup, Black (Dave Whitlock)
Hook: TMC 7999, sizes 1/0 and 4
Thread: Red single strand nylon floss
Snag Guard: Mason hard nylon, 20 lb.
Rib: Copper wire
Body: Black rabbit
Tail/Back: Black rabbit hide, 1/8" wide, 3-4" long, tied Matuka style
Collar: Black deer
Throat: Red Flashabou
Head: Black deer
Eyes: Red and black solid plastic

Hare Waterpup, Olive (Dave Whitlock)
Hook: TMC 7999, sizes 1/0 and 4
Thread: Red single strand nylon floss
Rib: Copper wire
Body: Black rabbit
Tail/Back: Black rabbit hide, Matuka style
Collar: Pale yellow (bottom), olive (sides, front, top), and black (top, back) deer body hair
Throat: Red Flashabou
Head: Same as collar
Eyes: White and black solid plastic

Hare Waterpup, Purple (Dave Whitlock)
Hook: TMC 7999, sizes 1/0 and 4, weighted
Thread: Red single strand nylon floss
Snag Guard: Mason hard nylon, 20 lb.
Rib: Copper wire
Body: Purple rabbit
Tail/Back: Purple rabbit hide, Matuka style
Collar: Purple deer
Throat: Red Flashabou
Head: Purple deer
Eyes: Red and black solid plastic

Hare Worm, Black (Dave Whitlock)
Hook: TMC 8089, size 2
Thread: Black single strand nylon floss
Snag Guard: Mason hard nylon, 20 lb.
Tail/Body: Black rabbit hide, 1/4" wide, 7" long; cut slit in hide at 5-1/2" mark, slide over hook eye, secure in front of eyes (see Hare Grub)
Eyes: Amber and black plastic, Zap-A-Gap in place

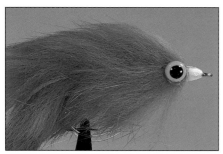

Hare Worm, Electric Blue *(Dave Whitlock)*
    Hook: TMC 8089, size 2
    Thread: White single strand nylon floss
Snag Guard: Mason hard nylon, 20 lb.
    Tail, Body: Bright blue rabbit hide, 1/4"
        wide, 7" long; cut slit in hide
        at 5-1/2" mark, slide over hook
        eye, secure in front of eyes (see
        Hare Grub)
    Eyes: White and black plastic, Zap-
        A-Gap in place

Hare Worm, Yellow *(Dave Whitlock)*
    Hook: TMC 8089, size 2
    Thread: Yellow single strand nylon
        floss
Snag Guard: Mason hard nylon, 20 lb.
    Tail, Body: Yellow rabbit hide, 1/4" wide,
        7" long; cut slit in hide at 5-
        1/2" mark, slide over hook eye,
        secure in front of eyes (see
        Hare Grub)
    Eyes: White and black plastic, Zap-
        A-Gap in place

Lemming *(Mike Mercer)*
    Hook: TMC 8089, size 2
    Thread: Black single strand nylon floss
    Tail: Black round rubber, knotted
    Body: Natural deer, tied in stages
    Legs: Black round rubber, knotted
        and tied in stages between deer
        body stages
Underbody: Reddish brown Australian opos-
        sum hide slipped over hook
        point
    Head: Tapered foam with amber and
        black plastic eyes

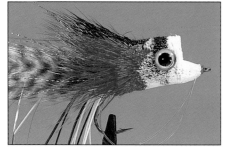

Lucky Wiggler *(Jim Stewart)*
    Hook: TMC 811S, sizes 1/0 or 2
    Thread: Fluorescent red SSNF
Snag Guard: Mason hard nylon, 20 lb., double
    Tail: White rubber (6), gray rubber
        (4), grizzly hackle (6), silver
        Flashabou, silver Krystal Flash
    Butt: Fluorescent red chenille
    Head: Natural brown (top rear), red
        (sides), black and gray bands
        (top center, and white (front)
        deer, trimmed to shape
    Eyes: White and black plastic

Mega Diver, Chartreuse *(Larry Dahlberg)*
    Hook: TMC 811S, size 1/0
    Thread: Chartreuse SSNF
Snag Guard: Mason hard nylon, 20 lb.
    Tail: Chartreuse Big Fly Fiber, gold
        Flashabou, 5" long
    Collar: Chartreuse deer, trimmed and
        cemented on bottom
    Head: Chartreuse deer, spun and
        trimmed as a diver and
        cemented on the bottom
    Eyes: Amber and black plastic, glued
        on each side of head

Mega Diver, Orange and Black *(Larry Dahlberg)*
    Hook: TMC 811S, size 1/0
    Thread: Black, 3/0
Snag Guard: Wire or Mason hard nylon, 20
        lb.
    Tail: Black Big Fly Fiber and orange
        Flashabou
    Collar: Black deer, trimmed on bottom
    Head: Black and orange deer

Mega Diver, White *(Larry Dahlberg)*
    Hook: TMC 811S, size 1/0
    Thread: White, 3/0
Snag Guard: Wire or Mason hard nylon, 20
        lb.
    Tail: White Big Fly Fiber and pearl
        Flashabou
    Collar: White deer, trimmed on bottom
    Head: White deer
    Eyes: Amber and black plastic

Mega Slop Slider, Black *(Larry Dahlberg)*
    Hook: TMC 811S, size 1/0
    Thread: Black, 3/0
Snag Guard: Wire
    Tail: Purple Flashabou, black Big
        Fly Fiber, red marabou
    Collar: Black deer
    Head: Black deer
    Eyes: Yellow and black plastic

Messinger Frog *(Joe Messinger, Jr.)*
    Hook: TMC 8089, sizes 6-10
    Thread: White, 3/0, or Kevlar
Snag Guard: Mason hard nylon, 20 lb.
    Rump: Green and yellow deer
    Legs: Green over yellow bucktail
    Body: Black stacked over green deer
        body hair stacked over yellow
        and white, trimmed as shown
    Eyes: Amber and black plastic

Mouserat, Black (Dave Whitlock)
Hook:	TMC 8089, size 6
Thread:	Black, 3/0
Snag Guard:	Mason hard nylon, 20 lb.
Tail:	Black chamois
Body:	Black deer
Ears:	Same as tail
Head:	Same as body
Eyes:	Black Pantone
Whiskers:	Black moose

Mouserat, Natural (Dave Whitlock)
Hook:	TMC 8089, size 6
Thread:	White, 3/0 (back); black, 3/0 (front)
Snag Guard:	Mason hard nylon, 20 lb.
Tail:	Tan chamois
Body:	Natural deer
Ears:	Same as tail
Head:	Same as body
Eyes:	Black Pantone
Whiskers:	Black moose

Multicolor Muddler, Gold (Dave Whitlock)
Hook:	TMC 300, sizes 2-4
Thread:	Fl. fire orange single strand nylon floss
Body:	Gold mylar tubing, medium
Wing:	White and yellow marabou, yellow and fl. yellow Krystal Flash, fl. orange marabou, red Krystal Flash, brown marabou, peacock
Collar:	White (bottom), yellow, fl. orange, brown, dark olive (top) deer
Head:	Same as collar; trim to shape
Eyes:	Fl. green and black plastic

Multicolor Muddler, Silver (Dave Whitlock)
Hook:	TMC 300, sizes 2-4
Thread:	Yellow single strand floss
Body:	Silver mylar tubing, medium
Wing:	Pearl Flashabou, white marabou, yellow marabou, green and yellow Flashabou, olive marabou, peacock
Collar:	White (bottom), yellow (sides and top), dark green and black (top) deer
Head:	Same as collar; trim to shape

Near Nuff Sculpin, Olive (Dave Whitlock)
Hook:	TMC 5263, sizes 4-10
Thread:	Fluorescent green, 6/0
Eyes:	Lead, painted
Tail:	Olive grizzly hen hackles
Rib:	Olive thread, 6/0
Body:	Olive dubbing
Thorax:	Black dubbing
Head:	Same as body
Hackle:	Olive grizzly, soft, palmered
Highlights:	Olive Krystal Flash

Near Nuff Sculpin, Tan (Dave Whitlock)
Hook:	TMC 5263, sizes 4-10
Thread:	Tan, 6/0
Eyes:	Lead, painted black with white, red, and black center, using epoxy paint
Tail:	Two tan grizzly hen hackles
Rib:	Tan thread, 6/0
Body:	Tan dubbing
Head:	Same as body
Hackle:	Tan grizzly, soft, palmered
Highlights:	Orange Krystal Flash

Pike
Hook:	TMC 811S, size 3/0
Thread:	White and fl. fire orange, 6/0
Snag Guard:	Mason monofilament, 30 lb.
Tail:	Chartreuse Crystal Hair, chart. Icelandic sheep, yellow saddle, pearl saltwater Flashabou, chart. and green grizzly saddles
Fins:	Red neck hackle tips
Skirt:	Chart. hackle and Crystal Hair
Head/Collar:	White, chartreuse, black, green deer
Eyes:	Orange and black plastic

Rabbit Strip Diver, Black (Larry Dahlberg)
Hook:	TMC 811S, sizes 1, 4
Thread:	White, 3/0
Snag Grd.:	Mason hard nylon, 20 lb.
Tail:	Black rabbit fur strip
Body:	Black cross-cut rabbit fur strip
Wing:	Silver Flashabou
Collar:	Black deer trimmed to a diving collar/head, cemented on bottom
Head:	Black deer body hair trimmed to form a diving collar and head, cemented on bottom

Rabbit Strip Diver, Chartreuse (Larry Dahlberg)
Hook:	TMC 811S, sizes 1, 4
Thread:	White, 3/0
Snag Guard:	Mason hard nylon, 20 lb.
Tail:	Olive rabbit fur strip
Body:	Chartreuse cross cut rabbit strip, palmered and trimmed flush on bottom
Wing:	Lime green Flashabou
Collar:	Chartreuse deer body
Head:	Chartreuse deer

Rabbit Strip Diver, Mullet/Sucker (*Larry Dahlberg*)

Hook:	TMC 811S, size 1/0
Thread:	Gray, 3/0
Tail:	Natural gray rabbit strip
Collar:	Dyed gray or dark brown deer
Head:	Dyed gray or brown deer
Eyes:	Yellow 4-1/2 mm solid plastic

Rabbit Strip Diver, Olive (*Larry Dahlberg*)

Hook:	TMC 811S, sizes 1, 4
Thread:	Olive, 3/0
Snag Guard:	Mason hard nylon, 20 lb.
Tail:	Olive rabbit fur strip
Body:	Olive cross cut rabbit strip, palmered and trimmed flush on bottom
Wing:	Black Flashabou
Collar:	Olive deer, trimmed on bottom
Head:	Olive deer

Rabbit Strip Diver, Red and White (*Larry Dahlberg*)

Hook:	TMC 811S, size 1/0
Thread:	White, 3/0
Tail:	White rabbit strip, red Flashabou
Collar:	Red and white deer
Head:	Red and white deer
Eyes:	Yellow 4-1/2 mm solid plastic

Rabbit Strip Diver, Rust and Orange (*Larry Dahlberg*)

Hook:	TMC 811S, size 1/0
Thread:	White, 3/0
Tail:	Rust rabbit strip and copper Flashabou
Collar:	Rusty brown deer, top only
Head:	Brown and orange deer
Eyes:	White 4-1/2 mm solid plastic

Rabbit Strip Diver, White (*Larry Dahlberg*)

Hook:	TMC 811S, sizes 1 and 4
Thread:	White, 3/0
Snag Guard:	Mason hard nylon, 20 lb.
Tail:	White rabbit fur strip
Body:	White cross cut rabbit strip, palmered and trimmed flush on bottom
Wing:	Light blue Flashabou
Collar:	White deer, trimmed on bottom
Head:	White deer

Rabbit Strip Diver, Yellow (*Larry Dahlberg*)

Hook:	TMC 811S, sizes 1 and 4
Thread:	Yellow, 3/0
Snag Guard:	Mason hard nylon, 20 lb.
Tail:	Yellow rabbit fur strip
Body:	Yellow cross cut rabbit strip, palmered and trimmed flush on bottom
Wing:	Gold Flashabou
Collar:	Yellow deer, trimmed on bottom
Head:	Yellow deer

Red Head, Red and Green (*Dave Whitlock*)

Hook:	TMC 8089, sizes 2-6
Thread:	White and fl. fire orange SSNF
Snag Guard:	Mason hard nylon, 20 lb.
Tail:	Lime KF, chartreuse marabou, grizzly hackle, and chartreuse saddle hackle
Skirt:	Chartreuse marabou, lime KF
Body:	Chartreuse, black, red, and orange deer
Legs:	Chartreuse rubber and lime KF
Eyes:	Yellow and black plastic

Red Head, Red and Orange (*Dave Whitlock*)

Hook:	TMC 8089, sizes 2-6
Thread:	White, fl. fire orange SSNF
Snag Guard:	Mason hard nylon, 20 lb.
Tail:	Red and orange KF, yellow or pale orange marabou, orange saddle hackle, orange grizzly hackle
Skirt:	Orange marabou, red KF
Body:	Lt. orange, burnt orange, lt. orange, black, red, lt. orange deer
Legs:	Orange rubber and orange KF
Eyes:	Yellow and black plastic

Red Head, Red and White (*Dave Whitlock*)

Hook:	TMC 8089, sizes 2-6
Thread:	White, fl. fire orange SSNF
Snag Guard:	Mason hard nylon, 20 lb.
Tail:	White rubber, pearl KF, white and grizzly hackle
Skirt:	White hackle, pearl KF
Body:	White, black, red, and bright orange deer
Legs:	Red, white, and black rubber; pearl KF
Eyes:	Yellow and black plastic

Red Head, Red and Yellow *(Dave Whitlock)*
Hook: TMC 8089, sizes 2-6
Thread: White, fl. fire orange SSNF
Snag Guard: Mason hard nylon, 20 lb.
Tail: Fl. yellow rubber, fl. yellow KF, yellow marabou, grizzly and yellow hackle
Skirt: Yellow marabou, fl. yellow KF
Body: Fl. yellow, black, red, and orange deer
Legs: Fl. yellow rubber and fl. yellow KF
Eyes: Yellow and black plastic

Red Head, Red Roach *(Dave Whitlock)*
Hook: TMC 8089, sizes 2-6
Thread: White, fl. fire orange SSNF
Snag Guard: Mason hard nylon, 20 lb.
Tail: Gold and silver KF, grizzly marabou, grizzly and cree hackle
Skirt: Brown hackle, gold KF
Body: Natural brown-gray, black, red, and bright orange deer
Legs: White, black, and brown rubber; silver and gold KF
Eyes: Yellow and black plastic

Sheep, Deep, Bluegill *(Dave Whitlock)*
Hook: TMC 9395, sizes 2 and 6
Thread: Yellow, 6/0
Head: Fluorescent red yarn
Underwing: Yellow Krystal Flash, yellow Icelandic sheep, olive Krystal Flash, olive Icelandic sheep, peacock Krystal Flash
Outerwing: Yellow grizzly and pheasant rump; Pantone black
Overwing: Yellow Krystal Flash, yellow and orange Icelandic sheep hair
Eyes: Silver bead chain or lead

Sheep, Deep, Crappie *(Dave Whitlock)*
Hook: TMC 9395 bent to shape, 2 and 6
Thread: White, 6/0
Head: Fluorescent red yarn
Underwing: Pearl Krystal Flash, white Icelandic sheep, pearl blue Krystal Flash, yellow and gray Icelandic sheep, peacock Krystal Flash
Outerwing: Grizzly hackle, pearlescent mylar, mallard breast feather
Overwing: Pearl Krystal Flash, white Icelandic sheep
Eyes: Silver bead chain or lead

Sheep, Deep, Shad *(Dave Whitlock)*
Hook: TMC 9395, sizes 2 and 6
Thread: White, 6/0
Head: Fluorescent red yarn
Underwing: Pearl Krystal Flash, white Icelandic sheep, pearl blue Krystal Flash
Outerwing: Pale badger hackle and mallard breast or flank feather marked with black Pantone marker
Overwing: Red wool fibers, pearl Krystal Flash, white Icelandic sheep
Eyes: Silver bead chain or lead

Sheep, Swimming, Bluegill *(Dave Whitlock)*
Hook: TMC 9395, sizes 2-6
Thread: Yellow, 6/0 or 8/0
Head: Red Antron
Underwing: Yellow Krystal Flash, yellow Icelandic sheep, yellow Krystal Flash, olive Icelandic sheep, peacock Krystal Flash
Outerwing: Light olive grizzly hackle, ringneck pheasant rump
Overwing: Yellow Krystal Flash, yellow and orange Icelandic sheep hair
Eyes: Amber and black plastic

Sheep, Swimming, Crappie *(Dave Whitlock)*
Hook: TMC 9395, sizes 2-6
Thread: White, 6/0
Head: Red Antron
Underwing: White, gray Icelandic sheep, yellow Krystal Flash, yellow Icelandic sheep, smolt blue Krystal Flash
Outerwing: Grizzly hackle, pearlescent mylar, and mallard breast or flank
Overwing: Pearl Krystal Flash, white Icelandic sheep hair
Eyes: White and black plastic

Shineabou Shad, Deer Hair *(Jimmy Nix)*
Hook: TMC 811S, sizes 1/0 and 4
Thread: White, 3/0
Snag Guard: Mason hard nylon, 20 lb.
Body: Silver gray Antron
Wing: Gray marabou; pearl, silver, and gold Accent Flash; peacock herl; mallard flank
Throat: Red marabou
Collar: Dyed gray deer body hair
Head: Same as collar
Eyes: Amber and black plastic

Shineabou Shad, Wool Head *(Jimmy Nix)*
Hook: TMC 811S, sizes 1/0 and 4
Thread: Gray Kevlar
Snag Guard: Mason hard nylon, 20 lb.
Eyes: Lead, painted white and black
Innerwing: Gray marabou
Outerwing: Natural mallard flank
Overwing: Peacock, pearl and silver Flashabou and peacock herl
Throat: Red marabou
Head: Gray lamb's wool, spun and trimmed to shape

144

Shineabou Shiner, Deer Hair (*Jimmy Nix*)
- Hook: TMC 811S, sizes 1/0 and 4
- Thread: White, 3/0
- Snag Guard: Mason hard nylon, 20 lb.
- Tail: White bucktail, 8 blue dun saddles, gold and silver Flashabou
- Body: Silver gray Antron
- Gills: Red marabou
- Wing: Gray marabou, pearl KF, peacock
- Collar: Dyed gray deer
- Head: Dyed gray deer
- Eyes: Black and white plastic

Shineabou Shiner, Woolhead (*Jimmy Nix*)
- Hook: TMC 811S, sizes 1/0 and 4
- Thread: Gray, 3/0, or Kevlar
- Snag Guard: Mason hard nylon, 20 lb.
- Eyes: Lead, painted white and black
- Tail: White bucktail, silver gray hackle; silver, gold, pearl Accent Flash
- Body: Silver gray Antron
- Wing: Gray marabou; pearl, silver, Accent Flash; peacock
- Gills: Red hackle fluff or marabou
- Collar: Gray lamb's wool
- Head: Gray lamb's wool

Skipper, Frog (*Larry Dahlberg*)
- Hook: TMC 811S, size 1/0
- Thread: White, 3/0, or Kevlar
- Snag Guard: Mason hard nylon, 20 lb. (optional)
- Tail (legs): Green grizzly and yellow hackle, green and fluorescent yellow round rubber
- Collar: Green deer, trimmed on top
- Head: Green and white deer
- Eyes: Yellow and black plastic

Softshell Crayfish, Brown (*Dave Whitlock*)
- Hook: TMC 300, sizes 2-8, weighted
- Thread: Orange, 3/0
- Eyes: Mono at back; lead at front
- Antennae: Black moose
- Tail: Rusty brown deer
- Claws: Rusty brown and brown hen saddle; Flexament together
- Rib: Copper wire, medium
- Legs: Golden or rust grizzly saddle
- Body: Rust Antron, picked out
- Back, Tail: Rust Swiss Straw; black Pantone

Softshell Crayfish, Sandy (*Dave Whitlock*)
- Hook: TMC 300, sizes 2-8, weighted
- Thread: Gray, 3/0
- Eyes: Mono at back; lead at front
- Antennae: Black moose
- Tail: Gray squirrel or deer body
- Claws: Light brown and white hen saddle; Flexament together
- Rib: Copper wire, medium
- Legs: Grizzly saddle hackle
- Body: Gray Antron or SLF, picked out
- Back, Tail: Gray Swiss Straw; black Pantone highlight

Spent Damsel-Dragon, Blue (*Dave Whitlock*)
- Hook: TMC 8089, sizes 6-10
- Thread: White single strand nylon floss
- Snag Guard: Mason hard nylon, 20 lb.
- Underbody: Foam (Evazote) or quill stem
- Legs: Rubber hackle (optional)
- Wing: Med. blue and nat. gray br. deer
- Rib: Blue mono or Kevlar thread
- Body: Dark blue (top) and light blue (underneath) bucktail, tied reverse (bullet head) style

Note: A black version is also popular.

Sunfish, Deerhair (*Jimmy Nix*)
- Hook: TMC 8089 NP, size 2
- Thread: Olive, 3/0 or Kevlar
- Snag Guard: Mason hard nylon, 20 lb.
- Rib: Copper wire, medium
- Body: Olive Antron
- Wing: Dyed olive grizzly hen
- Gills: Red marabou
- Collar: Olive and orange deer
- Overwing: Olive marabou, sparse
- Head: Olive, orange, black deer
- Eyes: Solid plastic

Sunfish, Wool Head (*Jimmy Nix*)
- Hook: TMC 8089 NP, size 2
- Thread: Olive, 3/0, or Kevlar
- Snag Guard: Mason hard nylon, 20 lb.
- Rib: Copper wire, medium
- Body: Olive Antron
- Wing: Olive grizzly hen hackle, Matuka style, top and underside
- Gills: Red marabou
- Overwing: Olive wool and olive marabou
- Head: Olive, orange, black lamb's wool
- Eyes: Lead, painted yellow, black

Umpqua Swimming Baitfish, Red and White (*Dave Whitlock*)
- Hook: TMC 811S, size 1/0
- Thread: White, 3/0 and red, 3/0
- Snag Guard: Mason hard nylon, 20 lb.
- Tail: Pearl Krystal Flash, 4 white and 2 grizzly saddle hackles
- Throat: Pearl and red Flashabou
- Collar: White deer overlaid with natural dark deer; trim bottom
- Head: White, orange, and red deer
- Eyes: Yellow and black plastic

Umpqua Swimming Baitfish, Red and Yellow *(Dave Whitlock)*

Hook:	TMC 811S, size 1/0
Thread:	White, 3/0 (back) and red, 3/0 (front)
Snag Guard:	Mason hard nylon, 20 lb.
Tail:	Pearl KF; white, yellow, grizzly saddle hackles; fl. yellow KF
Throat:	Red Flashabou
Collar:	White hackle
Head:	Fluorescent yellow, natural dark, orange, and red deer
Eyes:	White and black plastic

Umpqua Swimming Baitfish, Shad *(Dave Whitlock)*

Hook:	TMC 811S, size 1/0
Thread:	White, 3/0
Snag Guard:	Mason hard nylon, 20 lb.
Tail:	Pearl KF; white, light dun, and dark dun saddle hackles, one pair each; smolt blue KF
Throat:	Red Flashabou
Body:	White rabbit, white hackle
Collar:	White and natural dark deer
Head:	Nat. lt., dark, pale green deer
Eyes:	Yellow and black plastic

Umpqua Swimming Frog, Orange Belly *(Dave Whitlock)*

Hook:	TMC 8089, sizes 2 and 6
Thread:	Fluorescent fire orange SSNF
Snag Guard:	Mason hard nylon, 20 lb.
Tail:	Pearl KF; orange, orange grizzly, yellow grizzly, olive grizzly hackle
Collar:	Orange hackle overlaid w/black, chartreuse, bright green deer
Head:	Bright green, chartreuse, and black, alternate bands
Legs:	Red, fl. green, green rubber
Eyes:	White and black plastic

Umpqua Swimming Frog, White Belly *(Dave Whitlock)*

Hook:	TMC 8089, sizes 2 and 6
Thread:	White, 3/0
Snag Guard:	Mason hard nylon, 20 lb.
Tail (legs):	Pearl KF, 2 ea. white, nat. grizzly, lt. olive grizzly, and dk. olive grizzly
Collar:	White deer, topped with yellow, black, and dark olive deer
Head:	White, black, yellow and olive deer (top); white underside
Legs:	Gray, white, and yellow rubber
Eyes:	Yellow and black plastic

Umpqua Swimming Frog, Yellow Belly *(Dave Whitlock)*

Hook:	TMC 8089, sizes 2 and 6
Thread:	Olive, 3/0
Snag Guard:	Mason hard nylon, 20 lb.
Tail:	Fl. yellow KF; yellow, yellow grizzly, olive grizzly hackle
Collar:	Yellow marabou
Head:	Fl. yellow, black, green olive, alternating bands and fl. yellow deer
Legs:	Green, fl. green, and fl. yellow rubber
Eyes:	White and black plastic

Umpqua Swimming Waterdog, Black and Chartreuse *(Dave Whitlock)*

Hook:	TMC 8089, size 2
Thread:	Fluorescent green SSNF
Tail:	Black rabbit strip with 1" section of fl. green rabbit glued onto end at tail; lime green KF; chartreuse grizzly hackle
Collar:	Black deer
Head:	Black deer
Legs:	Black and chartreuse round rubber
Eyes:	Yellow and black plastic

Umpqua Swimming Watersnake, Black *(Dave Whitlock)*

Hook:	TMC 8089, size 2
Thread:	Black, 3/0, or single strand nylon floss
Snag Guard:	Mason hard nylon, 20 lb.
Tail:	Black rabbit fur strip
Collar:	Black deer
Head:	Black deer
Eyes:	Yellow and black plastic

Umpqua Swimming Watersnake, Brown *(Dave Whitlock)*

Hook:	TMC 8089, size 2
Thread:	Brown, 3/0
Snag Guard:	Mason hard nylon, 20 lb.
Tail:	Brown rabbit fur strip
Collar:	Brown (top) and tan (bottom) deer
Head:	Brown, tan, black, and white deer
Eyes:	Yellow and black plastic

Wigglelegs Frog *(Dave Whitlock)*

Hook:	TMC 8089, sizes 2-6
Thread:	White, 3/0
Snag Guard:	Mason hard nylon, 20 lb.
Legs:	Chartreuse and white bucktail, green grizzly hackle
Body:	White (bottom) and alternating bands of chartreuse, green, and black (top) deer
Legs:	Black, white, chartreuse, and fluorescent yellow rubber
Eyes:	Yellow and black plastic

Chapter 7

Saltwater

Lefty Kreh

The first fly fishing I did was for smallmouth bass on the Potomac in Washington, D.C., and other rivers of the region in 1947. There were no other fly fishermen in my area, and I soon considered many of the flies of that time to be poor fish producers. In 1948 I began trying to tie my own. "Try to tie" is an apt description. There was a Herter's book about fly tying; that was about all I could find. In some ways that was fortunate—although I did not think so at the time.

About 1950, I began writing a local outdoor column. In about three years I was writing for several regional papers and began to seriously think about being an outdoor writer. Since I was one of the first fly fishermen-fly casters in my region, I was traveling around doing demonstrations. Others shared their fly fishing ideas, and my experience in the field grew. Outdoor writing usually requires photos to illustrate the articles, so it was necessary to become involved in photography, which became one of my greatest pleasures.

I began doing slide shows and seminars in the late 1950s. Clubs and groups around the country would pay me to travel to their areas to make presentations. Local anglers would take me fishing. Through the kindness of many great anglers around the United States and the world, I was lucky enough to fish virtually everywhere and was able to obtain a broad overview of fly fishing.

From these observations I began to realize several things. One: fly fishing is mainly presentation. If you can present a fly to a fish so that it arrives naturally, free of any suspicious sounds or actions, that's more than half the game. Two: if you cannot shoot, you cannot hunt. If you cannot cast, your fly fishing is going to suffer. I became a student of fly casting. Three: fish basically want food. Most of the time, in most fishing situations, a limited number of fly patterns will do well—if the presentation is good.

It helps to have a pattern that is near the size of the flies on the water and, perhaps, one close to the color of insects prevailing at the time. Presentation remains the main key. Learning all the insects, when they hatch, and all the assorted technicalities is grand sport. It will increase your knowledge, catch, and fun. It is not necessary to know all of the Latin names of creatures and have a fly box loaded with hundreds of flies. Have a few choice patterns that work consistently in your region and make good presentations, and you will score frequently.

This same thing applies to fly fishing in saltwater—perhaps even more so. There are few hatches in saltwater, but there are innumerable numbers of food (prey) for predators. Keeping it simple, using a few basic patterns, and making good presentations are the keys to catching fish in fresh or saltwater.

Today, I have been an active outdoor writer for more than 40 years. I have written for almost every major outdoor magazine in this country and abroad. I am the retired outdoor editor of the *Baltimore Sun* newspaper, and I hold a staff position on six outdoor magazines. I have participated in a number of videos and television shows.

I have written several books: *Fly Casting With Lefty Kreh, Salt Water Fly Fishing, Spinning Tips, Advanced Fly Fishing Techniques, Longer Fly Casting, L. L. Bean Guide To Outdoor Photography,* and *Salt Water Fly Patterns*. I created *Lefty's Little Library*, which is a series of individual books, each devoted to a particular area of fly fishing. I have also co-authored several other books. However, my most profound accomplishment is that I have been married for over 40 years to my wife, Evelyn.

In 1958, I lived in Maryland and fished in Chesapeake Bay for striped bass. A constant companion in those days was Tom Cofield, outdoor editor of the *Baltimore News-American* newspaper. Tom and I discussed what the desirable features of a good fly for salt water work would be. We determined that it should have a baitfish shape. It should not foul and should be easy to cast—even long distances in a breeze. It should have good action. It should appeal to the fish.

It was this experience and discussion that gave birth to the Lefty's Deceiver. It was a simple all-white fly with a feather wing and a bucktail collar. It was about four inches long and attempted to imitate alewives, the baitfish so prevalent in the shallows of the Chesapeake. After about a year of fishing, I began to modify the color combinations, adding a little red at the throat to imitate gills (I believe this is an attack trigger) and some peacock herl to the top. I also started tying it in various lengths to match different baitfish. It is important that the tip ends of the collar flow well behind the hook bend, which helps prevent the wing from underwrapping and also gives the body its fish-like shape.

The fly can be tied in many ways. The Lefty's Deceiver is not really a strict pattern but a method of tying. It can have various shapes, lengths, and colors. The fly can be tied as short as two inches and longer than a foot for billfish, amberjack, and other species demanding a large offering. It can be tied in a bend-back fashion or with the hook reversed. It has caught everything from striped bass to baramundi and billfish. To get full benefit from the Lefty's Deceiver, you need to analyze what you are trying to do and match the type of fly to the conditions.

Not all Lefty's Deceivers imitate baitfish. Some are tied in bright colors. For example, one of the best attractor types is a white and chartreuse combination that has worked for me around much of the world. A favorite of many experienced anglers is an all-black pattern. I favor black with a dash of either dark blue or purple bucktail. The first time I fished the Northern Territories of Australia, I was amazed to find the overwhelming choice was a black Lefty's Deceiver. One reason was that the flats there experience six- to nine-foot tides, which means many areas contain slightly roiled or dirty water; the black fly showed well.

Author's Note: Lefty Kreh is one of the best known and respected personalties in fly fishing. Lefty loves to fish, but he also loves to teach and share with others his hard earned knowledge. His casting seminars are legendary, as are his rapid-fire jokes and one-liners. If you have a chance to meet him, do it!

Lefty Kreh
Hunt Valley, Maryland
May, 1994

Bob Popovics

In 1970 I started fly fishing salt water. I joined the Saltwater Flyrodders of America, International, serving as president of my local Seaside Park, New Jersey, chapter and on the national executive board. In addition, I founded the Atlantic Saltwater Flyrodders in Seaside Park in 1992. I'm an adviser to that club, which now has an active membership of over 160. I teach fly tying, fly casting and do many saltwater fly fishing workshops, and am a member of the Sage team.

My beginning in fly tying is due solely to Butch Colvin. On my birthday in 1971, he gave me a vise, some materials and thread, and, most of all, a lot of time and patience. He helped me to always keep an open mind in solving fly tying and fishing problems. That was a great start! Butch was always willing to share information; that influences me to this day.

I never really liked to tie just for fun. I tie to have fishing flies. I would much rather be fishing than tying. For me, fishing is the hobby— fly tying simply is a necessary part of it. That's why durability is a top priority in many of my fly designs. It helps me fish more while tying less! My fishing and tying philosophies are the same: "Keep it simple and enjoy it—all of it!"

Fly fishing has affected my life for almost 25 years. Many memorable days and nights have been spent along the Jersey shoreline fishing for bass, blues, and other species. They're all great sport, offering many challenges to the fly fisher. Designing flies to effectively catch them has been particularly gratifying to me.

The Surf Candy and Bob's Banger flies were probably the most rewarding. Bluefish are toothy predators and can destroy almost any fly. With specific use of five-minute epoxy, the Surf Candies were coming back ready to battle another blue. I've caught as many as 30 bluefish on one Surf Candy made with Ultra Hair and epoxy. Durability was established!

The Bangers were every bit as successful as the Candies. No longer did one bluefish destroy the popper. Even an outboard motor running into my forward cast did not blow out the face of my Banger and make it into a slider. The Bangers were also designed to be made quickly and easily, without paint, glue, or special tools.

That's keeping it simple. . .

Author's Note: Bob Popovics has been an active saltwater fisher and tyer for over 30 years and presents national seminars on the subject. He is one of the most innovative saltwater tyers today and is a fanatical bluefish and striper angler. Bob is a renowned chef at his Shady Rest Italian Restaurant in Bayville, New Jersey, which has been in the family for 28 years.

Bob Popovics
Bayville, New Jersey
July, 1994

149

Baitfish Fly, Blue Pearl (Dave Whitlock)
Hook:	TMC 811S, size 1/0
Thread:	White single strand nylon floss covered with Aquaseal
Snag Guard:	Hard Mason nylon
Tail:	White, mist green, and light blue marabou; light blue grizzly hackle; silver and blue Flashabou
Collar:	Blue grizzly hackle; blue, silver and red Flashabou
Body:	White SSNF covered w/ Aquaseal
Eyes:	Solid plastic, glued in place with Aquaseal

Baitfish Fly, Chartreuse Pearl (Dave Whitlock)
Hook:	TMC 811S, size 1/0
Thread:	White SSNF covered w/ Aquaseal
Snag Guard:	Hard Mason nylon
Tail:	White and chartreuse marabou; chartreuse grizzly hackle; gold and lime green Flashabou
Collar:	Chartreuse grizzly hackle; red, pearl, gold, lime green Flashabou
Body:	White SSNF covered w/ Aquaseal
Eyes:	Solid plastic, glued in place with Aquaseal

Baitfish Fly, Emerald Pearl (Dave Whitlock)
Hook:	TMC 811S, size 1/0
Thread:	White SSNF covered w/ Aquaseal
Snag Guard:	Hard Mason nylon
Tail:	White and pale emerald marabou; grizzly hackle; silver and green Flashabou
Collar:	Grizzly hackle; pearl, green, silver and pearl Flashabou
Body:	White SSNF covered w/ Aquaseal
Eyes:	Solid plastic, glued in place with Aquaseal

Baitfish Fly, Yellow Pearl (Dave Whitlock)
Hook:	TMC 811S, size 1/0
Thread:	White SSNF covered w/ Aquaseal
Snag Guard:	Hard Mason nylon
Tail:	White and yellow marabou; yellow-olive grizzly hackle; lime green, yellow, and gold Flashabou
Collar:	Yellow-olive grizzly hackle; pearl, gold, yellow and red Flashabou
Body:	White SSNF covered w/ Aquaseal
Eyes:	Solid plastic, Aquaseal in place

Bally-Hoo (Bob Veverka)
Hook:	TMC 9394, size 4/0
Thread:	Dark Brown, 3/0
Body:	White marabou; blue and black Icelandic sheep; silver, pearl, and copper Accent Flash; cover with five-minute epoxy
Eyes:	Gold and black Prismatic stick-on
Gills:	Red paint
Head:	Color thread head area with reddish-brown Pantone and epoxy

Banana Peel (Moana Kofe)
Hook:	TMC 811S, sizes 4-6
Thread:	Light orange, 6/0
Eyes:	Gold bead chain
Tail:	Yellow Accent Flash
Body:	Yellow chenille
Wing:	Light tan calftail and Yellow Accent Flash

Banana Sunday (Moana Kofe)
Hook:	TMC 811S, sizes 4-6
Thread:	Yellow, 6/0
Eyes:	Chrome bead chain
Tail:	Pearl Flashabou
Body:	Yellow chenille
Wing:	White calftail and pearl Flashabou

Banger, Chartreuse (Bob Popovics)
Hook:	Eagle Claw 6655, size 4/0
Head:	Live body foam cylinder with chartreuse prismatic tape covering
Thread:	White Gudebrod size D rod winding thread
Tail:	Chartreuse bucktail
Body:	Chartreuse Estaz
Eyes:	Silver and black stick-on, large prismatic

Banger, Orange (Bob Popovics)
Hook:	Eagle Claw 6655, size 4/0
Head:	Live body foam cylinder with orange prismatic tape covering
Thread:	White Gudebrod size D rod winding thread
Tail:	Orange bucktail
Body:	Orange Estaz
Eyes:	Silver and black stick-on, large prismatic

Banger, Silver (Bob Popovics)
Hook: Eagle Claw 6655, size 4/0
Head: Live body foam cylinder with silver prismatic tape covering
Thread: White Gudebrod size D rod winding thread
Tail: White bucktail
Body: Pearl Estaz
Eyes: Silver and black stick-on, large prismatic

Bend Back Muddler
Hook: TMC 411S, size 1/0
Thread: Brown, 3/0
Body: Tan sparkle blend dubbing
Wing: Golden tan FisHair, dyed orange saddles (four), and bronze Flashabou
Head: Dyed brown antelope; tips form collar

Bend Back, White and Blue
Hook: TMC 411S, size 1/0
Thread: Black, 3/0
Body: White chenille
Wing: White bucktail, two grizzly hackles, pearl and electric blue Flashabou, sky blue FisHair and eight strands of peacock herl
Eyes: Painted white with black pupil and red circle

Bend Back, White and Green
Hook: TMC 411S, size 1/0
Thread: Black, 3/0
Body: White chenille
Wing: White bucktail; lime, pearl, and silver Flashabou; Green FisHair and two grizzly hackles
Eyes: Painted white with black pupils and red circle

Bend Back, Yellow
Hook: TMC 411S, size 1/0
Thread: Fluorescent fire orange, 6/0
Body: Yellow chenille
Wing: Yellow bucktail; pearl and silver Flashabou; Peacock herl and two grizzly hackles
Eyes: Painted white with black pupil with red circle

Big Eye Tarpon Fly, Blue and Grizzly (Bob LeMay)
Hook: TMC 800S, size 3/0
Thread: Black single strand flat floss
Tail: Black calftail
Wing: Royal blue and LeMay blue (aqua) saddles with pearl Krystal Flash
Collar: Royal blue and LeMay blue saddles
Eyes: Painted white with black pupil, epoxied

Big Eye Tarpon Fly, Furnace and Squirrel (Bob LeMay)
Hook: TMC 800S, size 3/0
Thread: Fluorescent orange single strand flat floss
Tail: Furnace neck hackles with fox squirrel tail and pearl Krystal Flash
Wing: Furnace neck hackles
Collar: Well-marked fox squirrel
Eyes: Painted yellow with black pupils, epoxied

Big Eye Tarpon Fly, Orange and Blue (Bob LeMay)
Hook: TMC 800S, size 3/0, weighted
Thread: Fluorescent fire orange single strand flat floss
Tail: Royal blue bucktail and pearl Krystal Flash
Wing: Blue grizzly neck hackles
Collar: Bright orange saddles (from base—soft)
Eyes: Painted white with black pupils, epoxied

Big Eye Tarpon Fly, Orange and Grizzly (Bob LeMay)
Hook: TMC 800S, size 3/0
Thread: Fluorescent orange single strand flat floss
Tail: Burnt orange calftail and pearl Krystal Flash
Wing: Orange grizzly neck hackles
Collar: Orange grizzly hackle fluff (from base—soft)
Eyes: Painted yellow with black pupils, epoxied

Big Eye Tarpon Fly, Red and Grizzly (Bob LeMay)

Hook:	TMC 800S, size 3/0, weighted
Thread:	Red single strand flat floss
Tail:	Red calftail with pearl Krystal Flash
Wing:	Red and grizzly neck hackle
Collar:	Red and grizzly hackle fluff (from base—soft)
Eyes:	Painted white with black pupils, epoxied

Big Eye Tarpon Fly, Sand Devil (Bob LeMay)

Hook:	TMC 800S, size 3/0, weighted
Thread:	Fluorescent orange single strand flat floss
Tail:	Burnt orange or rusty calftail with ginger variant neck hackles and pearl Krystal Flash
Wing:	Ginger variant neck hackles
Collar:	Ginger variant saddles (from base—soft)
Eyes:	Painted yellow with black pupils, epoxied

Big Fish Fly, White and Blue

Hook:	TMC 800S, size 4/0
Thread:	White single strand nylon floss
Tail:	White FisHair
Wing:	White and blue FisHair with gold, silver, and pearl Flashabou

Big Fish Fly, White, Green, and Blue

Hook:	TMC 800S, size 4/0
Thread:	White single strand nylon floss
Tail:	White FisHair
Wing:	White, green, and blue FisHair with gold, silver, green, and pearl Flashabou

Billfish Fly (Billy Pate)

Hook:	TMC 800S, size 4/0, front; size 2/0, rear
Thread:	White single strand nylon floss
Tail:	White saddle hackles, long, and pearl Flashabou
Wing:	White and blue saddle hackles, white bucktail, and pearl Flashabou
Body:	White deer, clipped
Eyes:	10 mm. yellow doll eyes

Note: Pattern has a trailer hook dressed with 20 white saddle hackles and pearl Flashabou.

Black Death

Hook:	TMC 811S, sizes 2/0-3/0
Thread:	Black, 3/0
Tail:	Black (four) and red (two) hackles, and black marabou
Body:	Black thread, coated with epoxy
Eyes:	Painted yellow with black pupil

Blue Grizzly

Hook:	TMC 800S, sizes 4/0-3/0
Thread:	Fluorescent blue single strand nylon floss
Tail:	Four blue saddle hackle tips, enclosed by four grizzly hackle tips
Hackle:	Blue and grizzly
Body:	Mylar thread coated with epoxy

Bonefish Bitters, Amber (Craig Mathews)

Hook:	TMC 811S, sizes 6-8
Thread:	Tan, 6/0
Eyes:	Gold bead chain
Head:	Molded amber epoxy or hot glue around eyes
Legs:	Tan Sili or speckled flake rubber
Wing:	Natural deer over tan Z-Lon underwing

Bonefish Bitters, Chartreuse (Craig Mathews)

Hook:	TMC 811S, sizes 6-8
Thread:	Chartreuse, 6/0
Eyes:	Gold bead chain
Head:	Molded chartreuse epoxy or hot glue around eyes
Legs:	Chartreuse Sili or speckled flake rubber
Wing:	Chartreuse deer over chartreuse Z-Lon underwing

Bonefish Bitters, Orange (*Craig Mathews*)
Hook: TMC 811S, sizes 6-8
Thread: Orange, 6/0
Eyes: Gold bead chain
Head: Molded orange epoxy or hot glue around eyes
Legs: Orange Sili or speckled flake rubber
Wing: Orange mottled deer over orange Z-Lon underwing

Bonefish Bugger, Pink and White
Hook: TMC 800S, sizes 2-4
Thread: Gray, 3/0
Eyes: Nickel steel
Tail: White marabou and two grizzly hackle tips
Hackle: Grizzly, palmered
Body: Pink chenille
Wing: Pearl Accent Flash and fine black monofilament

Bonefish Bugger, Tan and Orange
Hook: TMC 800S, sizes 2-4
Thread: Maroon, 6/0
Eyes: Nickel steel
Tail: Orange marabou and two furnace hackles
Hackle: Ginger, palmered
Body: Tan chenille
Wing: Pearl Accent Flash and fine black monofilament

Bonefish Critter (*Tim Borski*)
Hook: TMC 800S, sizes 2-4
Thread: Tan, 3/0
Eyes: Non-toxic, for weight
Snag Guard: Clear monofilament
Eyes: Burned monofilament (60 lb. hard Mason)
Butt: Hot orange Crystal Chenille
Body: Tan wool, spun and tinted on top with Pantone 147M
Legs: Tan or olive grizzly hackle, wide and webby

Bonefish Special
Hook: TMC 811S, sizes 4-6
Thread: Black, 3/0
Tail: Orange marabou
Body: Yellow monofilament over flat gold mylar
Wing: White calftail and two grizzly hackles

Bonefish Slider (*Tim Borski*)
Hook: TMC 811S, sizes 2-4
Thread: Tan, 3/0
Eyes: Steel, painted yellow with black pupils
Tail: Tan Craft Fur marked with dark brown Pantone pen, with six strands of orange Accent Flash
Hackle: Brown-grizzly variant
Head: Clipped deer; dark brown Pantone stripes on underside

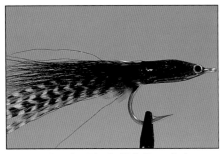

Bonita Candy, Black (*Bob Popovics*)
Hook: TMC 800S, size 2
Thread: Black, 3/0
Body: Epoxy, tapered (Devcon 5-minute)
Wing: Black bucktail with grizzly hackles
Eyes: Silver and black stick-on, prismatic

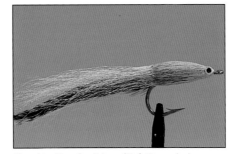

Bonita Candy, Lime (*Bob Popovics*)
Hook: TMC 800S, size 2
Thread: Chartreuse single strand nylon floss
Body: Epoxy, tapered (Devcon 5-minute)
Wing: Lime bucktail, green grizzly hackle, and fluorescent lime Krystal Flash
Eyes: Lime and black stick-on, prismatic

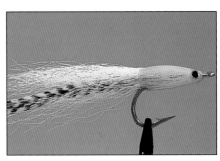

Bonita Candy, Pearl (*Bob Popovics*)
Hook: TMC 800S, size 2
Thread: White single strand nylon floss
Body: Epoxy, tapered (Devcon 5-minute)
Wing: White bucktail, grizzly hackle, and pearl Krystal Flash
Eyes: Silver and black stick-on, prismatic

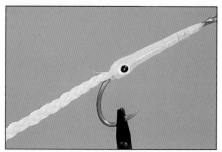

Braided Barracuda Fly, Fluorescent Green
Hook: Eagle Claw 66SS, size 2/0
Thread: Fluorescent green single strand nylon floss
Tail: Fluorescent green FisHair, braided
Body: Tying thread, coated with epoxy
Eyes: Painted white with black pupil

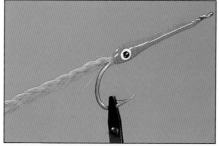

Braided Barracuda Fly, Orange
Hook: Eagle Claw 66SS, size 2/0
Thread: Fluorescent orange single strand nylon floss
Tail: Fluorescent orange FisHair, braided
Body: Tying thread, coated with epoxy
Eyes: Painted white with black pupil

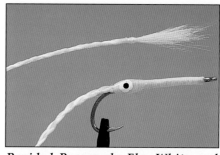

Braided Barracuda Fly, White and Green
Hook: Eagle Claw 66SS, size 2/0
Thread: Fluorescent green single strand nylon floss
Tail: White and fluorescent green FisHair, braided
Body: Tying thread, coated with epoxy
Eyes: Painted white with black pupils

Candy Eel, Brown (Bob Popovics)
Hook: TMC 811S, size 1/0
Thread: White, 3/0
Wing: Cream or white Ultra Hair with wide Flashabou stripe
Body: Epoxy, tapered (Devcon, 5-minute)
Gills: Red paint
Eyes: Silver and black stick-on

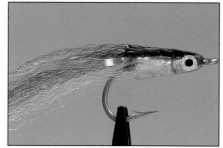

Candy Eel, Olive (Bob Popovics)
Hook: TMC 811S, size 1/0
Thread: White, 3/0
Wing: Brown or white Ultra Hair with wide Flashabou stripe
Body: Epoxy, tapered (Devcon, 5-minute)
Gills: Red paint
Eyes: Green and black stick-on

Chernobyl Crab (Tim Borski)
Hook: TMC 811S, sizes 1/0-2
Thread: Tan, 3/0
Eyes: Steel, painted yellow and black
Tail: White calftail, gold Accent Flash, brown hackle, and natural gray deer
Hackle: Brown, wide and webby, palmered through head
Head: Natural gray deer, clipped

Chili Pepper (Moana Kofe)
Hook: TMC 811S, sizes 4-6
Thread: Burnt orange, 3/0
Eyes: Gold bead chain
Tail: Gold Accent Flash
Body: Clear V-Rib over gold flat mylar
Wing: Orange bucktail or calftail
Overwing: Pearl Accent Flash

Christmas Island Special, Orange (Randall Kaufmann)
Hook: Mustad 3407, sizes 4-8
Thread: Fluorescent fire orange, 6/0
Eyes: Gold plated non-lead, painted white, fluorescent orange, black
Tail: Fluorescent orange Krystal Flash
Body: Fluorescent orange Krystal Flash
Wing: Fluorescent orange Krystal Flash with tan craft fur

Christmas Island Special, Pearl (Randall Kaufmann)
Hook: Mustad 3407, sizes 4-8
Thread: Fluorescent fire orange, 6/0
Eyes: Gold plated non-lead, painted white, fluorescent orange and black
Tail: Pearl Krystal Flash
Body: Pearl Krystal Flash
Wing: Pearl Krystal Flash and tan craft fur

Christmas Island Special, Pink (*Randall Kaufmann*)
- Hook: Mustad 3407, sizes 4-8
- Thread: Fluorescent red, 6/0
- Eyes: Gold plated non-lead, painted white, fluorescent red, and black
- Tail: Fluorescent pink Krystal Flash
- Body: Fluorescent pink Krystal Flash
- Wing: Fluorescent pink Krystal Flash and tan craft fur

Christmas Island Special, Yellow (*Randall Kaufmann*)
- Hook: Mustad 3407, sizes 4-8
- Thread: Fluorescent yellow, 6/0
- Eyes: Gold plated non-lead, painted white, fluorescent yellow, and black
- Tail: Fluorescent yellow Krystal Flash
- Body: Fluorescent yellow Krystal Flash
- Wing: Fluorescent yellow Krystal Flash and tan craft fur

Chub Darter (*Jim Stewart*)
- Hook: TMC 511S, size 2/0
- Thread: Fluorescent orange single strand flat floss
- Tail: Orange and chartreuse grizzly hackle with chartreuse Accent Flash and orange and copper Flashabou
- Snag Guard: Clear monofilament
- Butt: Fluorescent orange Chenille
- Body: Chartreuse and reddish-orange deer
- Eyes: Solid plastic

Chugger (*Greg Miheve*)
- Hook: TMC 511S, size 1/0
- Thread: Red, 3/0
- Body: Gold Diamond Braid
- Wing: Yellow bucktail and gold Flashabou
- Head: Red deer
- Eyes: Yellow and black Audible

Note: A chartreuse and a white version are also popular.

Cockroach
- Hook: TMC 811S, sizes 3/0-4/0
- Thread: Black, 3/0
- Tail: Grizzly hackles (six), bronze Flashabou, and brown bucktail
- Body: Black thread coated with epoxy
- Eyes: Painted, white with black pupil; optional

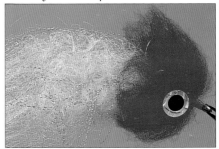

Cotton Candy (*Bob Popovics*)
- Hook: TMC 800S, size 4/0
- Thread: Fluorescent red single strand nylon floss
- Tail: Gray-silver Big Fly Fiber with silver Krystal Flash
- Body: Wool, spun and cut to shape
- Eyes: Large Prismatic

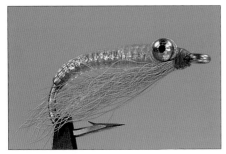

Crazy Charlie, Brown
- Hook: TMC 811S, sizes 4-8
- Thread: Brown, 3/0
- Eyes: Chrome bead chain
- Body: Clear V-Rib over pearl Flashabou
- Wing: Brown calftail

Crazy Charlie, Pink
- Hook: TMC 811S, sizes 4-8
- Thread: Pink, 3/0
- Eyes: Chrome bead chain
- Body: Clear V-Rib over pearl Flashabou
- Wing: Pink calftail

Crazy Charlie, Tan
- Hook: TMC 811S, sizes 4-8
- Thread: Tan, 3/0
- Eyes: Chrome bead chain
- Body: Clear V-Rib over pearl Flashabou
- Wing: Tan calftail

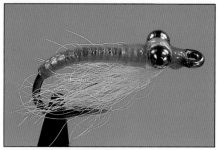

Crazy Charlie, White
Hook: TMC 811S, sizes 4-8
Thread: White, 3/0
Eyes: Silver bead chain
Body: Clear V-Rib over pearlescent
          flat tinsel
Wing: White calftail

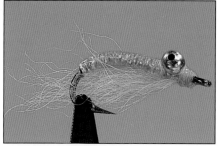

Crazy Charlie, Yellow
Hook: TMC 811S, sizes 4-8
Thread: Yellow, 3/0
Eyes: Chrome bead chain
Body: Clear V-Rib over pearl
          Flashabou
Wing: Yellow calftail

Deer Hair Squid, Pink (Scott Walker)
Hook: TMC 800S, size 4/0
Thread: White single strand flat floss
Tail: Pink rubber and saddle hackle
Body: Pink deer, lacquered
Eyes: Silver bead chain

Deer Hair Squid, White (Scott Walker)
Hook: TMC 800S, size 4/0
Thread: White single strand flat floss
Tail: White rubber and saddle hackle
Body: White deer, lacquered
Eyes: Silver bead chain

Epoxy-Backed Shrimp (Jimmy Nix)
Hook: Mustad 34011, sizes 1/0, 4
Thread: White, 3/0
Eyes: Heavy mono; dip in Spar Varnish
Antennae: Tan and brown Ultra Hair and
           pearl Accent Flash
Body: Pinkish Angora goat and rabbit
Rib: Copper wire
Tail: An extension of the back with
           pearl Accent Flash
Back: Clear plastic straw with pearl
           Accent Flash underneath
Snag Guard: Wire

Epoxy Charlie, Brown (Joe Branham)
Hook: TMC 811S, sizes 4-8
Thread: Brown, 6/0
Eyes: Stainless bead chain
Body: Gold Kreinik braid
Epoxy: Devcon 2 Ton
Wing: Brown calftail, cree hackle tips,
          and pearl Krystal Flash

Epoxy Charlie, Pink (Joe Branham)
Hook: TMC 811S, sizes 4-8
Thread: Pink, 6/0
Eyes: Stainless bead chain
Body: Star pink Kreinik braid
Epoxy: Devcon 2 Ton
Wing: Pink calftail, pink grizzly hack-
          le tips, and pearl and pink
          Krystal Flash

Epoxy Charlie, Tan (Joe Branham)
Hook: TMC 811S, sizes 4-8
Thread: Tan, 6/0
Eyes: Stainless bead chain
Body: Pearl Kreinik braid
Epoxy: Devcon 2 Ton
Wing: Tan calftail, tan grizzly hackle
          tips, and pearl Krystal Flash

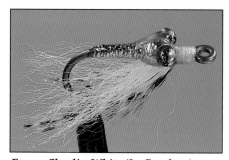

Epoxy Charlie, White (Joe Branham)
Hook: TMC 811S, sizes 4-8
Thread: White, 6/0
Eyes: Stainless bead chain
Body: Silver Kreinik braid
Epoxy: Devcon 2 Ton
Wing: White calftail, grizzly hackle
          tips, and pearl Krystal Flash

Epoxy Charlie, Yellow *(Joe Branham)*
Hook: TMC 811S, sizes 4-8
Thread: Yellow, 6/0
Eyes: Stainless bead chain
Body: Star yellow Kreinik braid
Epoxy: Devcon 2 Ton
Wing: Yellow calftail, yellow grizzly hackle tips, and yellow and pearl Krystal Flash

Epoxy Fly, Clear *(Jimmy Nix)*
Hook: TMC 811S, sizes 4-8
Thread: White, 6/0
Tail: Cream marabou, pearl Accent Flash, and two ginger variant hackles
Snag Guard: Stiff monofilament, two pieces
Body: Devcon 2-part, 5-minute epoxy
Eyes: Painted black

Epoxy Fly, Pink *(Jimmy Nix)*
Hook: TMC 811S, sizes 4-8
Thread: White, 3/0
Tail: Pink marabou, pink Accent Flash, and two pink grizzly hackles
Snag Guard: Heavy monofilament
Body: Devcon 2-part, 5-minute epoxy
Eyes: Painted black

Epoxy Fly, Root Beer *(Jimmy Nix)*
Hook: TMC 811S, sizes 4-8
Thread: White, 3/0
Tail: Cream marabou, pearl and gold Krystal Flash, and two grizzly hackle tips
Snag Guard: Heavy monofilament
Body: 5-minute epoxy, tinted brown
Eyes: Burned monofilament

Epoxy Moe Squirrel Tail
Hook: TMC 811S, sizes 4-8
Thread: White single strand flat floss
Tail: Red squirrel and orange Accent Flash
Snag Guard: Mason monofilament, 20 lb.
Body: Epoxy
Eyes: Black paint

Everglades Deceiver *(Flip Pallot)*
Hook: TMC 811S, sizes 1/0 and 4
Thread: Red, 3/0
Snag Guard: Wire
Tail: Grizzly hackle with pearl Accent Flash
Body: Silver braid
Wing: White calftail
Throat: Red calftail
Eyes: Painted white with black pupil

Feather Crab *(Jimmy Nix)*
Hook: TMC 811S, sizes 4-6
Thread: Red, 3/0
Tail: Copper Accent Flash
Legs: Rubber bands
Claws: Pheasant body; Flexament to shape
Body: White saddle hackle, clipped
Back: Pheasant rump

Flashtail Whistler, Orange and Yellow
(Dan Blanton)
Hook: TMC 800S, sizes 2/0, 3/0, weighted
Thread: Red single strand flat floss
Eyes: Silver bead chain
Tail: Yellow bucktail and silver Flashabou with multi-colored Krystal Flash and hot orange neck hackle
Body: Fluorescent red chenille
Hackle: Hot orange and yellow saddle

Flashtail Whistler, Red and White *(Dan Blanton)*
Hook: TMC 800S, sizes 2/0, 3/0, weighted
Thread: Red single strand flat floss
Eyes: Silver bead chain
Tail: White bucktail and silver Flashabou with multi-colored Krystal Flash and grizzly neck hackles
Body: Red chenille
Hackle: Red saddle

Flashtail Whistler, Red and Yellow *(Dan Blanton)*
Hook: TMC 800S, sizes 2/0 and 3/0, weighted
Thread: Red single strand flat floss
Eyes: Silver bead chain
Tail: Yellow bucktail and silver Flashabou with multi-colored Krystal Flash and grizzly neck hackle
Body: Red chenille
Hackle: Red saddle

Flashtail Whistler, White and Grizzly *(Dan Blanton)*
Hook: TMC 800S, sizes 2/0 and 3/0, weighted
Thread: Red single strand flat floss
Eyes: Silver bead chain
Tail: White bucktail and silver Flashabou with multi-colored Krystal Flash and grizzly neck hackle
Body: Red chenille
Hackle: Red saddle

Fur Shrimp *(Tim Borski)*
Hook: TMC 811S, sizes 2-4
Thread: Tan, 3/0
Eyes: Steel, painted yellow with black pupil
Tail: Tan Craft Fur, marked with black Pantone pen, with orange Accent Flash
Hackle: Natural grizzly, wide and webby, palmered
Snag Guard: Stiff monofilament

Glass Minnow *(Dennis Goddard)*
Hook: Mustad 34011, size 1
Thread: Clear, fine monofilament
Tail: Black hackle inside small pearlescent Flat Braid tube
Underbody: Pearlescent Flat Braid
Overbody: Pearlescent Flat Braid
Body: Epoxy and pearlescent flakes
Eyes: Silver and black Prismatic stick-on
Note: Underbody and overbody forms shape of body

Glass Minnow, White
Hook: TMC 811S, size 1/0
Thread: White, 3/0
Body: Silver flat tinsel under clear monofilament (20-30 lb.)
Wing: White FisHair with silver Flashabou
Eyes: Painted yellow with black pupil; fluorescent fire orange stripe at back; epoxy head

Glass Minnow, White and Brown
Hook: TMC 811S, size 1/0
Thread: Orange, 3/0
Body: Silver flat tinsel under clear monofilament (20-30 lb.)
Wing: White FisHair and red squirrel tail
Eyes: Painted white with black pupil over orange paint; epoxy head

Glass Minnow, White and Green
Hook: TMC 811S, size 1/0
Thread: Dark olive, 3/0
Body: Silver flat tinsel under clear monofilament (20-30 lb.)
Wing: White and chartreuse FisHair, with silver Flashabou and peacock herl
Eyes: Painted white with black pupil; epoxy head

Gold and Brown Shrimp
Hook: TMC 811S, sizes 4-6
Thread: Black, 6/0
Body: Golden tan sparkle dubbing
Wing: Natural brown bucktail and two cree hackles

Greg's Flat, Tan *(Greg Miheve)*
Hook: TMC 811S, sizes 4-8
Thread: Brown, 6/0
Eyes: Silver or chrome bead chain
Tail: Tan calf and pearl Accent Flash
Legs: Ginger variant hackle, palmered and trimmed on top
Body: Alternating bands of pearl tinsel and brown thread; epoxy and install hackle before epoxy dries

Herring (*Bill Catherwood*)
Hook:	*TMC 800S, size 3/0*
Thread:	*White, 3/0*
Wing:	*White, pearl gray, pink, pale blue marabou; pale blue and pearl gray hackle, four each*
Overwing:	*Hot pink, ice blue, and blue charm Krystal Flash, four strands each*
Collar:	*White deer*
Head:	*White deer, pale blue or lavender deer at hook eye*
Eyes:	*Amber and black glass, 6 mm.*

Herring Sprat (*Bill Catherwood*)
Hook:	*TMC 800S, size 2*
Thread:	*Blue, 3/0*
Snag Grd.:	*Monofilament*
Wing:	*White, pink, pearl gray, and pale blue marabou; pale blue and pearl gray saddle hackle*
Overwing:	*Hot pink, four strands; ice blue and blue charm KF; peacock*
Eyes:	*Amber and black plastic*

Horror
Hook:	*TMC 811S, sizes 4-6*
Thread:	*Black, 6/0*
Wing:	*Brown hackle tips over natural brown bucktail*
Head:	*Yellow chenille*

Interceptor, Pink (*Randall Kaufmann*)
Hook:	*Mustad 3407, sizes 4-8*
Thread:	*Fluorescent pink, 6/0*
Eyes:	*Nickel plated steel, painted pink with white and black centers*
Tail:	*Pink, wine, and pearl Krystal Flash*
Body:	*Pearl Diamond Braid*
Wing:	*Pink, wine, and pearl Krystal Flash*

Keel Eel (*Bob Popovics*)
Hook:	*Mustad 34011, size 1/0*
Thread:	*White, 3/0*
Tail:	*Brown and white Ultra Hair*
Underbody:	*Pearl mylar*
Body:	*Epoxy, tapered (5 minute Devcon)*
Eyes:	*Gold and black stick-on*

Lefty's Deceiver, Black (*Lefty Kreh*)
Hook:	*TMC 811S, size 2/0*
Thread:	*Black single strand nylon floss*
Tail:	*Black hackles (6) and copper Accent Flash*
Body:	*Tying thread*
Wing:	*Black bucktail, top and bottom*
Throat:	*Red Accent Flash*
Eyes:	*Painted white with black pupil*

Lefty's Deceiver, Cockroach (*Lefty Kreh*)
Hook:	*TMC 800S, sizes 4/0, 2/0, 1/0, or 2*
Thread:	*Black, 3/0*
Tail:	*Grizzly saddle hackles (6); copper Flashabou, silver Accent Flash*
Body:	*Silver flat tinsel or tying thread*
Wing:	*Natural brown bucktail or gray squirrel*
Head:	*Red thread stripe; optional*
Eyes:	*Painted yellow or white with black pupils*

Lefty's Deceiver, Red and White (*Lefty Kreh*)
Hook:	*TMC 811S, sizes 2-4/0*
Thread:	*Fluorescent fire orange SSNF*
Tail:	*White hackle (6) and pearl Accent Flash*
Body:	*Tying thread*
Wing:	*Red bucktail, top; white bucktail, bottom*
Throat:	*Red Accent Flash*
Eyes:	*Painted white with black pupils*

Lefty's Deceiver, Red and Yellow (*Lefty Kreh*)
Hook:	*TMC 800S, sizes 4/0, 2/0, 1/0, 2*
Thread:	*Fluorescent fire orange SSNF*
Tail:	*Yellow saddle hackle (6), with red Accent Flash and red Flashabou*
Body:	*Silver flat tinsel or thread*
Wing:	*Red bucktail, top; yellow bucktail, bottom*
Throat:	*Red Accent Flash*
Eyes:	*Painted white with black pupil*

Lefty's Deceiver, White (Lefty Kreh)
Hook: TMC 811S, sizes 2-4/0
Thread: White single strand nylon floss
Tail: White saddle (6) and pearl Accent Flash
Body: Tying thread
Wing: White bucktail, top and bottom
Throat: Red Accent Flash
Eyes: Painted white with black pupils

Lefty's Deceiver, White and Blue (Lefty Kreh)
Hook: TMC 800S, sizes 4/0, 2/0, 1/0, 2
Thread: White single strand nylon floss
Tail: White saddle hackle (6), with pearl Accent Flash and pearl Flashabou
Body: Silver flat tinsel or tying thread
Wing: Blue bucktail, top; white bucktail, bottom
Throat: Red Accent Flash
Head: Painted blue
Eyes: Painted white with black pupil

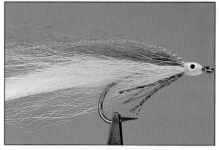

Lefty's Deceiver, White and Green (Lefty Kreh)
Hook: TMC 811S, sizes 2-4/0
Thread: Fluorescent green single strand nylon floss
Tail: White hackle (6) and pearl Accent Flash
Underbody: Tying thread
Wing: Green bucktail, top; white bucktail, bottom
Throat: Red Accent Flash
Eyes: Painted white with black pupils

Lefty's Deceiver, Yellow and Green (Lefty Kreh)
Hook: TMC 800S, sizes 4/0, 2/0, 1/0, 2
Thread: Black single strand nylon floss
Tail: Yellow saddle hackle (6), with gold Accent Flash and silver Flashabou
Body: Silver flat tinsel or thread
Wing: Green bucktail, top; yellow bucktail, bottom
Throat: Red Accent Flash
Eyes: Painted white with black pupils

Lemon Shark (Jim Stewart)
Hook: TMC 811S, size 2
Thread: Fluorescent orange SSNF
Tail: White and hot orange marabou and chartreuse rabbit strip with chartreuse marabou over top
Snag Guard: Clear monofilament
Butt: Fluorescent pink chenille
Body: Natural deer top and sides (tips form collar); white deer bottom and front; chartreuse deer top center
Eyes: Solid plastic

Major Bunker (Tom Kintz)
Hook: TMC 811S, size 4/0 weighted
Thread: White, 6/0
Tail: White saddle, gray bucktail, brown streamer hair, and pearl Flashabou
Body: Pearl braided mylar
Wing: Black and brown streamer hair
Underwing: Gray bucktail and pearl Flashabou
Collar: Gray bucktail, brown streamer hair, and pearl Flashabou
Eyes: White plastic, 12 mm

Mangrove Critter (Tim Borski)
Hook: TMC 811S, size 1/0
Thread: Tan, 3/0
Eyes: Non-toxic (for weight)
Snag Guard: Clear monofilament
Tail: Tan Craft Fur, topped w/orange KF
Eyes: Burnt monofilament (60 lb. hard Mason)
Butt: Pearlescent Crystal Chenille
Legs: Olive or tan grizzly hackle
Body: Tan wool, spun, tint with Pantone 147M

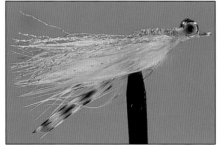

Marabou Shrimp, Pink (Randall Kaufmann)
Hook: Mustad 3407, sizes 4 and 6
Thread: Pink, 6/0
Eyes: Gold steel, painted pink with red and white centers
Body: Pink Diamond Braid
Wing: Pink and white marabou; pearl, fluorescent pink, and pink Krystal Flash; and two pink grizzly hackles

Marabou Shrimp, Tan (Randall Kaufmann)
Hook: Mustad 3407, sizes 4-6
Thread: Tan, 6/0
Eyes: Gold steel painted tan with black centers
Body: Orange Diamond Braid
Wing: Tan marabou; pearl and orange Krystal Flash; and tan grizzly hackles

Marabou Shrimp, White *(Randall Kaufmann)*
    Hook: Mustad 3407, sizes 4-6
    Thread: White, 6/0
    Eyes: Gold steel, painted white with black centers
    Body: Pearl Diamond Braid
    Wing: White marabou with pearl and light orange Krystal Flash and two grizzly hackles

Marabou Shrimp, Yellow *(Randall Kaufmann)*
    Hook: Mustad 3407, sizes 4-6
    Thread: Yellow, 6/0
    Eyes: Gold steel painted yellow, white, and black
    Body: Yellow Diamond Braid
    Wing: Yellow over white marabou; pearl and yellow Krystal Flash; and two yellow grizzly hackles

McCrab *(George Anderson)*
    Hook: TMC 811S, sizes 1/0-4, weighted
    Thread: Brown, 3/0
    Tail: Tan marabou, pearl Accent Flash, and two brown hackle tips
    Eyes: Mono, plus black steel eyes
    Body: Antelope, marked with dark brown Pantone pen
    Legs: Rubber bands, marked like body
Underbody: Lead, held in place with white tile sealer

Menemsha Minnow, Blue and Silver *(Page Rogers)*
    Hook: TMC 511S, sizes 2-2/0
    Thread: White single strand flat floss
    Tail: White calftail and blue, silver, and gold Flashabou
    Body: Witchcraft tape No. 101, topped with No. 68 and marked with black Pantone
    Gills: Painted red
    Eyes: Silver-black stick-on

Menemsha Minnow, Herring *(Page Rogers)*
    Hook: TMC 511S, sizes 2-2/0
    Thread: Black single strand flat floss
    Tail: Black calftail
    Body;   Witchcraft tape No. 101, topped with No. 34
    Gills: Black Pantone marking pen
    Eyes: Silver-black stick-on

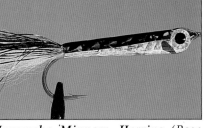

Menemsha Minnow, Mackerel *(Page Rogers)*
    Hook: TMC 511S, sizes 2-2/0
    Thread: White single strand flat floss
    Tail: White calftail and kelly green Flashabou
    Body: Witchcraft tape No. 101, topped with No. 24, marked with black Pantone
    Gills: Painted red
    Eyes: Silver-black stick-on

Mini Puff, Orange
    Hook: TMC 800S, size 4
    Thread: Orange, 6/0
    Eyes: Silver bead chain
    Wing: Tan calftail, with pearl Krystal Flash and grizzly hackle tips
    Head: Orange chenille

Mini Puff, Pink
    Hook: TMC 800S, size 4
    Thread: Pink, 6/0
    Eyes: Silver bead chain
    Wing: Tan calftail with pearl Krystal Flash and grizzly hackle tips
    Head: Pink chenille

Mini Shrimp, Chartreuse *(Randall Kaufmann)*
    Hook: Mustad 3407, size 8
    Thread: Fluorescent green, 6/0
    Eyes: Silver mini bead chain, optional
    Body: Chartreuse Hare-Tron or lime Holographic Fly Flash
    Wing: Fluorescent green Krystal Flash, yellow pheasant rump, and chartreuse grizzly hackle tips

Mini Shrimp, Tan *(Randall Kaufmann)*
Hook: Mustad 3407, size 8
Thread: Brown, 6/0
Eyes: Silver or gold mini bead chain or lead, optional
Body: Tan Hare-Tron
Wing: Pearl Krystal Flash, natural brown pheasant rump, and cree hackle tips

Mullet *(Jimmy Nix)*
Hook: TMC 811S, size 1/0
Thread: Gray, 3/0
Snag Guard: Heavy monofilament
Tail: White bucktail, flanked by 6 blue dun saddles and tipped with silver Accent Flash
Body: Gray yarn
Wing: Gray marabou, peacock herl, pearl Accent Flash, red marabou
Collar: Deer
Head: Natural deer, clipped
Eyes: White 4 mm. solid plastic

Needlefish *(Bill Catherwood)*
Hook: Mustad 34011, sizes 4/0
Thread: Green A
Wing: Light blue (4), sea foam green (2), and pearl gray (2) saddle hackles; and white, pearl gray, pink, sea foam green, and pale blue marabou (one each)
Eyes: Amber and black glass, 6 mm., or solid plastic

Needlefish *(Greg Miheve)*
Hook: TMC 811S, size 2
Thread: White single strand flat floss
Tail: White, fluorescent chartreuse, and green Streamer Hair, with peacock, lime, green, and pearl Krystal Flash
Head: White thread painted peacock green on top
Gills: Red paint
Eyes: White and black paint
Leader: Wire

Orange Butt Tarpon *(Tim Borski)*
Hook: TMC 800S, sizes 1/0 and 2/0
Thread: Black, 3/0
Tail: Tan Craft Fur, barred with Pantone 147 M and topped with orange Accent Flash
Body: Hot orange chenille
Collar: Gray squirrel

Orange Grizzly
Hook: TMC 800S, sizes 3/0 and 4/0
Thread: Fluorescent orange single strand nylon floss
Butt: Orange chenille
Body: Tying thread coated with epoxy
Tail: Orange hackles (four), enclosed by four grizzly hackles
Hackle: Orange and grizzly

Pearly Bait *(Page Rogers)*
Hook: Mustad 34011, size 2
Thread: White single strand flat floss
Tail: White marabou
Body: Pearl mylar piping, covered with 5-minute epoxy
Eyes: Silver-black stick-on

Permit Crab *(Del Brown)*
Hook: TMC 811S, sizes 1/0-2
Thread: Fluorescent green single strand nylon floss
Tail: Cree hackle tips, four, and pearl Flashabou
Eyes: Nickel plated steel
Body: Alternating bands of tan and brown yarn
Legs: White rubber; paint tips red

Pink Sands *(Randall Kaufmann)*
Hook: Mustad 3407, sizes 4-8
Thread: White, 6/0
Eyes: Gold steel, painted white, pink, and black
Body: Pink Diamond Braid
Wing: Pink calftail, pink and pearl Krystal Flash, and two white hackle tips

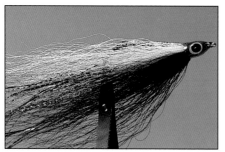

Prince of Tides (Flip Pallot)
Hook: TMC 411S, sizes 1/0 and 4
Thread: Tobacco brown, 3/0
Body: Copper Flashabou and green bucktail wound on shank and overwrapped with clear monofilament
Wing: White, green and brown bucktail with copper Krystal Flash and Flashabou
Eyes: Painted yellow with black pupil, epoxied

Punch, Lime (Dan Blanton)
Hook: TMC 811S, sizes 2/0 and 3/0
Thread: Fluorescent green SSNF
Eyes: Chrome bead chain
Tail: Lime bucktail and lime Flashabou
Body: Green Polyflash or Diamond Braid
Wing: Green grizzly hackles (2), with lime Flashabou and Krystal Flash
Hackle: Lime
Head: Fluorescent green chenille

Punch, Sabalo (Dan Blanton)
Hook: TMC 811S, sizes 2/0 and 3/0
Thread: Fluorescent fire orange SSNF
Eyes: Chrome bead chain
Tail: White bucktail and silver Flashabou
Body: Silver Polyflash or Diamond Braid
Wing: Grizzly hackles (2), peacock herl, and pearl green Accent Flash
Hackle: Orange
Head: Fluorescent red chenille

Punch, Tropical (Dan Blanton)
Hook: TMC 811S, sizes 2/0 and 3/0
Thread: Fluorescent fire orange SSNF
Eyes: Chrome bead chain
Tail: Yellow bucktail and gold Flashabou
Body: Gold Polyflash or Diamond Braid
Wing: Orange grizzly hackles (2), with peacock herl, yellow Accent Flash, and gold Flashabou
Hackle: Yellow
Head: Fluorescent red chenille

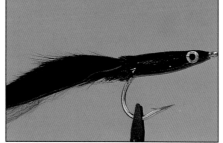

Rabbit Candy, Black (Bob Popovics)
Hook: TMC 800S, sizes 1/0-3/0
Thread: Black, 3/0
Tail: Black rabbit strip
Body: Black Ultra Hair over silver mylar coated with black epoxy
Eyes: Silver-black stick-on

Rabbit Candy, Lime (Bob Popovics)
Hook: TMC 800S, sizes 1/0-3/0
Thread: White, 3/0
Tail: Lime rabbit strip
Body: Lime Ultra Hair over silver mylar, coated with lime epoxy
Eyes: Silver-black stick-on

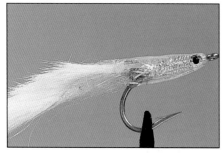

Rabbit Candy, White (Bob Popovics)
Hook: TMC 800S, sizes 1/0-3/0
Thread: White, 3/0
Tail: White rabbit strip
Body: White Ultra Hair over silver mylar, coated with white epoxy
Eyes: Silver-black stick-on

Sailfish, Anchovy (Trey Combs)
Hook: TMC 811S, size 4/0; trailer hook connected w/60 lb. mono
Thread: White single strand flat floss
Tail: White bucktail and saddle; pearl Flashabou; chartreuse and blue KF; chartreuse, pale blue, aqua, and white bucktail; peacock; pearl Flashabou; silver KF
Head: Pearlescent mylar tube; ends form collar; epoxy entire head
Eyes: Silver/black Prismatic stick-on

Sailfish, Flying Fish (Trey Combs)
Hook: TMC 811S, size 4/0; trailer hook connected w/60 lb. mono
Thread: White single strand flat floss
Tail: White saddle, white bucktail, pearl Flashabou, lt. blue bucktail, lt. blue, pearl, smolt blue, and royal blue KF, peacock, silver and pearl Flashabou
Head: Pearlescent mylar tube; ends form collar; epoxy entire head
Eyes: Silver/black Prismatic stick-on

Salt Crab *(Dave Whitlock)*
Hook: TMC 811S, sizes 1/0 and 4
Thread: White single strand nylon floss
Snag Grd.: Hard Mason nylon
Pinchers: Dark mottled brown and white hen hackle
Legs: Soft grizzly hackle
Body: Gray and white deer; make stripes on back with brown or tan Pantone pen
Eyes: Monofilament nymph eyes

Salt Shrimp, Gold *(Dave Whitlock)*
Hook: TMC 811S, sizes 1/0, 4, or 8, weighted
Snag Guard: Monofilament
Thread: White, 6/0
Tail: Gold deer
Antennae: Gold hackle stems, stripped
Back: Clear plastic
Eyes: Monofilament nymph eyes
Rib: Fine gold wire
Body: Gold Antron
Legs: Gold grizzly hackle

Salt Shrimp, Gray *(Dave Whitlock)*
Hook: TMC 811S, sizes 1/0, 4, or 8, weighted
Snag Guard: Monofilament
Thread: Gray, 6/0
Tail: Gray deer
Antennae: Grizzly hackle stems, stripped
Back: Clear plastic
Eyes: Monofilament nymph eyes
Rib: Fine gold wire
Body: Gray Antron
Legs: Grizzly hackle

Salt Shrimp, Olive *(Dave Whitlock)*
Hook: TMC 811S, sizes 1/0, 4, or 8, weighted
Snag Guard: Monofilament
Thread: Olive, 6/0
Tail: Olive deer
Antennae: Olive grizzly hackle stems, stripped
Back: Clear plastic
Eyes: Monofilament nymph eyes
Rib: Fine gold wire
Body: Olive Antron
Legs: Olive grizzly hackle stems

Sand Eel *(Dave Whitlock)*
Hook: TMC 811S, size 2/0
Thread: White single strand nylon floss
Snag Grd.: Hard Mason nylon
Tail: Olive grizzly thin saddle hackles (4-6) and lime green Accent Flash
Body: Pearl mylar tinsel and olive grizzly saddle hackle
Throat: Red and lime green Accent Flash
Eyes: Solid plastic

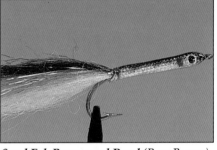

Sand Eel, Brown and Pearl *(Page Rogers)*
Hook: Mustad 34011, sizes 1-4
Thread: White single strand flat floss
Tail: Pearl white FisHair, topped with light pink Fly Fur, 2 strands silver Flashabou, 8 strands pink Fly Flash and auburn Fly Fur
Body: Pearl mylar piping tinted with pink and brown Pantone
Gills: Painted red
Eye: Silver-black stick-on

Sand Eel, Green and Pearl *(Page Rogers)*
Hook: Mustad 34011, sizes 1-4
Thread: White single strand flat floss
Tail: Pearl-white FisHair topped w/fl. Day-Glo chartreuse FisHair, 2 strands silver Flashabou, 6 strands olive-pearl Flashabou, moss green Fly Fur
Body: Pearl mylar piping, tint w/olive-green, yellow-chartreuse Pantone
Gills: Red paint
Eyes: Silver-black stick-on

Sar-Mul-Mac, Anchovy *(Dan Blanton)*
Hook: TMC 811S, size 3/0
Thread: White single strand nylon floss
Tail: White bucktail
Wing: White hackles (6), white bucktail, silver Flashabou, royal blue bucktail, peacock Accent Flash, and peacock herl
Head: Red chenille (2 turns), white chenille with peacock topping
Eyes: Amber 7 mm. solid plastic

Sar-Mul-Mac, Mullet *(Dan Blanton)*
Hook: TMC 811S, size 3/0
Thread: White single strand nylon floss
Tail: White bucktail
Wing: White saddles (6), white bucktail with silver Flashabou, gray marabou, and grizzly hackles (2)
Head: Red chenille and white chenille, topped with gray chenille
Cheeks: Teal flank
Eyes: Amber 7 mm. solid plastic

Sea Arrow Squid (Dan Blanton)
  Hook: Eagle Claw 66SS, size 3/0
  Thread: White single strand nylon floss
  Tail: White hackles (10), w/purple buck-
           tail, purple Accent Flash, white
           marabou
  Body: Medium white chenille
  Fin: White calftail and pearl Accent
           Flash
  Eyes: Orange solid eyes, 7 mm.
  Tag: Gold embossed tinsel
Note: Use orange, rust, gold, and black
Pantone markings.

Sea Bunny, Gray and Yellow (Mike
Wolverton)
  Hook: TMC 811S, size 3/0
  Thread: Brown, 3/0
  Tail: Yellow-olive rabbit strip, yel-
           low Accent Flash, and natural
           gray rabbit
  Body: Tying thread coated with
           epoxy
  Eyes: Painted yellow with black
           pupil

Sea Bunny, Red and Black (Mike
Wolverton)
  Hook: TMC 811S, size 3/0
  Thread: Red, 3/0
  Tail: Black rabbit strip, pearl Accent
           Flash, and red rabbit
  Body: Tying thread coated with
           epoxy
  Eyes: Painted yellow with black
           pupil

Sea Bunny, Red and White (Mike
Wolverton)
  Hook: TMC 811S, size 3/0
  Thread: White, 3/0
  Tail: White rabbit strip, pearl
           Accent Flash, and red rabbit
  Body: Tying thread coated with
           epoxy
  Eyes: Painted yellow with black
           pupil

Sea Bunny, Rust (Mike Wolverton)
  Hook: TMC 811S, size 3/0
  Thread: Fluorescent fire orange, 6/0, or
           single strand nylon floss
  Tail: Rust rabbit strip, gold Accent
           Flash, and rust rabbit fur
  Body: Tying thread coated with
           epoxy
  Eyes: Painted yellow with black
           pupil

Sea-Ducer, White and Red
  Hook: TMC 800S, size 2/0
  Thread: Red, 3/0
  Tail: White saddle hackles (6), and
           silver Flashabou
  Body: White hackle, palmered; red
           hackle front

Sea-Ducer, White, Yellow, and Grizzly
  Hook: TMC 811S, size 2/0
  Thread: White, 3/0
  Tail: Yellow, white, and grizzly
           hackles (2 each), with silver
           Flashabou
  Body: White, yellow, and grizzly
           hackle wound together

Sea-Ducer, Yellow and Red
  Hook: TMC 811S, size 2/0
  Thread: Red, 3/0
  Tail: Yellow saddle hackles (6), with
           silver Flashabou
  Body: Yellow hackle, palmered; red
           hackle front

Sea Habit Bucktail, Anchovy (Trey Combs)
  Hook: TMC 800S, size 2/0
  Thread: White single strand flat floss
  Tail: Pearl Flashabou
  Wing: Pearl Flashabou, white FisHair,
           pearl Flashabou, lime green AF,
           fluorescent lime green FisHair,
           pearl blue AF, royal blue FisHair,
           peacock AF; silver KF on each side
  Head: Pearl mylar piping, coated w/epoxy;
           blue-green Pantone on top
  Eyes: Pearlescent-black prismatic

Sea Habit Bucktail, Flying Fish (Trey Combs)
Hook: TMC 800S, size 2/0
Thread: White single strand flat floss
Tail: Pearl Flashabou
Wing: Pearl Flashabou, white FisHair, pearl blue AF, royal blue FisHair, royal blue AF, and black FisHair; silver AF on each side
Head: Pearl mylar piping, coated with epoxy; medium blue Pantone on top
Eyes: Pearl-black prismatic

Sea Habit Bucktail, Herring (Trey Combs)
Hook: TMC 800S, size 2/0
Thread: White single strand flat floss
Tail: Pearl Flashabou
Wing: Pearl Flashabou, white FisHair, pearlescent purple AF, pearl blue AF, sky blue FisHair, mouse-gray FisHair, black FisHair; silver AF on each side
Head: Pearl mylar piping coated with epoxy; gray Pantone on top
Eyes: Pearlescent-black prismatic stick-on

Sea Habit Bucktail, Sardine (Trey Combs)
Hook: TMC 800S, size 2/0
Thread: White single strand flat floss
Tail: Pearl Flashabou
Wing: Pearl Flashabou, white FisHair, olive AF, emerald green FisHair, moss-green FisHair, and peacock AF
Head: Pearl mylar piping, coated with epoxy; olive-green Pantone on top
Eyes: Pearl-black prismatic stick-on

Sea Habit, Green Machine (Trey Combs)
Hook: None—tie on hollow clear plastic tube
Thread: White single strand nylon floss
Wing: White and chartreuse FisHair base, surrounded with 20-30 chartreuse saddle hackles, four dark blue saddles, some dark olive and chartreuse bucktail, and electric blue Accent Flash
Body: Chartreuse live foam cylinder, 1" diameter
Eyes: Silver and black stick-on

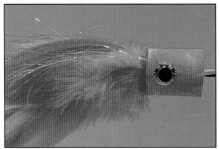

Sea Habit, Pink Squid (Trey Combs)
Hook: None—tie on hollow clear plastic tube
Thread: White single strand nylon floss
Wing: White bucktail, pink Flashabou, white FisHair, pink bucktail, hot pink FisHair, and 15 long hot pink saddles on each side
Body: Hot pink foam cylinder, 1" diameter, painted with fluorescent neon pink squiggles paint
Eyes: Silver and black stick-on

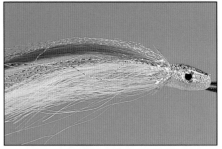

Sea Habit Tube Fly, Anchovy (Trey Combs)
Hook: Tie on hollow clear plastic tube
Thread: White single strand nylon floss
Body: White FisHair, pearl Flashabou, silver KF, lime green AF, fluorescent lime green FisHair, pearl blue AF, royal blue FisHair, and peacock AF, w/silver KF on each side
Head: Pearl mylar piping, painted green on top and epoxied
Eyes: Silver and black stick-on

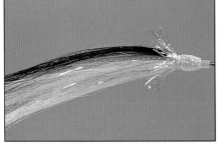

Sea Habit Tube Fly, Ballyhoo (Trey Combs)
Hook: Tie on hollow clear plastic tube
Thread: White single strand nylon floss
Body: White FisHair, pearl Flashabou, silver AF, pearlescent purple AF, pearl blue AF; sky blue FisHair; veiled w/mouse gray FisHair and black FisHair; silver AF on each side
Head: Pearl mylar piping, painted blue and epoxied
Eyes: Silver and black stick-on

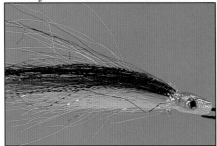

Sea Habit Tube Fly, Flying Fish (Trey Combs)
Hook: Tie on hollow clear plastic tube
Thread: White single strand nylon floss
Body: White FisHair, pearl Flashabou, silver AF, pearl blue AF, veiled w/royal blue FisHair, topped w/few strands of royal blue AF and black FisHair; silver AF on each side
Head: Pearl mylar piping, painted blue on top and epoxied
Eyes: Silver and black stick-on

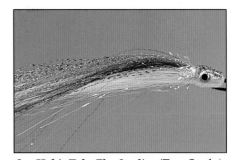

Sea Habit Tube Fly, Sardine (Trey Combs)
Hook: Tie on hollow clear plastic tube
Thread: White single strand nylon floss
Body: White FisHair, pearl Flashabou, silver AF, olive AF, few strands emerald green FisHair, moss green FisHair; topped w/peacock AF
Head: Pearl mylar piping, painted green on top and epoxied
Eyes: Silver and black stick-on

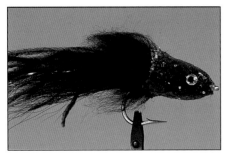

Siliclone, Black *(Bob Popovics)*
Hook: TMC 811S, size 3/0
Thread: Black, 3/0
Wing: *Black ostrich herl over black bucktail with blue, gold, and silver Flashabou*
Body: *Black fleece, trimmed, with GEII Silcone and glitter flakes*
Eyes: *Silver and white stick-on*

Siliclone, Chartreuse *(Bob Popovics)*
Hook: TMC 811S, size 3/0
Thread: Chartreuse, 3/0
Wing: *Chartreuse ostrich herl over chartreuse bucktail with blue, gold, and lime Flashabou*
Body: *Chartreuse fleece, trimmed, with GEII Silcone and glitter flakes*
Eyes: *Silver and white stick-on*

Siliclone, Yellow *(Bob Popovics)*
Hook: TMC 811S, size 3/0
Thread: Yellow, 3/0
Wing: *Yellow ostrich herl over bucktail with blue, gold, and yellow Flashabou*
Body: *Yellow fleece, trimmed, with GEII Silcone and glitter flakes*
Eyes: *Silver and white stick-on*

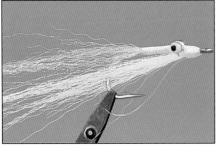

Skinny Water Clouser Minnow, Chartreuse and White *(Bob Clouser)*
Hook: TMC 811S, sizes 2, 6
Thread: White, 3/0
Eyes: *Non-toxic, painted black with yellow pupils, epoxied*
Snag Guard: Monofilament
Wing: *Chartreuse Super Hair, chartreuse Accent Flash over white Super Hair, or substitute same color bucktail with pearl Accent Flash*

Skinny Water Clouser Minnow, Gray and White *(Bob Clouser)*
Hook: TMC 811S, sizes 2 and 6
Thread: White, 3/0
Eyes: *Non-toxic, painted white with black pupils, epoxied*
Snag Guard: Monofilament
Wing: *Light gray Super Hair with pearl Accent Flash over white super Hair with pearl Accent Flash*

Skinny Water Clouser Minnow, Red and White *(Bob Clouser)*
Hook: TMC 811S, sizes 2 and 6
Thread: White, 3/0
Eyes: *Non-toxic, painted black with red pupils, epoxied*
Snag Guard: Monofilament
Wing: *Red Super Hair with pearl Accent Flash over white Super Hair with pearl Accent Flash*

Skinny Water Clouser Minnow, Tan and White *(Bob Clouser)*
Hook: TMC 811S, sizes 2 and 6
Thread: White, 3/0
Eyes: *Non-toxic, painted white with black pupils, epoxied*
Snag Guard: Monofilament
Wing: *Red Super Hair with pearl Accent Flash over white Super Hair with pearl Accent Flash*

Snapping Shrimp
Hook: TMC 811S, sizes 4-6
Thread: Black, 3/0
Butt: *Orange sparkle dubbing*
Body: *Tan sparkle dubbing*
Wing: *Brown FisHair*

Snook-A-Roo *(Jim Stewart)*
Hook: TMC 811S, size 1/0
Thread: Fluorescent fire orange SSNF
Snag Guard: Monofilament
Tail: *White bucktail, grizzly hackles, silver Flashabou, lime green AF, and red marabou fibers*
Butt: *Shell pink chenille*
Head: *Spun white deer, natural deer with black center*
Wing: *White deer*
Eyes: *Blue solid plastic, 9 mm.*

Super Swimming Shrimp (Tim Borski)
Hook: TMC 800S, sizes 2-4
Thread: Tan, 3/0
Legs: Tan or white rubber, front
Eyes: Non-toxic, painted yellow and black
Tail: Tan calftail with orange Accent Flash
Legs: Tan or white rubber, back, Pantone alternating bands
Body: Golden brown bucktail, flared on top (bottom)

Surf Candy, Light Blue (Bob Popovics)
Hook: TMC 800S, size 1/0
Thread: White, 3/0
Tail: Badger hackle feather, cut to shape, attached with Zap-A-Gap to pearlescent mylar tube, with white and light blue Ultra Hair
Body: Epoxy tapered (Devcon, 5 minute)
Gills: Red paint
Eyes: Pearl and silver stick-on

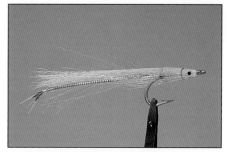

Surf Candy, Lime Green (Bob Popovics)
Hook: TMC 800S, size 1/0
Thread: White, 3/0
Tail: Badger hackle feather, cut to shape, attached with Zap-A-Gap to pearlescent mylar tube, with white and green Ultra Hair
Body: Epoxy tapered (Devcon, 5 minute)
Gills: Red paint
Eyes: Green and black stick-on

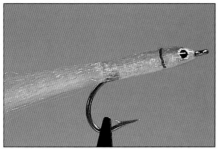

Surf Candy, Olive (Bob Popovics)
Hook: TMC 800S, size 1/0
Thread: White, 3/0
Tail: Badger hackle feather, cut to shape, attached with Zap-A-Gap to silver mylar tube, with white and olive Ultra Hair
Body: Epoxy tapered (Devcon, 5 minute)
Gills: Red paint
Eyes: Green and black stick-on

Surf Candy, Yellow (Bob Popovics)
Hook: TMC 800S, size 1/0
Thread: White, 3/0
Tail: Badger hackle feather, cut to shape, attached with Zap-A-Gap to pearlescent mylar tube with white and yellow Ultra Hair
Body: Epoxy tapered (Devcon, 5 minute)
Gills: Red paint
Eyes: Pearl and black stick-on

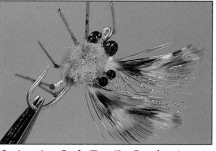

Swimming Crab, Tan (Joe Branham)
Hook: TMC 800S, sizes 2, 4
Thread: Tan, 3/0
Weight: Led eyes
Body: Tan wool, spun and trimmed to shape, covered with epoxy after all other parts are in place
Claws: Grizzly hackle tips, pearl Krystal Flash secured on top w/Zap-A-Gap
Legs: Tan speckle flake rubber, knotted, secured onto top w/Zap-A-Gap
Eyes: Burned monofilament, secured on top w/Zap-A-Gap

Swimming Shrimp (Tim Borski)
Hook: TMC 811S, size 6
Thread: Pink or white, 6/0
Eyes: Extra small steel eyes painted black over white
Tail: Gold Accent Flash over tan calftail with grizzly hackle
Head: Spun antelope
Snag Guard: Monofilament

Tarpon Glo, Bad Crab (Jonathon Olch)
Hook: TMC 811S, size 4/0
Thread: Burnt orange, 3/0
Butt: Orange chenille
Tail: Orange and furnace hackles over red squirrel tail enclosed with pheasant feathers
Hackle: Orange and furnace hackle (one each)
Body: Orange tying thread, coated with epoxy
Eyes: Painted yellow and black pupil

Tarpon Glo, Green (Jonathon Olch)
Hook: TMC 800S, sizes 4/0 and 3/0
Thread: Fluorescent green SSNF
Butt: Fluorescent green chenille
Tail: Peacock blue FisHair, w/four olive grizzly hackles enveloped by four green hackles
Hackle: Green grizzly, natural grizzly
Body: Fl. fire orange single strand nylon floss and fl. green single strand nylon floss, coated w/epoxy
Eyes: Painted white with black pupil

Tarpon Glo, Orange (Jonathan Olch)
Hook: TMC 800S, sizes 4/0 and 3/0
Thread: Fluorescent fire orange single strand nylon floss
Tail: Natural brown bucktail and four grizzly hackles enveloped by four red grizzly hackles
Hackle: Grizzly and red grizzly
Body: Fluorescent green single strand nylon floss and fluorescent fire orange single strand nylon floss, coated with epoxy
Eyes: Painted black w/white pupil

Tarpon Glo, Squirrel (Jonathan Olch)
Hook: TMC 811S, size 4/0
Thread: Claret, 3/0
Tail: Grizzly hackles (six) and gray squirrel tail
Body: Tying thread, coated with epoxy
Eyes: Painted yellow with black pupils

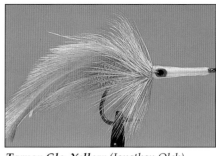

Tarpon Glo, Yellow (Jonathan Olch)
Hook: TMC 811S, size 4/0
Thread: Yellow, 3/0
Tail: Yellow and orange hackles (four each) over orange bucktail enclosed with natural mallard breast
Body: Tying thread, coated with epoxy
Hackle: Orange and yellow hackle (one each)
Eyes: Painted red with black pupil

Tarpon Shrimp, Nix's (Jimmy Nix)
Hook: TMC 800S, sizes 3/0 and 2/0
Thread: White single strand nylon floss
Eyes: Burned heavy monofilament (50-100 lb.), dipped in Spar Varnish
Tail: Grizzly hackle stem, one, trimmed closely; woodchuck; and six grizzly hackles
Body: Pearl Flashabou or Diamond Braid

Tinker Mackerel (Bill Catherwood)
Hook: TMC 800S, size 3/0
Thread: White single strand flat floss
Tail: Aqua, pale blue, and grizzly saddle hackle; aqua, light blue, white, and pink marabou
Collar: Lavender deer
Head: Lavender, light blue, blue/gray, and green deer
Eyes: Amber and black glass

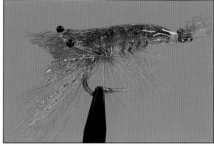

Ultra Shrimp (Bob Popovics)
Hook: TMC 811S, sizes 1/0 and 4
Thread: Tan, 3/0
Tail: Gold Krystal Flash and tan Ultra Hair
Eyes: Burned monofilament, colored with black Pantone pen
Antennae: Tan Ultra Hair
Body: Tan Ultra Hair, cut to shape and epoxied, over tan thread palmered with brown hackle

White Sands (Randall Kaufmann)
Hook: Mustad 3407, sizes 4-8
Thread: White, 6/0
Eyes: Gold steel, painted white, orange and black
Body: Pearl Diamond Braid
Wing: White rabbit with pearl and orange Krystal Flash

Wobbler, Gold (John Cave)
Hook: Mustad 34007, size 2/0 and 2
Thread: Light orange, 3/0
Snag Guard: Wire
Tail: Orange bucktail and gold Accent Flash
Body: Gold mylar tubing flattened and covered with epoxy
Eyes: Black plastic bead chain

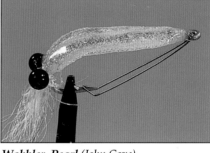

Wobbler, Pearl (John Cave)
Hook: Mustad 34007, size 2/0 and 2
Thread: White single strand flat floss
Snag Guard: Wire
Tail: White bucktail and mixed pearlescent Krystal Flash
Body: Pearlescent mylar tubing flattened and covered with epoxy
Eyes: Black plastic bead chain

Index

Note: Bold type indicates photo.